P9-BHR-948

How Your Pet's Feelings Hold the Key to His Health and Happiness

UNLOCKING THE ANIMAL MIND

FRANKLIN D. McMILLAN, D.V.M.
WITH KATHRYN LANCE
Foreword by Bob Barker

RODALE

© 2004 by Franklin D. McMillan and Kathryn Lance

Printed in the United States of America

Book design by Tara Long
Illustrations provided by the author
Photographs © Dirk Westphal/Getty Images, except: © PhotoDisc/Getty Images, pp. 38, 64, 76, 81, 90, 106, 119, 122, 162, 190, 211, 228, 244, 252, 276; © Duncan Smith/Getty Images, pp. 98, 258

Library of Congress Cataloging-in-Publication Data

McMillan, Franklin D.
    Unlocking the animal mind : how your pet's feelings hold the key to his health and
happiness / Franklin D. McMillan, with Kathryn Lance ; foreword by Bob Barker.
       p.   cm.
    Includes index.
    ISBN 1–57954–880–6 paperback
    1. Pets—Psychology. 2. Pets—Behavior. 3. Pets—Health. 4. Emotions in animals.
I. Lance, Kathryn. II. Title.
SF412.5.M39 2004
636.088'7'019—dc22   2004017570

Distributed to the trade by Holtzbrinck Publishers

2 4 6 8 10 9 7 5 3 1   paperback

This book is dedicated to some very special members of the animal kingdom.
First, to my Mom, Dad, and brothers Bob and Mike.
No one could have a more loving and supportive family.

To Lauretta Dennis, who saw something in me worth taking a chance on
and gave me my start in the greatest profession I could ever hope to be part of.

To Tammy Stevenson, my lighthouse in any storm and the most caring
animal doctor I have ever known.

And, finally, to some very special animals I have had the great honor
to have shared my life with . . .
Birdie, Boo, Dana, Brandy, Leo, Zorro, General, Snowball, and Butch.
And especially to Meebs and Gooby, whose lives would have been
so much happier if I had known then what I know now.
I'll make it up to you when we are together again.

CONTENTS

FOREWORD

MANY OF US SINCERELY LOVE our pets. We consider them full-fledged members of our families. We happily provide them with all of life's necessities and strive to do much more than just that. We are devastated when they are ill or injured, and we seek the best possible medical care for them. We buy them toys, we take them for walks, and we love to have them in the car with us. We play in the yard with our pets, reassure them when they are frightened, and we heap praise on them for the smallest accomplishments. We are happy when our pets are happy, and when they are less than happy we are deeply concerned.

In short, our pets are a very important part of our lives, and because they are, I know that *Unlocking the Animal Mind* will become a very important part of your life.

Unlocking the Animal Mind is a fascinating, original study and explanation of animals' "feelings" by Franklin D. McMillan, D.V.M., a sensitive, compassionate veterinarian who has treated many animals for me during the last 20 years.

Dr. McMillan sums up *Unlocking the Animal Mind* succinctly and perfectly when he says, "The purpose of this book is to offer you the knowledge and tools to make your own pet feel good."

Bob Barker
Hollywood, California
July 8, 2004

ACKNOWLEDGMENTS

I WISH TO THANK Michel Cabanac, Jaak Panksepp, Marc Bekoff, and Robert Sapolsky for their invaluable advice on portions of the scientific content of this book. I would also like to thank our team at Rodale, Ellen Phillips, Jennifer Reich, and Jennifer Kushnier, for making this project a pleasure to work on. And my great appreciation to our agent, Linda Konner, for her unwavering support of this book.

INTRODUCTION: SPECIAL PETS

I'M AN ANIMAL DOCTOR. People rely on me to make their sick or injured pets well. People expect me to have the medical knowledge and skills to run the proper diagnostic tests, prescribe the most appropriate medications, and perform surgery when it is necessary. In society's eyes, I am a healer of the animals.

But I'm going to show you why what I am doing may not be what you think I'm doing. For starters, no matter what diagnostic lab test I run, x-ray I take, antibiotic I prescribe, or surgical procedure I do, I am not directing my efforts at fixing what's wrong with your pet's body. In fact, it will likely surprise you to hear that my ultimate concern is not your pet's health. Any what may be even more surprising is your pet doesn't care about his health. What he cares about—and what I want for him—is more important than health: He wants to "feel good." He wants to enjoy his life. He doesn't care how this comes about.

The truth is that the *only* thing your pet cares about is feeling good and being happy. My main job is to help your pet feel good. And, like your pet, I don't care how that comes about. My goal goes well beyond health—I am trying to help your pet achieve happiness.

Any time we humans care for an animal, we accept certain responsibilities. All animals in our care will, at some point or another, want or need something for their well-being that they lack the ability to obtain. It could be food or warmth. It might be safety, adequate living space, mentally engaging activities, play, or social companionship. Since we created their living arrangements, our responsibility is to do our best to fulfill the needs that these living arrangements either create or prevent the animals from obtaining on their own. If, for example, we confine a highly social animal like a dog or horse to a house or stable where there is no social interaction, then it is our duty to help the animal satisfy this unmet need.

Figuratively speaking, if the chimpanzee in my care has a 4-foot stick to reach a banana 6 feet away, I become the provider of a 2-foot extension for his stick. If my dog has the need to relieve herself outside, I become her hands to turn the doorknob so the door will open. And if my rabbit has a loose, infected tooth, I provide the manual dexterity that his paws lack to remove the painful tooth. In a very literal sense, I am answering nature's call for that animal.

LEARNING HOW TO HELP

How can we accurately know what animals need? And how do we help animals fulfill those needs? The simple answer, though it's not simple at all, is that we look at their behavior. Sometimes our task is easy, as when we recognize and fulfill the needs and desires associated with pain, thirst, hunger, and being too cold or hot. But sometimes it is not. How, for example, can we tell if a cat has a headache? What if she is lonely or suffering—and I do mean suffering—from severe boredom due to being home alone all day? What signs should we look for? This is one of the biggest challenges in animal care.

As I will show throughout this book, a dog doesn't care if he comes from a long line of grand champion Cavalier King Charles spaniels and was just awarded Best in Show at the Westminster Dog Show. A Norwegian elkhound doesn't mind that she's been contemptuously labeled "pet quality" because she has an underbite, the wrong coat coloring, a limp tail, or is fearful of show judges. The starving, homeless mutt rummaging around in garbage cans for a morsel of food, the once-proud German shepherd who now languishes in an animal shelter, the pampered Persian cat in the Beverly Hills mansion, the pet cat who was simply left to fend for herself when her family moved away, and the determined Labrador retriever Search and Rescue dog trying to locate survivors in the rubble of an earthquake all care about one thing only: leading an enjoyable, happy life. One free of hurts and filled with pleasures.

Unpleasant feelings come in many forms—some are health-related, most are not—but they all inflict some form of hurt. Consider just a tiny number of the animals I care for. There's Tiger, the young Boxer who was brought in with a broken leg and then abandoned by his owner because he decided that the postoperative nursing care would be "too much work"; or Princess, the German shepherd who faithfully served as the elderly Mrs. Bellings' sole loving companion in her final years, and was now showing signs of a canine Alzheimer's-like disease; or the unnamed stray kitten who was found by the roadside, suffering from multiple broken bones and skull fractures after being struck by a car.

And consider the animals with emotional pain, such as Winnie, the homeless mixed-breed dog who had been bounced from foster home to foster home and in her current home lived in terror every time her new owner left, almost certainly from the intense insecurity of potentially being abandoned once again. Or Bessie, the sweet little white female cat with large black spots that made her look like a Holstein cow. Bessie's first owner died when the cat was 3 years old; her second owner passed away when she was 10; her third owner had to give Bessie up when she checked into a nursing home. Now Bessie's fourth owner sat across from me because, for the 4 months he had been caring for her, she hid under the bed all the time and quite understandably behaved like a person with clinical depression.

I spend my life protecting animals like these from their hurts. There is nothing more gratifying. I go to my animal hospital every day feeling blessed that today I get the opportunity to make animals feel good. I get to go home every day knowing that today many animals feel better because of something that I have done for them. I can't think of a more rewarding life.

LOOKING AHEAD

The purpose of this book is to offer you the knowledge and tools to make your own pet feel good. That may seem so obvious that it hardly needs stating—much less an entire book written about it. But the obviousness and simplicity of this concept belies its enormous scope. Feeling good is far more than feeling good *health*. Feeling good encompasses every aspect of life that matters to your pet.

Every single thing that goes on in your pet's life that she cares about is associated with a pleasant or unpleasant feeling. This is because of a very basic fact of the evolved brain: Feelings are what make animals, including humans, *care* about things. This simple fact gives us a phenomenal new and powerful tool to enrich the positive feelings of our pets' lives, to protect them from the hurts of life, and to give them emotional fulfillment, a fun-filled existence, and true happiness.

In this book I will present some of the recent scientific discoveries indicating not only that animals have feelings but that their feelings function virtually identically to ours. I will show you how these feelings dominate nearly every aspect of the lives of animals, and how pleasure, desire, pain, distress, suffering, joy, fun, hope, and even "gut feelings" all show evidence of being experienced as powerfully by the so-called "lesser" creatures as by humans.

In our journey, we will look at the latest research into the workings of the animal mind. As complex as the animal brain is, you might find yourself surprised at the extraordinarily simple logic that governs it. As we see what an animal's life experience truly consists of, it will become clear how all of us who care for animals in any capacity are striving to achieve the same goal, through different means.

One of the most important themes of this book is that all feelings speak the same language. In the animal mind, the feeling of loneliness is weighed in the same units as the feeling of hunger, the feelings of fear and coldness, and the feelings of pain and joy. The scale on which all feelings are registered weighs not in units of pounds and ounces, but in units of *pleasure*.

In the coming chapters, I will show you how feelings are believed to guide behavior—ours and our animals'. You'll see how emotions evolved to protect us: how they reward us for doing things that are good for us and punish us for things that are bad or dangerous. Fear, for example, protects us from risks to life, while love bonds us to others for the sake of safety and reproduction.

In this book, you will learn that the importance of emotions and feelings goes even further than determining how an animal feels. You'll see the impact of emotions—both pleasant and unpleasant—on your pet's physical health, and you'll learn how to use this knowledge to help restore and maintain his health. You'll meet many of the patients I have treated in my practice. You'll get to know Shawnee, the Labrador retriever who developed severe gastric upsets whenever the teenagers of the house fought with one another; Maggie, the miniature poodle who actually developed diabetes when she was ignored after a new baby arrived in the house; and Gooby, my own cat, who learned to tolerate pill time when he found that a walk always followed.

I will explain why understanding animal feelings is essential in making all decisions that affect your pet's well-being, from whether to spay and neuter to the heartbreaking decision to euthanize a beloved pet. And I will show you how familiarity with animal feelings will enable you to improve your pets' lives—to make sure that they have the opportunity to experience the happiest, healthiest, most emotionally fulfilled, and enjoyable lives possible.

Chapter 1

WHY FEELINGS RULE

AN INTERESTING THING HAPPENED when I served as the scientific advisor for the movie *Dr. Dolittle*. We were using live animals along with animatronic, or robotic, animals. One day on the set we filmed a scene where Eddie Murphy—Dr. Dolittle—takes his dog, Lucky, to the vet. The crew lifted Lucky onto the examination table so Dr. Dolittle could look on as the actor playing the veterinarian did the exam. The director, Betty Thomas, called me aside and asked how to make the scene look realistic. When you examine a dog, do you start at the head and end with the tail, or the other way around? How should the veterinarian place the stethoscope on the dog's chest?

I turned back to watch as the film began to roll and soon found myself astonished at Lucky's performance. He responded precisely on cue and did everything absolutely flawlessly, from shooting a wary glance at the veterinarian to cocking his ear when Dr. Dolittle spoke to him. When the human actors screwed up, and the scene had to be reshot, Lucky performed perfectly again. I felt a pang of sympathy for all this little creature had to go through for the sake of his art.

As I stood there in awe of the dog's Oscar-worthy "Best Canine Performance in a Movie," I happened to glance over to the side of the set— and was flabbergasted to see the real Lucky patiently sitting next to his trainer's chair. I looked back at the dog on the table, then once again back at Lucky, and realized that while I was talking with the director, they had switched the animal Lucky with the animatronic Lucky. I had been admiring the intelligence of—and feeling sympathy for—a machine, a nonconscious collection of moving mechanical parts. I had been completely fooled.

This incident got me thinking. For decades, many scientists have maintained that live animals, like the animatronic dog in the film, are essentially unconscious machines. Our pets' demonstrations of love and loyalty, their fears and hurts, the very essence of their personalities, are— in the views of some—nothing more than programmed responses. The existence of animal consciousness, emotions, and feelings, these skeptics point out, has not yet met the strict standards necessary to establish scientific certainty. Although what they say about scientific certainty is true, I have built my professional career on my conviction that animals do indeed think and feel, and that their emotions are every bit as real to them as our human emotions are to us.

Indeed, for most of us, the existence of animal feelings is intuitively obvious. For example, I'm sure you have read or seen stories about animal rescues. A kitten is stuck in a drainpipe for 4 days as worried neighbors and emergency personnel devise ways to save it. A firefighter is lowered by helicopter above a frozen river in an attempt to save a trembling dog stranded on an ice floe. Dozens of other examples come easily to mind, from headlines about beached whales to stories on television news shows about otters covered in oil from a tanker spill. Most of these relatively common incidents require not just one but teams of rescuers, involve great expense, and often pose substantial risk to human life.

No one would take such pains and risks to rescue a robot—the very idea is ludicrous. Why, then, do we go to such trouble to save imperiled animals? We do it for one reason only: animal feelings. If animals did not have feelings, every one of these animals could simply be ignored. No feelings, no suffering. But we don't ignore them. We know that the brains of these imperiled animals are generating very powerful feelings of fear and distress, and we cannot simply leave them to suffer.

THE POWER OF FEELINGS

It is the motivation to deliver feelings of comfort to distressed and suffering creatures that drives the rescue of trapped or injured animals. It is what impels a firefighter to endanger his own life to save a terrified dog trapped in a burning building. It is the reason that dozens of people will spend large amounts of money and time trying to rescue stranded dolphins and whales. It is why many of us will stop and try to help an injured cat or dog by the side of the road. And it is the motivating force behind my and many others' decisions to go into veterinary medicine.

So whether we're conscious of it or not, what drives us to help these animals all comes down to the way they *feel*. They feel the pain, they feel the fear and panic, they feel the relief from discomfort when they are rescued. Indeed, the only thing that matters to any of these animals is to be rescued from the intense discomfort they are experiencing. They want to feel good. It is *feelings*—comfort, pleasure, discomfort, and suffering—that matter. Feelings are the only thing that matters.

This same incredibly simple concept is what this book is about. Everything important in our animals' lives is experienced in the form of feelings. Nothing else is of concern to them. In caring for them, your pets want you only to attend to their feelings. The main idea of this book can be put into two words: *Feelings rule.*

In the years that I have practiced veterinary medicine, it has become clear to me that providing comfort to animals not only applies to medical care but is the goal of *all* animal care. I did not always understand this, however. After graduating from veterinary medical school at Ohio State University, I was fortunate to be chosen as one of the few to receive the most advanced post-graduate clinical training at the University of California at Davis, one of the top university veterinary teaching hospitals in the country. I ultimately reached the highest level of achievement in veterinary medicine: board-certified specialization in internal medicine. I represented the cutting edge of medical knowledge.

But something was missing from that knowledge. I was seeing many patients with disorders that weren't making sense. Diseases would come on, reoccur, and even go away for no known reason. The medical textbooks couldn't explain it. So I began asking the pet owners questions that also weren't in the textbooks—questions about their pets' living circumstances and emotional states when their illnesses began or went away.

Putting the Puzzle Together

An amazing picture began to emerge as I continued to gather information. I had owners keep diaries of their pets' symptoms. With their help, I discovered that one of the most powerful influences in all of animal health and disease was not a physical entity at all but a mental factor: the emotions deep inside the animals' minds. Once I began asking pet owners the right questions, that missing piece of the puzzle revealed itself.

For instance, there was the Great Dane whose skin periodically broke out in terrible boils. It was only after his owners began keeping a diary that we discovered the boils occurred only after his owners had loud arguments. Ginger, a tortoiseshell cat, had frequent diarrhea and vomiting—

A Vet's-Eye View

I cannot recall making the decision to become a veterinarian. It actually predates my earliest memories. I never wanted to be anything else. I'd have to say that being a veterinarian was always in me—as much as a person can be instilled at birth with a calling, that's what happened to me. Having the opportunity to live out my dream has been a blessing that I am grateful for every day, because caring for animals is the greatest privilege I could possibly know.

Including the time before attending veterinary school, I have worked in an animal hospital for the past 30 years. There are few places on earth where one can be closer to animals or develop a better feel for what goes on in their complex minds. I encounter every kind of distress and suffering—in the form of illness, injury, abandonment, homelessness, emotional disturbance, and all types of physical and emotional abuse. I also see happy, well-cared-for animals who are living enjoyable, fun, and fulfilling lives. In all of this, I witness the incredible emotional bond between pets and their human companions.

For three decades, I have sat face to face with animals who have needs and desires. And what these years of experience have taught me is that *animals want what we want.* They want comfort, peace of mind, and happiness. Everything they do is designed to achieve those goals. Knowing this is the key to enjoying a wonderful, rewarding relationship with the pets you love.

---

but only when her owners left home for a few days. Another cat, Cosby, experienced bladder problems when Chaz, the other, more dominant, cat in the house, picked on him. Even obesity—which most vets and pet owners assume is simply due to overeating—often turns out to be a result of emotional problems, just as it is in people. And I encountered many animals that developed a variety of illnesses when a companion—

human or animal—died. Unfortunately, the "cutting edge" of medicine did not address the role of the animal mind in illness. When I started tending to the emotional lives of my patients, I found that I could help many health disorders more successfully than when I used only the standard textbook approaches. But something else—far more important— also occurred. My animal patients' enjoyment of life was greatly improved. Making their lives fun and relieving the painful emotions of loneliness, boredom, fear, and anxiety resulted in much happier animals.

I came to see that focusing on the animals' feelings is more than an important aspect of animal care—it is the *only* aspect of care that matters. By ignoring the immense importance of the feelings that animals experience every moment of their lives, all fields of animal care had been missing the boat. As logical as it seems, though, putting feelings back into animal care isn't an easy task. In fact, it was only recently that the mind was even considered as a part of *human* health.

This separation of the mental aspects of animals and people from the physical began some 400 years ago with the philosopher Rene Descartes. At that time, Descartes wanted to study the human body, but the Catholic Church disapproved of any close examination of God's handiwork. Descartes responded by dividing human existence into two realms: the physical, which he would study, and the mental/spiritual, which would remain the exclusive domain of the Church. This artificial construct, dividing the mental from the physical, has dominated virtually all scientific and medical thought to this day.

The situation with regard to animals has been an almost complete split between the physical, observable animal body and the animal mind, which many people continue to deny experiences any feelings at all. If you're like most pet owners, by now you're probably exclaiming, "But that's not true!" After all, you've seen a whole range of feelings in your beloved animal companions. And, as we shall see, this time it's you, not the "experts," who are correct.

CONSCIOUSNESS AND FEELINGS

As far as we know now, feelings are conscious mental experiences, and to have them requires consciousness. Let's look at one common mental experience: the feeling of pain. Few people—either nonscientists or scientists—would deny that animals feel pain. The lion cub I held in my arms who whimpered sadly was expressing pain. His owner had been feeding him an unbalanced diet, which resulted in brittle bones that were broken in many places. He was in pain in virtually every part of his body.

The 90-pound dog lying in the middle of the street was in pain. When I tried to pick her up to take her to my animal hospital, she whipped her head around and bit hard into my face, tearing open my cheek. We found out later that she had a broken back from being hit by a car, and I had touched her fractured spine. Twenty-eight years later, the scar on my face remains glaring testimony to the existence of animal pain.

In every way we can tell, pain in animals acts virtually identically to pain in people. In the course of my day, I might pull a big thorn out of dog's paw, give an injection, squeeze an abscess on a cat's toe, feel the swelling around a broken bone, put pressure on an overly full bladder, press against a loose tooth, bend a swollen knee joint, touch the surface of an eye, and feel the back of a dog with a slipped disc. In every case, the animal will respond in a way that is very similar to the way a person would respond under the same conditions: by flinching, protecting the painful body part, crying out, moaning, or remaining inactive. In all but speech, an animal's reaction to pain is virtually indistinguishable from a person's.

Ironically, the scientists who deny that animals feel pain are often the

The Black Box of the Mind

Today mind/body medicine is on the leading edge of the healing arts—for humans. Unfortunately for animals, many still regard animals as having very limited mental lives. This situation is partly due to concern by early 20th-century researchers in psychology and animal behavior that their fields were not accepted as "hard" or "real" science.

In a hugely influential paper addressing animal and human behavior, the famous psychological theorist J. B. Watson entreated his fellow psychologists to abandon concern with such a vague and nonscientific concept as consciousness. Unlike the objects of study in physics and chemistry, consciousness and its associated notions (mind, emotions, feelings) could not be directly observed, measured, or verified. Watson thus implored those in his field to concentrate solely on behavior, which *could* be seen, measured, and verified. In other words, Watson proposed that all animal—as well as human—behavior should be treated exclusively as a simple stimulus-response reaction, and animals should be regarded as simple machines without thought or feelings.

To this day, emotions and feelings in animals are too often ignored. Animal trainers, animal behaviorists, and animal psychologists rarely discuss feelings in animals, even while they work very closely with the animal mind. Clinical animal behaviorists—professionals who work with animals showing unusual or undesirable behavior—often use principles based on a school of psychology called Behaviorism, which involves a stimulus and response but pays little (if any) regard to what goes on in the so-called

ones who, through their work, affirm the existence of animal pain. Pain researchers who use animals to study and develop better ways to treat human pain are basing their research on the assumption that animals do feel pain as we do (if they didn't, then applying this research to humans would be completely useless). Today, with the mountain of evidence accumulated from animal pain research, denying that animals feel pain—that they *hurt*—is simply absurd.

black box of the mind. For example, hold a piece of meat in front of your dog, and the dog follows you. Stimulus: food; response: follow. For strict Behaviorists, it simply is not necessary to know that in the "black box," a feeling of hunger motivates the dog's response.

Trainers, clinical behaviorists, and animal psychologists use these well-known principles of learning theory—and they get results. In their lectures and books, there is little if any discussion about feelings. Instead, the focus is on stimulus and response, reward and punishment, conditioning and counterconditioning. If you peruse the indexes of the vast majority of animal behavior books, you will turn up precious little under the word "emotion," and the word "feeling" is found about as often as "telepathy."

Although some scientists have recently begun to study mental states in animals, the animal behavior departments of virtually every university in the world and every veterinary college have focused almost exclusively on observable behavior and the physical body. Scientists are warned to avoid anthropomorphism—attributing human feelings, thoughts, or emotions to animals, particularly ones that they study or work with. Furthermore, many scientists—and others in industries that make use of animals—have a personal stake in denying that animals have feelings: After all, if animals do not have feelings, they cannot suffer, so the use of animals in medical research, circuses, rodeos, bullfights, zoos, and intensive farming would pose no moral problems.

Given that animals feel pain, is there any likelihood that pain is the *only* feeling that they experience? What about fear, loneliness, anger, love, joy, anticipation, or any of the myriad other emotions we all feel every day? What of hunger, thirst, and exhaustion? That evolution would have created just one feeling in nonhuman animals defies any reasonable logic. And, as we will see, the rich variety of animal feelings serves an amazing number of important functions.

We know, of course, that people have all these feelings. And we know that *our* feelings are the most prominent guides for our behavior. So much of what we do is because of the feelings we experience—we eat because we are hungry; we care for our children because we love them. Now consider this: If animals are doing all the things they do *without* feelings, why and how, in the course of evolution, did feelings arise in human beings? In other words, if things were working so well without feelings, why did they evolve at all in any species? And why would they pop up only when humans arrived on the evolutionary scene?

Animal Emotions

Recently, animal emotions have begun to receive some long-overdue attention. Books such as Jeffrey Masson and Susan McCarthy's *When Elephants Weep,* Masson's *Dogs Never Lie about Love* and *The Nine Emotional Lives of Cats,* Marc Bekoff's *The Smile of a Dolphin* and *Minding Animals,* and veterinary behaviorist Nicholas Dodman's *The Dog Who Loved Too Much* and *The Cat Who Cried for Help* have provided a first look at the rich emotional lives of animals.

But, as is true of so many supposedly "modern" concepts, the idea of emotions in animals is not new. More than 2,000 years ago, Aristotle confronted the issue when he stated, "Any organism that has senses has pleasure and pain. Desire resides in these organisms that experience pleasure and pain. Desire is an appetite for the pleasant."

The mere existence of animal emotions is not the main idea of this book—it is the starting point. In the next chapters, we will take an extensive look at all feelings, of which emotions are only one source. We'll examine feelings that come from physical conditions, such as an itch, a cold blast of wind, the bloated feeling of overeating as well as the obvious thirst, hunger, and, of course, pain. We will be spending most of our time looking at the feelings of emotions—such as fear, loneliness, boredom, frustration, and grief. And of course, we'll examine the pleasurable feelings as well—the things that make your pet feel good.

We'll see how each of these feelings guides the everyday actions of your cat or dog, and how they all come together in your pet's mind to create his sense of well-being, his emotional fulfillment, and the very quality of his life. Most important, we'll see how being aware of your pet's feelings—*all* of them—will help you to really understand your furry companion and provide him with the best life possible.

HOW FEELINGS GAINED CONTROL OF THE ANIMAL MIND

To understand how feelings came to occupy such a dominant position in animal lives, we need to take a look at the evolutionary view of the animal brain (and don't forget—this includes *your* brain, too).

The chief driving force behind evolution is nearly unanimously considered to be the process of natural selection. This principle, simply put, states that the plants and animals that are best adapted to environmental demands survive to pass on their genes. Those that are less well adapted die off. Success in natural selection is defined by producing the largest number of offspring that themselves will produce offspring.

In the course of animal evolution, natural selection led to the development of a nervous system, which in the higher animals consists of the brain and the spinal cord (together called the central nervous system), and the outer nerves. This remarkable innovation enabled the different cells, organs, and systems of the body to communicate with one another, which in turn allowed animals with a nervous system to rapidly process and respond to threats and opportunities. The animals with the most complex nervous systems—especially its main component, the brain—are the vertebrates, which include mammals, fish, reptiles, amphibians, and birds.

When an animal with a central nervous system is faced with a real or perceived threat or opportunity, the central nervous system assesses the threat or opportunity's importance, and then organizes a response, which may include

❖ Physiological and immunological changes (attacking a virus with white blood cells, increased bloodflow to the extremities)

❖ Psychological responses (coping, adapting to a situation, falling in love)

❖ Behavioral responses (avoidance, escape, approach)

These responses further the goal of natural selection, enabling the animal to survive and reproduce. Over the course of evolution, those animals with brains that were best at these tasks produced the most offspring; these offspring had brains that were even better at it, and so on, until we have the animals of today—highly efficient self-protectors and reproducers.

CHOICES, CHOICES

As more complex organisms faced more complex environmental problems, behavior also had to become more complex. Simple reflex actions—such as an eye blink in response to something nearing the eye—were no longer enough to assure that the animal would thrive and reproduce. Instead, conscious decision-making became necessary, and the animal now needed guides to make the best decisions. These guides were the forerunners of what we now know as feelings.

On the surface, it might appear that logical thinking, which is the logical way of looking at the world, should be a valid and perhaps even superior way to make decisions. But bear in mind that every situation that we sentient (feeling) animals face—not just minute by minute, but second

The Computer in Your Dog's (or Cat's) Head

Conscious decision-making coincided with development of the mind, which—and this may come as a surprise until you really think about it—is different from the brain. The brain is an anatomical structure, consisting of specialized tissues (gray matter and white matter) that coordinate physiological and behavioral functions. The mind, on the other hand, is the part of the animal that we think of as the mental life, the entity that possesses thoughts, emotions, feelings, desires, and sufferings. In many ways, the mind can be viewed as the software within the hardware of the brain, largely "written" by natural selection to solve the problems of daily living. The mind uses feelings to guide the decisions involved in solving these problems.

by second—can be responded to in an infinite number of ways. Let's take an example. Say you are hiking in the woods, and an enraged 900-pound brown bear jumps into your path and starts after you. What should you do? You have an endless list of choices from which to choose. You could whistle "Dixie." You could snap a picture with your camera. You could count the hairs on your knuckles. You could ponder who might win the next World Series. Or you could run.

Of these and the countless other options, how do you know what to do? There has to be some mental process that rapidly narrows down your infinite options to one or two, guiding you to make an appropriate behavioral choice—and fast. There has to be something that prevents you from practicing your golf swing, or perfecting your Jack Nicholson impersonation. Because making the wrong choice or taking too long to decide could result in your becoming the bear's dinner. Now consider the brown bear. She's a mother bear, with her two infant cubs by her side.

She sees you getting closer and closer, and she senses a danger to her cubs. What should she do? Gaze at the sun? Shake her front foot in the air? Groom herself? Spin in circles? Chase you away? There needs to be something that narrows her choices to the right one, and fast.

Luckily for both you and the bear, her concern for her cubs leads her to chase you away, while your fear impels you to run as fast as you can. Considering the vast number of choices available, both of you have hit on the ones that offer the best possibility of survival for you, the bear, and her cubs.

For every situation a person or animal faces, there are a number of questions that must be asked.

- What should I do?
- How urgent is it?
- How hard should I work at doing it?
- How do I know when to stop doing it?
- How will I know that something else is now more important to do?

Although you may not be aware of it, your mind is constantly answering every one of these questions, but not by pondering each one and rationally arriving at the answer. (You'd be dead if that's how your behavior were guided.) Instead, your mind uses a message system that you can't help but listen to—the system of feelings.

THE GOOD SIDE OF FEELING BAD

Though we don't enjoy them, unpleasant feelings are simply one of the ways we protect ourselves. They are the signal that something important and potentially detrimental is happening and needs to be tended to.

Some threats, such as a viral infection, require a response that happens inside the body without conscious action. But many threats demand a behavioral response. For example, if the temperature outside is too cold, your cat will try to come inside or find a warmer spot. If your dog picks up a thorn in her foot, she'll shift more of her weight to the other feet— which will help keep the thorn from going further in. She will also lick at the thorn in an effort to relieve the pain, which may manage to dislodge it. Her actions are a response to the unpleasant feeling of pain. They are designed to solve the immediate problem and help to prevent further injury.

How did this important protective system evolve? Our best guess is that over the course of millions of years of threats to well-being—and millions of years of responses to these threats—the conscious mind became wired in such a way that threats that required a behavioral response became associated with unpleasant feelings. This quality of unpleasantness was crucial for two reasons. First, it commanded the animal's attention, which is critical when a threat appears. These feelings are *meant* to hurt so that the animal will care about them and not ignore their presence. Second, the very unpleasantness of the feelings motivates the animal to do whatever is necessary to lessen the intensity of the feeling. The greater the intensity of unpleasantness, the more intense the effort to address and correct the problem. The intensity also tells the animal when to stop focusing on the problem: When the intensity subsides, the effort can end. Once your cat has warmed up, he stops looking for a warmer place. When your dog's foot heals, she can stop limping and licking it. This all happens beneath the level of consciousness: By simply responding to unpleasant feelings, the animal lessens any threat to its well-being or life without even being aware of the ultimate goal of its action. Feelings act like the voice of a caring mother who tells her children what to do and not do for their own good, while thinking silently, "You'll thank me for this later."

A World without Feelings

To understand the immense importance of feelings in animal life, imagine two worlds on which very different types of animals evolved. On one, as on earth, the animals developed a conscious mind with a full array of feelings that guide their behavior. On the other, the animals developed a conscious mind *without* feelings. All of their behavior is guided solely by unfeeling thought or pure reason. These animals behave much as a robot might behave.

For the feeling animals, encounters with danger elicit fear and an immediate self-protective response. A torn ligament in the leg elicits pain and a shift of weight off the injured leg, while an approaching forest fire brings forth a different feeling of pain, prompting the animal to flee to a safe distance from the heat. Hunger signals the need to eat, and feelings of fullness signal when to stop eating. The feeling of a full bladder tells the animal it is time to relieve itself, and a sex drive pushes the animal to find a partner and mate. When a feeling animal is faced simultaneously with several situations that each require a response, his feelings alert him which is the most urgent. His behavioral choices are guided quickly, efficiently, and nearly flawlessly to benefit his survival and well-being. He makes very few mistakes.

For the unfeeling, robot-like animals, life is completely different. When a flying predator swoops down from the sky, the prey animal feels no fear;

HOW FEELINGS FOCUS ATTENTION

The conscious mind experiences feelings of some sort almost every waking moment. Even if something distracting happens, unpleasant feelings act as a continual reminder, with growing urgency, to tend to the cause of the feeling and thereby lessen the threat.

To illustrate, let's look at how human feelings work. Suppose you are hungry, but as you look for food, something else captures your attention.

instead, it needs to think about what this may mean and then ponder what the best response might be. A torn ligament causes no pain, so the animal must first somehow figure out that his leg is injured and needs to be rested, then somehow calculate how much weight to take off his leg as he steps. Without a feeling of pain as a guide, he must figure out when the healing is complete and he can stop limping. An animal that isn't able to feel the approaching fire must ponder the best course of action in response to this interesting-looking, bright orange, crackling phenomenon. If he takes too long to decide to flee, he can look down and watch his flesh burning, then decide if this is a reason to move along.

On the planet of robot-like animals, every behavioral choice must be pondered and reasoned out. If fast action is needed—such as fleeing a predator or protecting an injured body part—the animal had better be an extremely fast thinker. And he'd better not forget anything, like eating, drinking, or sleeping. On this planet, mistakes, slow responses, and harmful behavioral choices are common. Now imagine that the animals of these two worlds are suddenly put together on a third planet, placing them in competition for resources and survival. One group is armed with feelings; the other makes every behavioral choice by thinking the situation through and then acting. Which group of animals is more likely to survive and prosper?

You needn't worry that you'll now forget to eat because your feelings of hunger will continue to hound you until you do.

Thanks to feelings, you never have to worry about forgetting to drink, or sleep, or eliminate—these activities are far too important for evolution to have left in the hands (actually, mind) of the individual to figure out or to risk forgetting. Your mind is constructed to continuously direct your attention to what is important until you attend to it. As a given feeling increases in intensity, your attention is increasingly directed to *that* matter and less and less to other, less urgent matters.

Imagine that you're sitting on an airplane in the window seat, reading a book on a 5-hour flight. You feel the first urge of needing to visit the bathroom but don't want to wake up the two people asleep in the seats between you and the aisle. You continue reading, but as the feeling of a filling bladder intensifies, your mind more and more frequently causes you to check whether the people are still asleep. You find yourself trying to think up strategies of how to get to the bathroom. You try to go back to reading, but in a very short time, you are looking at your watch to see how much time is left before you land, and you wonder if you can hold out until then. Eventually, you can't read even one word of your book. Your mind is focused on one thing, and one thing only: "I've got to get relief!"

The feeling of a full bladder is a physical-based feeling. Emotion-based feelings work in the same way. Suppose it's late at night, and you're at home alone watching a movie. Suddenly you hear a loud thump in the next room. Or did you? Your heart rate jumps up a bit, and you're a little frightened, because there have been some break-ins in your neighborhood recently. You listen intently, but after a few minutes, you hear nothing more, so you go back to watching the movie.

A few minutes later you hear a shuffling sound—like footsteps, you think. Now your heart is racing. What to do? Call the police? If someone is in the next room, what if he hears the call? You frantically look around for something you may be able to use as a weapon. You're sweating, but again, after a few minutes of no new sounds, you try to return to the movie. But you can't follow it. Your mind is focused on the other rooms in your house, on high alert and intently trying to pick up on every little noise. Finally, upon seeing your cat wander in from the next room and realizing that he was the culprit making all the noise, your one-track mind is immediately allowed to relax and go back to focusing on the movie.

The same sort of thing happens all the time in nature. On the African savannah, the impala cautiously approaches a water hole to alleviate his thirst. Every little noise in the surrounding brush is a possible lion. So any sound elicits fear, which directs his attention away from the water to the more important noise. Only when it is quiet can the impala focus on the water to take his drink.

HOW FEELINGS SET PRIORITIES

The example of the impala and the lion illustrates a function of feelings very closely related to the focus of attention. When two or more matters compete for an animal's attention and require different behavioral responses, how does the animal know which one is most important? In the impala's case, two unpleasant feelings are guiding his behavior: thirst and fear. Should he drink, or should he flee?

Feelings sort this problem out for us. Unpleasant feelings, through the discomfort they inflict, prioritize the urgency of threats. Sometimes, as in the impala's case, the priority changes quickly, possibly second by second. One moment the priority is drinking, then, on hearing a sound, it shifts to fleeing.

This situation—changing priorities—is why the normally intense unpleasantness of pain may be overridden by other, more urgent, matters. If the impala were to slip on a rock and break a bone in his foot while leaning over to drink, the feeling of pain would command more immediate attention than his thirst. Following this behavioral guide, he would shift weight off that leg, relieving the pain, and thirst would once again be top priority. But if a lion then leaped from the bushes, in that instant,

Calculated Feelings

An interesting way of looking at how feelings work is presented by Steven Pinker, professor of psychology at Harvard University, in his book *How the Mind Works*. In Pinker's view, feelings represent the accumulated wisdom that our ancestors' genes used to build brains. Over the span of millions of generations, the brains of modern animals (including us) became wired to make cost/benefit evaluations for commonly encountered situations. For example, the benefit for a snowshoe hare in venturing out of its burrow to find food comes with the cost of potentially being killed by a coyote; the benefit for a male chimpanzee in mating with a nearby female comes with the cost of potentially being punished by the alpha male; the benefit for a cheetah in chasing a gazelle comes with the cost of energy expenditure in the chase.

Pinker believes that these cost/benefit calculations are automatically generated by the brain and delivered in the form of feelings. They are, quite literally, calculated feelings.

To see how this works, imagine that you're on a hike, and you come upon a cliff edge overlooking a 200-foot drop. Bam! Instantaneous cost/benefit calculations are performed in your mind. The action with the best odds for self-benefit: *Don't go near the cliff edge!* Feeling delivered to you: *fear.* In this instance, fear is the cost/benefit calculation of the best action to take when standing near a cliff edge: Keep your distance.

Or suppose you're jogging, and you twist your ankle. Bam! Instantaneous cost/benefit calculation: *Don't put full weight on this leg!* Feeling delivered to you: *pain.* In this instance, that's what the feeling of pain is: the cost/benefit calculation of what to do when tissues are damaged in your ankle joint. Finally, imagine that you're under water, and the breath you took is running out. Bam! Instantaneous cost/benefit calculation: *Get to the surface now!* Feelings delivered to you: *oxygen deprivation, terror, and panic.* These feelings are giving you the instructions to do what, in evolutionary history, has been the most successful behavioral choice: Get oxygen.

the most urgent matter for the impala becomes escaping certain death. The feeling of fear then takes command of his attention, thus shifting his priorities once again. He bounds off, with little notice of either his thirst or the pain in his foot. Once he has successfully eluded the lion and relaxes, the fear dissipates, and his attention is again directed toward his feelings of thirst and pain.

This shifting focus of attention appears to be one of the main reasons feelings evolved: to set priorities. Feelings focus the mind on the matter most urgent and important to well-being at that moment. Feelings prioritize through an internal system of reward and punishment that is wired into the brain. This system is no different from externally applied systems of reward and punishment, such as those used to train lab rats to run through mazes, or some methods of dog training, in which a dog is rewarded with a treat for the desired behavior and scolded or ignored for failing to perform. Unpleasant feelings deliver punishment from *within* in order to make sure that the animal does certain things and refrains from doing others.

The fact that the unpleasantness of the feelings closely coincides with the degree of threat to life is exactly the way the tinkerings of evolution constructed it to be.

FEELINGS: THE BRIGHT SIDE

The mental health field in humans has maintained, until quite recently, a very lopsided focus on the negative aspects of mental health and well-being. In fact, psychology's first century was dominated by studies of the negative life experiences of unhappiness, depression, despair, discontent, and grief, while largely ignoring the positive aspects of life. Recently, this lopsided focus has begun to change. A new generation of researchers has

Is Suffering a Bad Thing?

Unpleasant feelings are the source of all discomfort, misery, and suffering in the world, and it is tempting to wish the world could be free of them. In fact, eliminating suffering in the world is often viewed as the quintessential human dream. But would this really be a good idea? After all, the unpleasant feelings that constitute suffering are instrumental in protecting all conscious beings from harm.

This principle applies to all unpleasant feelings, even those that you may not think about. For example, why does it hurt your eyes to look directly at the sun? This reaction is no accident. The discomfort exists to prevent animals from staring at the sun, burning out their retinas, and going blind.

The value of unpleasant feelings is dramatically demonstrated in people who have a rare disorder called congenital analgesia. People with this condition are born without innate pain sensors, so they literally feel no pain. Without the crucial protection of pain, they experience cuts, burns, injuries—even broken bones—throughout their lives that the rest of us can easily avoid.

Without pain, these unfortunate people receive no messages that tissue is being damaged, so their joints become destroyed by continual overextension and stress. Without pain, they are not alerted to early infections, such as a tooth abscess or hepatitis, so the infections can become life-threatening before they are discovered. These individuals almost always die before they reach 30 years of age, a result of feeling no pain.

So, would you be helping or hurting the Earth's creatures if you were to eliminate the capacity to suffer? By taking away one of the most important survival mechanisms sentient animals have, your action would almost certainly lead to mass extinctions.

turned their attention to the positive side of life, to feelings of happiness and satisfaction. A new field, called Positive Psychology, has recently emerged and has led to a surge of new books in only the past 3 years, such as *Authentic Happiness: Using the New Positive Psychology to Realize Your Potential for Lasting Fulfillment; Flourishing: Positive Psychology and the Life Well-Lived;* and *What Happy People Know: How the New Science of Happiness Can Change Your Life for the Better.*

The situation with regard to the psychology of animals has a long way to go to catch up. Writings on psychological well-being in animals have until very recently focused exclusively on negative mental states, what causes them, and how to relieve them.

Relieving pain and discomfort are certainly an important part of animal care, but the positive side—mental wellness and the pleasant feelings of life—is equally if not more important in making an animal's life a thoroughly fulfilled, pleasurable, and fun experience.

Chapter 2

THE COMFORT ZONE

IN THIS CHAPTER, I'm going to introduce the first of two important concepts that redefine the way we relate to our pets. These concepts are the keys to understanding our pets' behavior—why they act the way they do in any given circumstance, what causes them to "misbehave," and what we can do about it. I call these concepts the Comfort Zone (which I discuss here) and The Pet Pleasure Principle (which I'll cover in Chapter 3).

THE COMFORT ZONE

To see most clearly what my concept of the Comfort Zone is, let's look at animals in their native habitats in the wild. First, picture the polar bear in his natural environment deep in the Arctic Circle. Temperatures here may drop lower than 100 degrees below zero. Yet he seems content and relaxed as he goes about his daily affairs. He lounges on an ice floe for a while, then meanders over to the icy waters, where he dives in and catches a fish in his mouth. He climbs back onto the ice floe and eagerly consumes the tasty morsel. With food in his stomach, he lies down again on the snowy surface. He's feeling good. This is a life of comfort.

Now picture the Bactrian camel in the searing heat of the Gobi Desert. He has not taken a drink of water in 3 weeks, well beyond the time when almost any other animal, including humans, would have perished from dehydration. But this is his home, and he's feeling good. For him, this is a life of comfort.

Finally, picture the little brown bat in his home: a cold, clammy, pitch-black cave. It is a sightless world in which he hangs upside down for the vast portion of each day, flying off to catch and eat juicy insects for his meals. Not a life for you or me, but this life feels good to him. It is a life of comfort.

Each of these animals has a life that consists predominantly of comfort. Yet if any of them were to be put in another's home, they would lose not only their feelings of comfort but also most likely their lives. Understanding the importance and nature of comfort is one of the prime lessons for us in caring for our pets.

HOME SWEET HOME

It makes sense that the best environment for an animal is the one that offers the best and largest choice of food, the best and safest places to hide, the best and most comfortable temperatures to live in, and the best and safest activities to engage in. In short, an animal generally feels the most comfort in its natural environment.

Each animal's body and brain have evolved to match its natural environment. This is the reason for the polar bear's very thick fur coat and foot pads—to neutralize the adverse effects of the intense cold. This is why he enjoys the taste of raw fish and likes to lounge on the ice. Putting a polar bear into the Gobi Desert or a Bactrian camel onto the Arctic ice floe would pose extreme dangers for the relocated animals. And that danger would be signaled through feelings of discomfort.

COMFORT AND THE COMFORT ZONE

The polar bear, the Bactrian camel, and the little brown bat are all comfortable in their natural environments because their good feelings correspond with the conditions in their preferred living space. This was no accident. Throughout the history of life on Earth, all animals have faced challenges specific to their home environments, and natural selection has guided them in adapting to meet those challenges. Over hundreds of thousands—and in some cases, millions—of years of fine-tuning, every species has become ideally fitted to its home environment.

Not only have animals developed such useful physical features as speed, acute sense of smell, night vision, camouflage coloring, quills, and sonar-guided navigation, they have also developed feelings that promote survival and reproduction. The result is that pleasant and enjoyable feelings have become linked to behaviors that are beneficial to life, while unpleasant feelings are linked to things and behaviors that are harmful. Every animal feels best in the environment his ancestors successfully thrived in. So the polar bear, the camel, and the bat, assuming no unusual threats or disease, each live a life of general comfort. Each enjoys plenty of time in its Comfort Zone.

The Comfort Zone is one of the most important concepts in the care of animals. I define comfort as the mental state that occurs when no unpleasant feelings—or discomforts—are occurring (or at worst, they're minimal). Comfort is a state of ease and peaceful contentment. Discomfort, on the other hand, consists of all unpleasant feelings, both physical and emotional. Common physical discomforts include pain, sick feelings, nausea, itching, oxygen deprivation, thirst, hunger, and temperature extremes. Emotional sources of discomfort include fear, anxiety, frustration, boredom, broken or impaired social bonds, loneliness, separation anxiety, grief, and depression.

It may seem strange to refer to unpleasant emotional feelings as discomforts. Touching a hot stove is a discomfort, a grain of sand in your eye is a discomfort, but loneliness? Or boredom? But consider what it feels like when you glance in your car's rearview mirror and see a police car following you closely. Or your feeling when it's been half an hour since your child was due home from school, and she hasn't arrived yet. These are feelings that, until they are gone, will effectively prevent you from being in a state of comfort. An emotional discomfort may not feel the same as a physical discomfort, but it can be every bit as unpleasant.

Comfort and discomfort can be seen as existing on a simple continuum, in which the state of comfort—what I am calling the Comfort Zone—is on the left, and discomfort is on the right. When an animal moves toward the right of the continuum, discomfort grows in intensity; moving toward the left lessens discomfort, until the Comfort Zone is reached.

The Comfort Zone is the area of peace of mind that all sentient animals—including people—desire. Seeking comfort is the means by which nature pushes animals to do things that are good for them and avoid those that are bad for them. When an animal can stay inside his Comfort Zone, he feels good mentally and physically. Life in the Comfort Zone is the good life.

To show how the Comfort Zone works, I've created the Comfort Zone Scale. At the far left of the Scale is comfort. Reaching this place is the goal of most animal behavior. By contrast, at the far right end of the Comfort Zone Scale is suffering. As a discomfort—such as hunger or fear—increases in intensity, the animal's position on the Comfort Zone Scale moves farther to the right. If it moves far enough, the animal

THE COMFORT ZONE SCALE

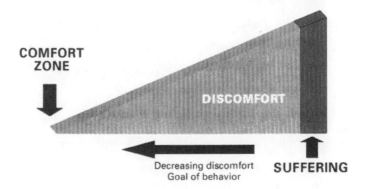

COMFORT ZONE

DISCOMFORT

Decreasing discomfort
Goal of behavior

SUFFERING

experiences suffering. The important thing to realize in caring for your pet is that the farther to the right he is on the Comfort Zone Scale, the greater the intensity of his discomfort and the greater the urgency to alleviate the discomfort. For all animal caregivers—pet guardians, veterinarians, zookeepers, and the like—our urgency in caring for an animal in discomfort rises correspondingly.

How the Comfort Zone Works

For all animals, the Comfort Zone is a kind of early-warning system that a potential threat exists. Whenever unpleasant feelings move your pet out of his Comfort Zone, he knows—actually, *feels*—that he must perform some action to return to a state of comfort. There are two main kinds of threats that the Comfort Zone alerts him to: needs and straightforward threats.

Needs

The Comfort Zone concept is intimately connected to needs, such as sleep, food, and water, which are required for mental and physical well-being. If needs are unmet, then the animal's well-being and possibly life are at risk. The animal's mind is wired to detect unmet needs and signal them in the form of negative feelings.

A good example of how unpleasant feelings signal unmet physical needs are the feelings of distress and panic caused by insufficient oxygen.

Discomfort Is Discomfort

For your pet, there is no meaningful distinction between physical and emotional sources of discomfort. Both are ultimately experienced as unpleasant feelings. Animals, like us, desire to be rid of unpleasant feelings, regardless of their origin.

Both physical and emotional sources of discomfort can be intense enough to constitute suffering. Both can be caused by external means, which is exactly what punishment, abuse, torment, and even torture really are: the external activation of an animal's (or human's) internally wired feeling mechanisms. Pain, loneliness (through solitary confinement), starvation, and fear have all been used by humans as methods of torture. All involve intentionally raising the individual's own self-protective feelings to an intolerably high level.

For any punishment to be effective, an animal must be mentally wired for the specific internal self-directed punishment. For example, using social isolation as a punishment would work for a chimpanzee but not for an orangutan. Unlike the highly social chimp, who would experience unpleasant emotions when denied companionship, the orangutan lives a solitary life in nature. It has no mental wiring for the unpleasant emotion of loneliness, which would otherwise motivate it to seek companionship.

Both physical and emotional discomfort can have long-term consequences. Just as in people, animals that go through a severe emotional trauma may suffer indelible psychological scars that can trouble them for their entire lives. This is just one reason why it's so important to keep your pet protected from these discomforts—secure in his or her Comfort Zone.

Thirst, hunger, salt cravings, and the discomfort of a full bladder are other obvious examples of feelings signaling unmet physical needs.

Unpleasant feelings also signal unmet emotional needs, such as the need for companionship or mental stimulation (which I discuss in detail in Chapter 4, "Soothing Hurt Feelings"). So another way to look at the Comfort Zone is that it is the place your pet is in when her physical and emotional needs are adequately met. When those needs aren't met, she is out of her Comfort Zone until her needs *can* be met.

All needs and their associated feelings vary from animal to animal. For example, some dogs thrive with a minimum of human companionship, whereas others need much more. Bobo, a super-affectionate, curly-haired little male dog that appeared to be a cross between a miniature poodle and a Chihuahua, was adopted from the animal shelter by the Brenners, clients of mine, after having been unsuccessfully placed in three previous homes. Prior to that, he had been found living in the streets.

Although Bobo was a loving addition to the household, the Brenners soon noticed that he never spent a minute away from at least one of his human family members, clinging to them and following them wherever they went. Mrs. Brenner became exasperated, and told me that she thought Bobo was insecure and needy. "It's as if he needs affection as much as food," she said.

"That's exactly it," I told her. "For Bobo, affection and companionship are needs, like food and air. But he's so insecure, he can't trust that your affection will last." I explained that dogs shuffled from home to home, where they can never develop a sense of stability, trust, and confidence, become more insecure with every change. They also can become needy. *Very* needy. "I've seen situations like Bobo's," I went on, "where the poor dog clings more tightly to each new adopter, seemingly in perpetual fear of being separated again from his current human companions."

I told the Brenners that Bobo's insecurity would gradually lessen as he gained trust in his new situation. And that's exactly what happened. It took almost a full year, but Bobo did regain his sense of security and trust in people, eventually showing a doggy confidence as if he owned the place. But during his traumatic shelter days and for some time after, his exceptionally high emotional need for stable companionship placed Bobo far, far outside his Comfort Zone. Mr. and Mrs. Brenner are now as happy as Bobo is that he lives a newly secure life in his Comfort Zone. (For more on dealing with insecure dogs, see Chapter 6, "Ain't Misbe-havin'.")

Straightforward Threats

A looming predator, the heat of a nearby fire, eating a toxic substance, excessive pressure against a body part, getting something caught in the windpipe—these situations do not involve needs, but they do trigger feelings of discomfort that move an animal outside his Comfort Zone.

One morning, I received a call from Josh, a graduate student in anthropology, about his male mixed breed cat, Mugsy. He told me that in the past few months, Mugsy, who was an indoor-outdoor cat, had begun acting afraid of cars. Whenever a car passed Josh's house, if Mugsy was inside, he would run behind the sofa, and if he was outside, he would bound inside through the pet door and into the laundry room behind the washer. Although his house wasn't on a particularly busy street, Josh said, there were enough cars during the day to keep Mugsy in a fairly continuous anxious state. I asked Josh the obvious question, "Was Mugsy ever hit by a car?"

"Never," Josh said, "At least not since I've had him." I told Josh to bring Mugsy in at his convenience for a checkup. Two weeks later, Josh showed up with Mugsy—and with an interesting story about him.

"A couple of days after our phone conversation," Josh told me, "Mugsy disappeared. I was in the middle of finals, but I put up notices all over the neighborhood with Mugsy's picture and my phone number. Mugsy came home by himself the next day, but I got a very interesting response to the posters. Right after I put them up, a woman called and said she didn't have Mugsy, but that she'd seen him about 4 months ago, when he got run over by a car."

My surprise must have shown on my face, because Josh said, "I was surprised, too. I asked her what she meant. She said she'd seen my cat in the street, the same one in the picture, freeze as a car came toward it. She said the cat went between the wheels of the car and didn't get hit by the tires, but ran off right afterward. She wanted to know if he had recovered from it."

"I'd say this explains Mugsy's fear of cars," I said. I told Josh that Mugsy's running and hiding was his way of trying to put himself back in his Comfort Zone. Our job was to help him do it. Over a period of months—and with the help of some anti-anxiety medication and an ultra-secure Safe Haven (I'll tell you more about both of these later in the book)—Josh managed to help his cat get over the lingering fear of the sound of cars. Now Mugsy spends his days happily inside with Josh, who gives Mugsy all the play he wants in the safety of his home.

In both situations—needs and straightforward threats—the system works the same way. There is a nearly endless supply of examples, since all unpleasant feelings push an animal outside of his Comfort Zone. Nausea, anxiety, intensely bright lights, hunger, dryness of the eyes, a torn cruciate ligament, being bullied by the two other dogs in the house—all create unpleasant feelings. The dog who scratches an itch, a cat who climbs a tree to escape a charging dog, an injured baboon licking his wounds, and a vampire bat sucking blood from a cow's neck are all examples of animals attempting to move themselves into their own Comfort Zone.

Multiple Discomforts

Sometimes an animal is moved out of his Comfort Zone by more than one discomfort. I will never forget Spanky, a blond male cocker spaniel I had cared for all 12 years of his life. He was always bouncy, animated, and outgoing, a dog who acted truly excited when he came to the animal hospital. But I almost didn't recognize him when his human companions, Jason and Broderick, brought him in one Monday morning. As Jason gently set Spanky on the examining table, I saw a very different dog. Spanky held his head down and watched me warily as I approached. He didn't jump up to lick me as he'd always done in the past, and when I got close to him, he flinched, and I heard a faint whimper. Spanky's soft brown eyes were wide open, and his pupils were widely dilated. He looked terrified.

"He's been like that all weekend," Jason told me. "Just staying in one spot and not moving."

"In fact," Broderick added, "he acts as if he doesn't want to move— you can see it in his eyes. When he does walk, he's very slow and stiff. And the worst thing is that he's been crying out in pain if we try to pick him up or touch him on his back."

I was extremely gentle in touching Spanky during my examination. The x-rays confirmed my suspicion—Spanky had a slipped disc. What he had been going through over the weekend and would continue to experience until our medicines began to help was a doubly severe discomfort. Not only did he experience intense back pain with any movement, but he also had an intense fear of moving, or being moved, which would heighten the pain. Both of these feelings, acting together, probably had Spanky as far out of his Comfort Zone as any animal—or human—could be. Spanky was doing all he could to reduce his discomfort and get back to his Comfort Zone by trying his hardest to remain motionless.

The pain medications I prescribed did the trick, and Broderick called me a week later to report that Spanky was his old self again, back in his Comfort Zone. The lesson for all animals is this: Do your utmost to avoid or lessen unpleasant feelings, and you will be sitting in the satisfying center of your Comfort Zone. The lesson for animal caregivers is this: Do your utmost to help your pet remain in or return to his Comfort Zone.

A Key to Your Pet's Behavior

Understanding the Comfort Zone is an important key to determining why animals do what they do. And it is key to changing any animal's behavior. Just keep this basic rule in mind: *An animal will always behave in a way that moves him to the left (toward comfort) on the Comfort Zone Scale.* Even

 Where Is the Comfort Zone?

The Comfort Zone is a mental place, not a physical location. It is created by the feelings in the conscious mind. When I say that a polar bear or a camel is in its Comfort Zone, I don't mean an Arctic ice floe or the Gobi Desert. Instead, I'm referring to the mental place that the animals' feelings form in their minds when they are in their adapted environments and relatively free from discomfort.

the little mouse in your basement—as he chews holes in your walls, tears open bags of dog food, and leaves little mouse turds all over—is not trying to make your life miserable. He doesn't care about you at all; he's simply seeking comfort and trying to avoid discomfort.

For those of us who care for animals, this principle helps us to understand the animals we deal with every day. When they bite, scratch, kick, try to escape, fail to cooperate with us, or "misbehave," they are almost always trying to minimize their unpleasant feelings of fear, anxiety, boredom, hunger, or pain. Whenever you notice your pet doing something unusual, she is probably doing it in an effort to return to the Comfort Zone.

Corby, a longtime client, brought his 10-year-old male Siamese cat, Aiko, to see me one afternoon. As always, the sleek chocolate-point gave me a disdainful once-over with his calm blue eyes. I noticed that the cat seemed thinner than usual as Corby told me of his concerns.

"Aiko seems to be less energetic than usual," he said, "and lately for some reason, he's been drinking water practically nonstop. I have to fill the water bowl once or twice a day, and he's using the litter pan way more than usual. He seems to be eating as much as ever, but I think he's lost a little weight."

I congratulated Corby on noticing important changes in Aiko's behavior and appearance and arranged for lab tests. As I suspected, they showed diabetes. "The high blood sugar level in diabetes causes an increase in water loss through the kidneys," I told Corby. "The result is that he needs much more water than usual." In other words, Aiko's excessive drinking was an attempt to get rid of the unpleasant feeling of thirst caused by the diabetes and return to his Comfort Zone.

Luckily, Aiko was still basically healthy, and Corby was able to give him daily insulin injections to control the diabetes and return his pet to the Comfort Zone. The following week, Corby told me that Aiko seemed to be back to his old self. "He still has the loudest purr you ever heard," he assured me. "And he's using it much more now."

The most important lesson for those of us who care for—and about—animals is this: Unpleasant feelings hurt. Animals want to be rid of them. Because minimizing discomfort is the single most important factor in your pet's well-being, the single most important duty you have toward your pet is to protect him against the discomforts, hurts, and unpleasantness that life can inflict. This is what your pet depends on you to do.

Chapter 3

THE PET PLEASURE
PRINCIPLE

IMPORTANT AS IT IS, the Comfort Zone is only part of the story
of animal care. The Comfort Zone explains how animals strive to eliminate the unpleasant feelings in life. Now, let's complete the picture of feelings by adding the pleasant feelings, and show how they work together
with the unpleasant feelings to form the concept I call The Pet Pleasure
Principle. This principle forms the foundation for all aspects of animal
well-being and is the ultimate guide for you as you care for your pet.

The Pleasure Principle had its origins in the work of philosopher Jeremy
Bentham in the late 18th century. The Pleasure Principle states that human
beings behave in such a way as to maximize pleasure and minimize pain. In
psychological terms, the Pleasure Principle can be used as a general guide
to explain most human behavior, and research now provides abundant evidence that this principle holds true for animals as well as humans.

INSTINCT OR EMOTION?

It was long believed in some scientific circles that instead of emotions,
all animal actions were motivated by blind, unfeeling instinct. (Many

(continued on page 40)

SCARLETT'S STORY

It began as a routine call for Hook and Ladder Company 175 of the New York City Fire Department. In a heavy snowfall, a four-alarm fire was raging in a single-story garage in Brooklyn. But the story surrounding this seemingly ordinary fire was soon to become news so extraordinary that it would move people to tears the world over. Foreign news crews from as far away as Japan would race to America to cover the story. It was a rare and sensational opportunity to look inside the mind of a creature who was not human, but who had acted with a nobility and courage any human would envy. What was it that so entranced the world and melted so many hearts? A cat.

A cat with no name, no owner, nothing to distinguish it from the tens of millions of other stray cats in every city the world over. This one happened to be a mother cat, nursing a litter of five tiny kittens only 4 weeks old. She happened to be quietly raising her small brood in this building when it was struck by fire. Recognizing the danger to her kittens, this mother cat began to remove the kittens from the flames and toxic fumes and carry them into the icy chill outside.

Able to carry only one kitten at a time, the mother cat had to repeatedly force her way back into the intensifying flames and heat to pull the crying kittens, who by now were suffering burns from the heat, out of the inferno. Her face was seared by the fire, her eyes had swelled shut, and she breathed in hot and poisonous smoke, but her maternal feelings kept pushing her to endure the pain of the fire to rescue each of her babies. Somehow, she managed to carry each of the five tiny kittens to safety. The firefighter who found them watched in awe as this mother cat, whose eyes were so blistered she could no longer open them to see, pressed her nose gently against each kitten, taking a sightless head count by touch and smell.

The fireman rushed the mother and kittens to the North Shore Animal

League shelter, where they received medical care, and all but one kitten survived. When the news hit the airwaves, more than 10,000 pleas came in from countries all over the globe to adopt this mother cat—now given the name Scarlett—and her kittens. The world was captivated by Scarlett's story, and several days later, the joyful reunion between her and her surviving kittens, who were being nursed by bottles because of the severe injuries to their mother, was broadcast across the nation.

Scarlett was an international sensation. She appeared on talk shows nationwide, from *Live with Regis and Kathie Lee* to *Oprah*. Yet 5 minutes before this fire, Scarlett was a very ordinary, nameless stray cat. What was it that transformed this undistinguished creature into a named, honored, and cherished paragon of heroism and devoted motherhood now beloved all over the world? Nothing about the cat had changed—she was the same cat she always was. What made the difference and riveted people's attention was the rare, eye-opening opportunity to see that an animal's mind contained something that has great meaning to us: qualities and noble values we ourselves aspire to. The 10,000-plus people wanting to adopt Scarlett weren't looking to adopt just any old cat, but a cat with an emotional makeup rivaling that of the most virtuous and principled human being.

Some observers dismissed Scarlett's show of devotion to her kittens as "maternal instinct," as if it were somehow automatic behavior, devoid of true emotion. Her heroic actions, however, demonstrate that "maternal instinct" is deeply *felt* by the mother cat. Without the motivation of very strong feelings—devotion to her babies—Scarlett would not have possessed the willpower to brave a life-threatening situation for them. Saving her babies was something she *had* to do because something inside her mind was more powerful than the suffering of third-degree burns. Something felt stronger to her than physical pain. This is the power of emotional feelings.

scientists still believe this.) Instinct *does* play a prominent role in animal—and human—behavior. Contrary to popular opinion, however, instinct is not purely automatic behavior, devoid of thought. Rather, instincts are the built-in emotions that an animal experiences in response to threats and opportunities in the environment. Put another way, feelings *are* instinct.

For example, fear is an instinct. *What* an animal or person fears is partially shaped by life experiences, but the emotion itself is instinct. A mouse's fear of barn owls is a good example. When a little mouse ventures into the barn to obtain some grain for a meal, he is alert for the slightest sense of sound, movement, or shadow signaling a predator overhead. The fear that he experiences at the sight or sound of anything resembling an owl is an instinct—a hard-wired fear—and it shows every sign of being strongly felt. Fear wouldn't be so successful if it weren't so strongly felt. It does much of its work through a powerful, unpleasant feeling that cannot be ignored.

Another well-known example is the instinctive drive to mate. Nipper, a foot-high male dachshund-Chihuahua mix, drove his owners crazy with his constant attempts to escape the yard whenever the female dog across the street came into heat. So strong was Nipper's feeling of desire for the neighboring dog that one afternoon he managed to climb over a 4-foot-tall chain-link fence—an amazing feat for such a small, short-legged dog. Luckily, the next-door neighbor spotted Nipper and returned him to his owners before he could run into traffic and be injured. Nipper's owners finally got the message and brought him in to be neutered.

Does the force of instinct mean that all activity by humans and other animals is simply programmed behavior? Not at all. For a human example, research in humans and our closely related primates has demonstrated that there is a strong inborn basis for our sense of justice. Observing an injustice, such as someone breaking into your home and making off with your things, or watching a trial in which a man who killed his ex-wife and her friend escapes punishment, or even being cut off in traffic, causes most of us to feel a deep sense of anger. Termed "moral anger" or "moral outrage," this emotion arises from being wronged or witnessing a wrong being committed. It also involves an urge to retaliate.

Evolutionary psychologists believe that the emotion of moral outrage helped social animals maintain order in their societies. Without widespread anger among their fellow society members, cheaters and wrongdoers would be able to get away with their misdeeds. Moral outrage makes you care—often quite passionately—when you hear of elderly people being swindled out of their life savings or a mother drowning her two children by driving her car into a lake. You feel a very strong desire to see the wrongdoer punished for his or her actions.

This emotion—this *instinct*—is precisely what Hollywood moviemakers exploit in their action movies. They know full well that the more wickedly their villain behaves, the more intensely you will want to see him brought to justice in the end. The more violently he is punished, the more satisfied you, the audience, will be. Your instinct for moral anger is the reason movie villains are so evil, and your emotional feelings about that evil are in a sense programmed. What you *do* about those feelings— cheering the villain's demise, writing a letter to the editor about a similar real-life case—is not programmed, however.

In thinking about the care of our pets, we need to remember how compelling all instinctive feelings can be. And it's not such a strange notion, after all: The fact that feeling and instinct are so deeply intertwined is intuitively obvious. The common advice to "follow your instincts" and "let your heart guide you" are both actually saying, "Listen to your feelings."

Here are four other examples of instincts/feelings.

- ❖ The delicious taste of sweetness instinctively craved by mammal babies. That delicious taste is a feeling. Liking sweet tastes is also an instinct, developed over the course of evolution to guide growing animals to rich sources of energy.

- ❖ The terror of a young foal separated from his mother. This painful feeling is a hard-wired genetic program that is designed to keep all mammal mothers and their young bonded tightly together until the young ones are capable of living on their own. It serves the purpose of making the foal do everything in its power to reunite with its mother. Instinct? Yes. *And* a feeling.

- ❖ The grief felt by an elderly dog who has lost his lifelong human companion to AIDS. This heartbreaking sense of loss shows all appearances of being felt as deeply by the dog as by any human who is mourning a loss. From an evolutionary perspective, his suffering probably stems from an instinct that promotes close bonds with packmates for self-protection.

- ❖ The self-sacrificing love felt by a mother cat for her kittens. This instinctive feeling appears to be experienced as strongly by a cat as by a human mother for her baby. (For more on the love of a mother cat, see "Scarlett's Story" on page 38.)

It appears that all of these instincts are experienced by the animals as intense emotional feelings. There is no reason to believe that these instinctive emotions are less powerful than the same emotions we humans have experienced since our species first emerged on the evolutionary scene.

CHOOSING PLEASURE

To think about what pleasure means to animals and how they decide to pursue it, let's again take an example from the wild. Picture a hungry fox

Reward and Punishment

One way to think about pleasant and unpleasant feelings is to see them as internal rewards and punishments. Pleasant feelings reward animals for engaging in activities that increase their chances of survival and reproduction.

Unpleasant feelings, on the other hand, are associated with threats to life and well-being. They discourage animals from repeating behaviors that, on average in the ancestral past, have resulted in a decreased chance of survival and reproduction.

Feelings at a Glance

	Pleasant Feelings	Unpleasant Feelings
Evolutionary Value	Reward animal for pro-survival actions	Deter animal from threatening actions, lessen risks to well-being
Physical Origin	Taste, physical contact with others, sexual activity, etc.	Lack of oxygen, thirst, hunger, illness, nausea, full bladder, itching, bright lights, loud noises, temperature extremes, etc.
Emotional Origin	Social companionship, mental stimulation, play	Fear, anxiety, loneliness, boredom, frustration, anger, depression, grief, helplessness

in the woods in winter. He spies the carcass of a rabbit on the other side of a river. The only way across is over a very shaky log; in deciding what to do, the fox's fear competes with his anticipation of a tasty reward.

Such mental competition between feelings occurs almost all the time in people and animals. The simplest day-to-day decisions involve weighing very different feelings against one another. Going shopping is weighed against the aggravation of fighting the crowds. Taking the pill that relieves your depression causes an unpleasant dryness in your mouth. It would feel so good to punch an obnoxious bully in the mouth, but you'd probably be beaten up or arrested. Your arthritis pain may be outweighed by the joy of playing catch with your son.

When you are weighing feelings against one another, sometimes it is two physical feelings, such as having to take a very unpleasant-tasting medicine to relieve your splitting headache. Sometimes it is two emotional feelings, such as suffering through your husband's boring corporate Christmas party versus the feeling of satisfaction for having done what makes your husband happy. Sometimes it is a physical feeling weighed against an emotional feeling, such as the agony felt when running a marathon against the pride and satisfaction at having completed the marathon. These mental calculations between feelings can work only if the feelings are evaluated using the same reference point. Without a standard unit of measurement—a common currency—comparing two feelings would be like comparing apples and oranges.

In 1992, the Canadian physiologist Michael Cabanac published research showing that animals weigh their decisions on the basis of which action results in the greatest net pleasure. In one experiment, lab rats were given a choice of eating regular lab chow in their own cages or a very tasty treat at the end of a long, frigid tunnel. Repeatedly, the rats opted for the tasty treat, even though they risked frostbite to do so. Clearly, the rats indicated that the pleasure of the tasty food outweighed the discomfort of the cold tunnel. When the tasty treats were replaced with less delicious food, the rats opted to stay in their cages.

It appeared as if the rats were making a cost/benefit analysis: "The pleasure of the tasty treats is greater, overall, than the unpleasantness of the extreme cold. Therefore, it is worth going after the treats. When the treats are less tasty, however, the discomfort of the cold is more important than the pleasure of the treats, so I'll stay in my den."

In fact, Cabanac and his colleagues suggest that a cost/benefit analysis of sorts is what animals do naturally whenever they rank pleasures and displeasures, choosing the behavior or behaviors that lead (or are most likely to lead) to the greatest overall degree of pleasure. Cabanac's studies also showed that when rats and humans were tested in the same way, the mental calculations performed by rats were virtually identical to those performed by humans.

It's important to understand that these mental calculations are done almost exclusively in the nonconscious part of the brain. The only thing the animal (or human) is aware of is the end result—the net increase in pleasure—delivered in the form of feelings.

This mental process of weighing feelings and choosing behavior on the basis of the greatest increase in net pleasure forms the underpinning of The Pet Pleasure Principle. Understanding and using it gives you the ultimate tool to make any animal's life—including your pet's—the happiest possible.

THE PLEASURE/DISCOMFORT SCALE

Earlier, we saw how animals strive to move from the right side (discomfort) to the left (comfort) side of the Comfort Zone Scale (see page 28) in order to eliminate unpleasant feelings and get into their Comfort Zone.

But the concept of the Comfort Zone deals only with unpleasant feelings and the desire to avoid them. It is *pleasant* feelings that give life its

THE PLEASURE/DISCOMFORT SCALE

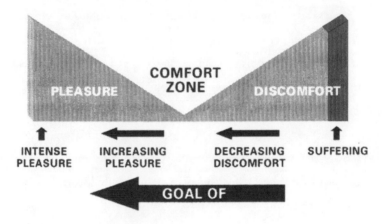

real savor. When we add pleasant feelings to the Comfort Zone Scale, we get the complete picture, as you can see in the Pleasure/Discomfort Scale above.

In the Comfort Zone Scale, the main aim is to achieve a state of comfort. With The Pet Pleasure Principle, the aim is expanded to include pursuit of the pleasurable feelings in life. The Pet Pleasure Principle is the behavioral guide that all conscious animals, including humans, follow during their waking hours. If your cat or dog is at the extreme right side of the Pleasure/Discomfort Scale, where he is suffering, his aim may be to minimize discomfort and simply move into comfort. If that same pet is already comfortable, he seeks to move toward pleasure. And if he is already experiencing pleasure, his natural motivation will be to move even farther to the left on the scale and experience even more pleasure. The Pet Pleasure Principle says that no matter where an animal is on the scale, the goal of his behavior is to move himself to the left.

A friend's 13-year-old Siamese cat offers a great example of an animal that is experiencing pleasure and seeks even greater pleasure. A strictly indoor cat, Ollie loves to go outside on his leash and pesters his "parents" to take him out each evening. Once outside, he begins to meow and rub against his mistress to be groomed. As she brushes him, Ollie purrs and murmurs as if he is in cat heaven. Following The Pet Pleasure Principle, here is a cat experiencing great pleasure (being outside), but making a behavioral choice to increase his pleasure (soliciting his mistress to add grooming).

Exceptions to the Rule

The Pet Pleasure Principle doesn't explain *all* animal behavior, but nearly all conscious behaviors appear to fall within its rule. (The same is true for the Pleasure Principle in human behavior—it is considered to be the main motivating force, but not necessarily the only one.) For example, last week when I was driving across town on the freeway, I became distracted and missed my exit. I got off at the next exit, circled around on city streets, and made my way back to the store I was headed to. A Martian anthropologist watching from a flying saucer might wonder: Why'd he take that round-about course to get where he was going? The answer is *not* that it was to increase my pleasure!

Unfortunately, the behavior that *does* result from The Pet Pleasure Principle is not always a good thing. While the principle serves as a good general guide for behavior in an animal's natural environment, man-made environments present choices not seen in nature, such as an overabundance of food. Choosing the greater pleasure isn't always what is best for long-term benefit. People (or lab rats) who are addicted to harmful substances may choose the substance again and again—to the extreme detriment of their long-term welfare. Or, in a far more common example, a dog (or her master) may try to increase her overall pleasure by eating as many tasty snacks as possible, which can result in obesity and its associated diseases and discomforts.

Why Do They Do That?

Below is a list of common behaviors that you may have seen in your own pets. To us, some of these seem good, some seem bad, and some seem neutral. But every one of these actions has something in common. Can you guess what it is?

- Your cat runs under the bed when you turn your vacuum cleaner on.
- Your dog brings his tug-of-war toy to you and drops it in your lap.
- Your cat is holding her swollen paw up and won't walk on it.
- Your hamster runs on his exercise wheel.
- Your dog keeps leaping over the fence and running around the neighborhood.
- Your cat spends lots of time lying on the warm top of your VCR.
- Your dog stands and puts his front paws on your kitchen counter and snatches a piece of fried chicken to carry off and eat.
- Your horse tries to kick the vet when he gives her an injection.
- Your non-neutered male dog keeps trying to hump your leg.
- Your two new puppies spend hours chasing and pouncing on one another.
- Your cat fights to avoid going into her carrier when you're taking her to see the vet, but fights to avoid coming *out* of her carrier once she's at the vet's.

Why do they do these things? In every case, it's to increase pleasure or diminish discomfort. To move closer to pleasure on the Pleasure/Discomfort Scale.

As you will see again and again in this book, The Pet Pleasure Principle not only explains most animal behavior, it is the fundamental guide to all our care of animals. Simply seeing to your pet's comfort, while essential, is *not* enough. For the most enjoyable life, every animal needs to spend plenty of time in the pleasure area of the Pleasure/Discomfort Scale, where the good feelings, excitement, and fun are all found.

HOW THE PET PLEASURE PRINCIPLE MOTIVATES YOUR PET

The Pet Pleasure Principle neatly explains why your pet prefers some activities to others. Here's how to use the Pleasure/Discomfort Scale (on page 46) to see how an animal's motivation level to do something is determined by two factors.

1. The distance moved from right (discomfort) to left (pleasure) on the Pleasure/Discomfort Scale. The starting point can be anywhere on the scale. For a behavior that causes a large movement to the left (a large increase in pleasure and/or decrease in discomfort), there is high motivation, while behavior that causes a small movement is associated with low motivation. A cat who is bored and lonely (on the right side of the scale) will be extremely motivated to interact and play with his human companion when she comes home (moving into the pleasure zone). If the cat spent the day in vigorous play with a cat companion, he would be closer to the left side of the scale, and his motivation to interact with his human playmate would be less intense. Conversely, the motivation level for resisting something that would move the animal to the right also appears to depend on the distance the animal would be moved. This is exactly what is happening as your cat fights to avoid being put in his carrier for a trip to the vet. (In Chapter 6, "Ain't Misbehavin'," I'll show you how to change your cat's perception of the carrier, so he will no longer resist it.)

2. How far to the right (discomfort) the pet begins on the Pleasure/Discomfort Scale. The farther to the right an animal is to begin with, the greater her motivation to move to the left. For example, a dog that has just eaten a meal will be much less motivated to seek food than a dog who hasn't eaten for several hours (farther to the right on the scale). A dog who is starving (at the extreme right end of the scale; suffering) will be extremely motivated to find food.

When an animal on the right side of the Pleasure/Discomfort Scale is *prevented* from performing a behavior that she is highly motivated to do, the animal continues to endure her unpleasant feelings. If this happens when she is on the far right side, she suffers. Consider these examples of highly motivated behavior.

- A rabbit fleeing a forest fire to avoid pain
- The intense efforts of a beaver caught in an underwater leg-hold trap to get to the surface when he begins to run out of air
- A squirrel attempting to flee a fast-approaching coyote
- A starving cat wolfing down a meal
- A bored dog digging holes in the backyard

If, however, the animal begins at the middle of the Pleasure/Discomfort Scale (a state of comfort) or on the left side (already in a state of pleasure), his behavior is still intended to move himself to the left, but in this case he seeks to increase pleasure. A common example is a dog who has just finished his dog chow and still begs for a piece of cheese. He is no longer hungry, but to him the cheese is a very tasty treat that gives him pleasurable feelings. Refusing him the cheese will not result in suffering. Whether blocking a highly motivated behavior results in suffering—and is unkind and possibly inhumane—always depends on where along the Pleasure/Discomfort Scale the animal is situated when events begin.

Here are some more examples.

- A dog who has an intense itch. Her attempt to scratch the itch is blocked by her veterinarian putting a big conical plastic "Elizabethan" collar on her. This leaves her outside her Comfort Zone and no way to get herself back into it.

Note: This is not to suggest that protective collars are wrong. When used appropriately, they may decrease pleasure temporarily, but by preventing self-harm to the animal, they ultimately contribute to an overall *increase* in pleasure through better health. For more on this topic, see Chapter 10, "The Veterinarian's Role."

❖ A dog chained outside who howls for human attention. This behavior is the dog's attempt to alleviate his unpleasant feelings of loneliness and move himself into the Comfort Zone. Blocking this behavior (or simply ignoring it) leaves the dog to endure his loneliness—with no way for him to reach his Comfort Zone.

❖ A dog who has been energetically playing fetch for an hour, at which time his owner has to quit so she can start her family's dinner. In this case, blocking the highly motivated behavior to continue playing fetch doesn't result in any discomfort or suffering because the dog is not currently in a state of discomfort. His behavior is aimed at raising (or at least maintaining) his level of pleasant feelings, not lessening unpleasant ones.

❖ A cat who spends the vast majority of her day at home alone with nothing to do. Now, with her owner home and watching TV, she is meowing loudly and dragging her string toy over to the owner in an attempt to get him to play with her. Her behavior is intended to lessen her unpleasant feelings of loneliness and boredom; by ignoring her behavior, her owner leaves her in a state of discomfort.

THE PET PLEASURE PRINCIPLE AND DECISION-MAKING

Although The Pet Pleasure Principle serves as your pet's guide to making behavioral choices, sometimes it's not obvious which of two possible actions will lead to the greater amount of pleasure. The result is indecision. In fact, it appears that the smaller the difference in total pleasure between two possible outcomes, the harder it is to decide which to do.

We see this type of indecision all the time in animals. A good example of this is my favorite little squirrel, who comes to my front door every day. He has a small notch out of the tip of his right ear, so I've named

Nature's Backup Systems

Some functions are so important to life that evolution appears to have made special assurances that they would not fail. It appears that, for some of life's activities, nature has guided the design of more than one motivational force. Thus, if one form of motivation malfunctions, the other will still function to safeguard the animal's well-being.

For example, consider the act of eating. This vital behavior is motivated by at least two feelings: the pleasurable feelings of taste, and the unpleasant feelings of hunger. If something causes one of these forces to falter, such as a chemical burn injury that damages all of the taste buds on an animal's tongue, then the other motivational force—the feeling of hunger—will still be there to make sure the animal eats well. Just as duplication and backup systems are built into the critical functions of complex structures such as submarines, jets, and space-flight vehicles, similar duplication has been wired into animals' minds in the form of feelings.

The workings of this backup system can be seen in the context of The Pet Pleasure Principle. For every important action an animal might take, *two* sets of feelings motivate him to move himself to the left (toward increased pleasure) on the Pleasure/Discomfort Scale. One set of feelings— pleasant—motivates the animal to seek increased pleasure, while the other set of feelings—unpleasant—pushes him to eliminate unpleasant-

---

him Notchy (this is at least as imaginative as naming a black cat Blackie). Even though I've been feeding him for several months, Notchy isn't totally at ease taking food from my fingers. In fact, his slowly advancing, approach-retreat, jerky motions, with his tail twitching, show the conflict he feels—pleasurable tasty treat versus fear. Advance or flee? When he gets close enough, in a flash he grabs the nut in his mouth and darts back to a safer distance to munch on his treat. When he has finished eating it, we go through the same thing again.

This nearly dead-even balance between Notchy's conflicted feelings ness. With two forces pushing in the same direction, the animal receives the strongest motivation nature could instill.

Another example is social bonding. Two sets of feelings promote social attachments: the unpleasant feeling of separation, and the pleasant feeling of emotional and physical interaction with a companion. If either system fails, the backup system will still operate. We all have experienced this at one time or another, whether through the parent-child bond, a best-friends bond, or a romantic-love bond. In each case, the feelings that motivate you to stay together—or get back together if you are separated—are the pleasant feeling of being with the other person and the unpleasant feeling of missing him or her. Scientific evidence, as well as innumerable anecdotes, strongly point to the very same backup system in many animals.

Sexual activity also appears to have been constructed this way. The sex drive, which can cause unpleasant urge-type feelings when it is ignored, works together with the pleasure of sexual activity to promote the very important activity of procreation.

One other need that appears to use nature's backup system is mental stimulation. Animals, including us, are motivated to seek mental stimulation by the rewarding feelings of mental engagement on the one hand and the unpleasant feelings (boredom) of insufficient stimulation on the other.

is very easily tipped in the direction of fleeing if I make any sudden movements. But even when I stay still, his mental calculator is unable to deliver a clear-cut message of which behavioral choice—advance or flee—will move him farther to the left (toward pleasure) on the Pleasure/Discomfort Scale. A similar dynamic may be seen in the common picture of the cat who can't decide whether to come inside, where it's warm and safe, or to stay outdoors, where there are many interesting things going on. Both choices increase his pleasure, but his mind cannot clearly determine which one will elicit the most pleasure.

Offering a dog her two favorite toys and allowing her to choose only one will also create this type of mental dilemma. Very often, you'll see a fair amount of vacillation before she finally picks one. (My neighbor's dog, Bruno, a big German shepherd with a rather large mouth, has another way of solving this dilemma: He simply crams both toys into his mouth at once.) If a husband and wife went to different doors of their house and called for the dog to go on a walk, the dog's mind would be in a state of conflict as to which equally pleasurable walk to go on.

As you can see, the mental life of your pets is very rich, and it directs almost all of their daily activities. In the next chapter, we'll take a closer look at the emotions responsible for some important unpleasant feelings and the best ways you can protect your beloved pet from the distress they cause.

Chapter 4

SOOTHING HURT FEELINGS

IMAGINE THAT A MONTH AGO you adopted a 9-week-old mixed-breed puppy from the animal shelter. You named him Bogie. Since he arrived at your home, you have been trying to housetrain Bogie. (If you're not familiar with the word "housetrain," it's what used to be called "housebreaking.") You have read a book on how to do it, and you like what the author says about using only positive techniques with rewards and praise and no punishment. But after all this time, you've seen no improvement.

You feel frustrated now, since you've been doing things literally "by the book." The book says that if you "catch him in the act" you should not punish him, but speak in disapproving tones and immediately get him outside to the desired "business" area. Every time you see Bogie squat and urinate, you rush over, pick him up, and carry him outside to the grass, along the way gently telling him, "No. That's a no-no." You set him down and every time, without fail, he shows no interest in doing anything other than jumping on your legs, nipping at your ankles and pants cuffs, and pulling on your shoelaces. You try using your foot to gently push him back over to the "bathroom" area, but he just becomes more energetic. After several minutes of this, you give up and carry the pup back inside.

Now you're starting to wonder, "What's Bogie's problem? Did I adopt a dumb dog? If this keeps up, I'm *never* going to get him housetrained!"

Not knowing what else to do, you lean over and look at the adorable, innocent little face staring up at you. And you ask him, "Why do you keep doing this? Why won't you do what I want you to do?"

After reading the first three chapters of this book, you already know the answer. "Because it makes me feel better when I do what *I* want," Bogie would say.

To continue this imaginary conversation, you might ask him, "How does it make you feel better? You don't get anything from it but my disapproval."

"Are you kidding?" Bogie responds. "Every time I piddle inside, my very best friend in the whole world drops everything and runs right over to me, gives me her undivided attention, picks me up and holds me, tells me over and over how much she loves me (at least that's what it sounds like she's saying), and then, best of all, she takes me outside to play!"

And now you get it. Bogie is doing what he's doing—piddling on the carpet—because in response, you've inadvertently been taking him way over toward pleasure on the Pleasure/Discomfort Scale. And that is *the* best way to get a dog to do something and keep doing it. (If you need a refresher on the Pleasure/Discomfort Scale, turn to the diagram on page 46.)

As we saw in the last chapter, The Pet Pleasure Principle—a pet's desire to move toward pleasure and away from discomfort—appears to explain nearly all pet behavior, both problem behaviors and desirable behaviors. It also explains why wild animals do what they do, from the raccoon that rummages through your trash cans, to the coyote that stalks your pet cat, to the gopher that digs holes all over your backyard. In virtually everything an animal does, its behavior seems to be motivated by the simple and understandable desire to feel good.

SCAREDY-CATS, BROKEN HEARTS, AND IDLE MINDS

Mental and emotional well-being in animals have long been neglected by scientists, pet caregivers, and even veterinarians. After all, the reasoning has been, if an animal is physically healthy and has plenty to eat, a soft bed, and a roof over its head, what more could it want?

The answer is simple—animals want what *we* want. They want comfort and pleasures. They want to be free from pain and discomfort. I've learned in my years as a veterinarian that emotional pains are every bit as important to your pet as physical discomforts, and research backs me up. Feelings can cause suffering just as intense as—or even more intense than—physical pains. Animals will do anything they can to relieve that suffering.

Once you understand how to evaluate your pet's life for potential and actual emotional discomforts, you'll have a much better idea why she acts the way she does. You'll be able to better protect her from enduring unpleasant feelings. And you'll be able to greatly increase her overall enjoyment and satisfaction with life. (Unpleasant emotions can also affect your pet's physical health through the mind/body connection. I'll have more to say about this topic in Chapter 8, "The Mind/Body Connection.")

As we saw in the last chapter, scientists believe that loneliness, fear, and boredom evolved for the same reason as physical discomfort: to help animals survive and reproduce. Like physical discomfort, emotional discomfort guides animals away from harmful actions or situations. Pleasant emotional feelings, on the other hand, like pleasant physical feelings, encourage animals to keep on doing things that are generally good for their well-being.

For example, the emotion of fear will cause a cat to run from a

It was a busy Monday morning when I walked into the examination room to greet Nancy Peterson, a paralegal in a busy law office, and her male Lhasa apso, Yanni. Mrs. Peterson was an attractive woman in her late forties, and every time I saw her, she was wearing several of the necklaces that in the 1960s we called love beads. Today, however, her worried face showed that she was far removed from thoughts of peace and love. "Yanni has been acting sick for the last 2 days," she told me. "He has no energy, and I can't get him to eat anything."

Gazing down at the 8-year-old dog, I had to admit he looked bedraggled and unwell. After examining Yanni, I explained to Mrs. Peterson that I would need to hospitalize him, put him on an IV fluid drip, and run some tests.

"Are you sure, Doctor?" she asked, fingering the beads at her neck. "My baby is very attached to me. I don't know how he'd do away from me."

I assured her that my staff would give Yanni lots of love and attention while he was hospitalized and encouraged her to come and visit him as often as she could.

"I'll try," she promised, "But I don't know if my boss will let me off early." She leaned over and kissed Yanni several times on top of his head and whispered something to him, then left, dabbing at her eyes with a tissue.

The next day, Mrs. Peterson called three times to check on Yanni's condition. And she called three times the day after that. Unfortunately, I had to tell her all six times that while he hadn't gotten any worse, Yanni hadn't

growling dog, just as the physical pain of being burned will motivate the cat to jump off a hot stove. Likewise, an enjoyable emotion will cause a cat to chase a feather toy, just as the physical pleasure of devouring his gourmet canned food treat will motivate the cat to come racing into the kitchen when he hears you open the can.

yet shown any improvement in response to my treatment. She always thanked me and said, "Please do all you can, Doctor."

When she called on Thursday morning, Yanni's fourth day in the hospital, I had to give Mrs. Peterson the same news. She was silent a few moments, then spoke with more force than I'd heard before. "I'm going to tell my boss I *have* to leave," Mrs. Peterson said. "I'll be there as soon as I can."

Mrs. Peterson arrived around 10:00 A.M. and spent the whole day with Yanni in our visitation room. She petted him, held him, and talked to him. She even brought the novel she had been reading and softly read it aloud so that Yanni would be soothed and comforted by her voice. She offered him his favorite foods to try to coax him to eat, but he had no appetite.

The next day she showed up when the clinic opened. "I called in sick today," she told me. "How is Yanni?"

I couldn't suppress a smile. "He is feeling *much* better," I told her. I watched as the little dog greeted her with bright, eager eyes, lots of little yips, a waggy tail, and licks to her face. When he wolfed down the food she had brought, we all knew it was time to send this little guy home.

To this day, I don't know exactly what forces were at work in Yanni's recovery, but I do know one thing: Yanni had missed his "mommy." Though we may never know what effected the healing of Yanni's condition in those last couple of days, in the end he was once again able to enjoy all the good feelings of life. And that's what mattered to him.

THE BIG THREE

Human psychologists have long recognized that there are many more unpleasant feelings than pleasant ones. This situation makes sense only when you remember that unpleasant feelings evolved to guide animals away from dangers, while pleasant feelings are meant to attract us to such life-affirming situations as food and sex. Unfortunately, the world offers more dangers than opportunities. For every possible mating partner, there may be a hundred predators; for every delicious, nutritious berry, there are dozens of plants that will make us sick or even kill us.

These unpleasant feelings may have saved the lives of your dog's or cat's ancestors, but the feelings that evolved to protect animals from the dangers in past environments may not be ideally suited for today's environment. After all, dogs have been domesticated for well over 10,000 years, but it is only in the past 50 of those years that we commonly began to bring dogs inside to live in our homes. In many cases, the feelings that are well constructed for self-preservation in a natural environment may cause your modern pet distress and suffering. Among these self-protective feelings are what I call the Big Three, and protecting your pet from them and the emotional suffering they cause can help you to make your pet's life the most enjoyable it can be. To understand what the Big Three are and how they work, let's look at each in turn.

Fear and Anxiety

Tramp, a 4-year-old gray male cat, was adopted by a client of mine, a screenwriter named Ron, who converted Tramp to an all-indoor pet. After living in Ron's hillside house for about 8 months, Tramp got outside by accident one morning and disappeared. Ron lives in the Hollywood Hills, where letting your cat outside usually means that the coyotes will soon have a tasty meal.

When Tramp didn't return after a few days, Ron was heartbroken. He assumed that the cat had been eaten by coyotes, and after a while, gave up hoping that he'd come back home. But 2 years later, Tramp showed up at Ron's front door.

"I couldn't believe my eyes," Ron told me the following week when he brought Tramp in for a checkup. "At first I thought it might be a lookalike cat, but I could tell after a couple of minutes that it was Tramp. He had the same scar on his ear, and the same way of rubbing first against my left leg and then the right." He paused, then gently and sadly pulled the cat from his carrier. "He's Tramp, all right," Ron repeated. "But in some ways, he's a completely different cat."

Familiar green eyes looked at me from a fuzzy gray face. But unlike the confident, friendly, social kitty I had come to know 2 years earlier, Tramp shrank away from me, trying to return to the safety of the carrier. "He's like this all the time now," Ron told me. "Tramp has become the ultimate scaredy-cat."

As I reached toward Tramp, he flattened himself against the wall, trying to evade me. For the first time ever, he trembled as I began my routine examination. It was very clear to me that Tramp was now terrified of people.

Ron sighed. "Something awful must have happened while he was away," he said.

"It's possible that he encountered some unkind people," I mused. "The important thing is to help him now."

"Will he ever get back to normal?" Ron asked.

"I can't promise anything," I said. "But he's young and healthy. For now, it's important to treat Tramp as lovingly and gently as possible. It's possible that simply being around you for a while will help the fear go away."

Luckily for Ron and Tramp, that's exactly what happened. As he began to realize that he had nothing to fear from Ron, Tramp gradually became less fearful of other people. He developed more confidence as he readjusted to his home. The last time Ron brought his pet in, he was all smiles. "It took more than 6 months," he told me. "But the fear seems to be completely gone. Tramp seems to be his old self—just like before he disappeared."

The Importance of Fear

The evolutionary importance of the emotion of fear cannot be over-stated. New York University neuroscientist Joseph LeDoux, a highly respected researcher of fear in animals, has pointed out that all animals must be able to escape from danger in order to survive. A system that detects danger and initiates rapid protective responses was an essential evolutionary development. LeDoux believes that the emotion of fear is such a system. The specific behavior that an animal uses to respond to fear varies depending on the animal. Some run, while others fly, curl up in a ball, or emit a horrible smell. No matter what the animal does in response to fear, the aim is the same: protection against danger. Fear is the emotion responsible for the "fight-or-flight response," which, as the name implies, is the rapid response of an animal's brain and body that prepares it to either escape or gear up to fight a looming danger. Fear's main functions are to recognize a threat, focus the mind's attention on that threat, and take the appropriate action on both a conscious and unconscious level.

Most researchers agree that because of its immense value for self-protection, fear was the first emotion to arise in the course of evolution. Studies have shown that the initial phases of the fear response occur extremely rapidly, below consciousness, and are not controlled by any feeling. You have probably experienced this yourself. For example, if a large shadow swoops down, you duck before you've had time to think or feel anything. This kind of immediate response was almost certainly wired into animal brains because even a fraction of a second's delay in responding to some dangers might get you killed.

The *feeling* of fear is what matters in our care of animals, because it is the feeling that is the unpleasant experience. You may never have realized how much of your pet's behavior is motivated by fear—from fleeing strange situations, to trembling and crying during the car ride to the vet's office, to biting the little boy who moves too quickly toward him while trying to pet him, to hiding under the bed.

One of the most dramatic experiences of fear in animals occurs during earthquakes. The sudden loss of life's most stable and reliable feature— the solid ground—can cause the wildest panic and terror in dogs, cats, and horses, often causing confined animals to hurl themselves through plate-glass windows and other barriers in their frantic attempts to escape. (For more on the devastating fear earthquakes can cause, see "Samson's Story" on page 81.)

Sometimes there is no obvious reason or cause for an animal's feelings of fear. Kai, a 2-year-old female shepherd-mix dog, was adopted by a pair of elderly sisters when she was a tiny 8-week-old puppy. As she grew older, Kai showed a steadily increasing fear of people and things. If the doorbell rang, Kai hid under the bed. A truck backfiring could send Kai into a trembling fit. For no clear reason and with no known emotional trauma, she finally reached the point where she acted terrified when anyone but her guardians approached her, or upon hearing seemingly innocuous sounds, such as a paper bag rustling.

It took several months, but behavioral therapy and anti-anxiety medications helped ease Kai's emotional distress. She continued to be a very anxious dog but was able to spend increasing amounts of time relaxed, in her Comfort Zone.

BOREDOM

The emotion of boredom is often dismissed as minor, trivial, or lightweight, a cutesy emotion to joke about ("I'm bored to tears"; "I was so

SHEP'S STORY

Sometimes the cause of an animal's fear may not be apparent to you, even though it's staring you right in the face. Roger, a longtime client, had been the caregiver for 6-year-old Shep since he'd adopted the Old English sheepdog as a puppy. Roger brought Shep in because, for a week, the dog had seemed terrified of everything around him. "This has never happened before," Roger told me. "When anybody approaches Shep, he snaps at them. I don't think he'd actually bite, but he's just a nervous wreck."

When I examined Shep, the dog cowered, but he checked out fine physically. I asked Roger if anything had changed recently, especially around the time Shep's fear started. Roger thought a moment, then told me that the only thing he could think of was that around that time, Shep went to the groomer. "His regular groomer was on vacation," Roger said. "This new gal cut the bangs much shorter than usual."

I thought back on Shep's previous visits and recalled that Shep had always worn the regular sheepdog look, with hair fully covering his face so his eyes weren't even visible. Now, for the first time, his face was uncovered by hair. And then it dawned on me why Shep was now so fearful: Up until the previous week, the sheepdog had viewed the world through a thick mass of hair. When his bangs were cut, all of a sudden, everything was clear—*too* clear.

"Put yourself in Shep's position," I advised Ron. "When things move toward him now, they're suddenly big, sharply visible, and scary. In other words, the world we're all used to seeing is frightening to him."

As a remedy, Roger agreed that he would have everyone in his household move very slowly when they were around Shep, giving him a chance to anticipate their actions. I predicted that when his bangs grew back, Shep would be fine—and he was. As his hair grew out, his fears faded. He was his loveable, confident self again in a few weeks.

bored I was climbing the walls"; "I was bored out of my skull"). But boredom is not trivial. It is very real, very powerful, and can be one of the most punishing of all the unpleasant emotions. Like any unpleasant feeling, boredom ranges from minor discomfort to the extreme discomfort associated with suffering. And scientists believe it, like all unpleasant feelings, is *meant* to feel unpleasant in order to motivate the individual to do whatever is necessary to alleviate the feeling.

It's hard to visualize boredom in animals, since they can't tell us exactly how they feel. But thinking about human boredom can probably give us a good idea of how our pets feel when they are bored. Think about those times when you haven't had anything (or enough) to do. An unpleasant, restless feeling begins to emerge. This is not your imagination. It is a very real feeling: the need to find stimulation. The feeling of restlessness continues until you find something to engage your mind.

Just as a 3-year-old child may fidget from boredom in church, pets receiving insufficient mental stimulation react in much the same way. They may fidget, pace, whine, or meow without an obvious reason. Cats who are allowed outside but are currently inside often show this restlessness, pacing and howling until somebody opens the door for them to go outside. Bored cats and dogs may groom themselves excessively, even to the point of creating sores, or become destructive to property by chewing or digging. If your pet is bored, she might bring you a toy to initiate play, or (depending on the pet's size) simply jump on you, paw at you, or nudge you. It's easy to imagine your pet's thoughts at these times to be something like, "Play with me!", "I'm bored!", or "Let's do something!"

Like the other unpleasant emotions, boredom appears to have evolved because it had survival advantages. The brains of higher animals are constructed to seek stimulation, which promotes alertness. The feeling of boredom appears to motivate animals to gather information and explore their environment, leading them to find food sources and potential mates as well as to remain mentally alert for possible dangers and predators. Looked at this way, it's obvious that animals that *weren't* motivated to seek stimulation, explore, search for new resources, and maintain mental alertness would be at a great disadvantage in terms of survival.

The Need for Mental Stimulation

Those of us who care for animals are only beginning to understand the importance of mental stimulation for their well-being. If you've been to a zoo in the past few years, chances are you observed that the exhibits have become more realistic-looking. In most zoos today, zookeepers strive to provide their charges with environments similar to the natural ones they would inhabit in the wild. Progressive and concerned zookeepers are beginning to specifically address boredom by providing animals with interactive toys, such as balls, mirrors, cardboard cartons, puzzles, and treat-stuffed logs.

The Los Angeles Zoo, among many others, has also begun to make mealtime a more natural experience for its animals. Zookeepers hide or disguise the animal's food (for example, by freezing fish for the polar bears in a block of ice, or hiding insectivores' food in a toilet-paper roll). In the wild, animals (including dogs and cats) would normally spend a large portion of each day hunting and searching for food. When in captivity and receiving their food already killed and prepared, they are left with very little to occupy their minds. The efforts of the Los Angeles Zoo, as well as several others with such feeding programs, give the animals something interesting to do. The results have been excellent. Zookeepers report that their charges are much more content and appear to be within their Comfort Zones.

Boredom is likely to be a serious problem for any animal confined to barren, monotonous environments such as boarding kennels, animal shelters, research laboratories, farm facilities, and even some private homes where their emotional needs aren't respected. Animals in these circumstances will do almost anything to provide a break from the unbearable monotony and get into their own Comfort Zone. Many scientists believe that stereotypic, repetitive behaviors represent animals' attempts to stimulate their own minds. These actions include pacing, rocking, biting the cage bars, masturbation, self-licking, tail- and flank-sucking, and even self-mutilation. Always keep in mind when you see stereotyped movements that they are likely indicators of emotional distress.

Animals who are forced to endure boredom are perpetually unable to return to their Comfort Zone. If they remain in the boring environment over a long enough period of time, they can actually lose the motivation or ability to respond to new stimulation.

Recent research on the effects of monotony on animals has revealed some disturbing findings. In the research laboratory, a mouse's entire life is spent in a metal box with a cage top. The box contains water, food, and bedding material, but no stimulation of any kind. Researchers had always believed that the mice lived a comfortable, contented life, until some bright young researchers wondered what these nocturnal animals were doing when all the lab personnel were at home asleep. Video cameras set up to tape the mice's overnight behavior revealed that the mice were far from content. During the night, these seemingly normal mice showed behavior one might see at a human psychiatric hospital. They repeatedly displayed senseless behaviors, such as flipping themselves over backward, climbing the walls to hang from the cage top, and gnawing at the wire. A scientist familiar with this research commented that it sounded as if the mice were losing their minds. If not that, it is certainly safe to conclude that they were emotionally disturbed.

Like all other intelligent animals, your pets can suffer boredom, too. They let you know it in a variety of ways that you may not have understood until now, from pacing and whining to destroying the carpets and woodwork. We'll discuss these symptoms, how to recognize them, and how to keep your pet from suffering from boredom in Chapter 6, "Ain't Misbehavin'." Because animals can't speak to us, much of what we believe about our animals' emotions is based on assumption as much as on science. However, the important take-home message here is that is boredom is almost certainly the most overlooked emotion in pet animals, and it's so simple to correct that no pet should have to endure its destructive effects.

Loneliness, Grief, and Feelings of Isolation

In social animals (including domestic cats, dogs, and humans), social attachments improve the odds of survival. There is safety in numbers. Bonded individuals can help and learn from each other. One member of a bonded group can watch out for danger while the others feed. These crucial bonds are reinforced not just with warm fuzzy feelings of love and affection, but also with the painful emotional punishments experienced when those bonds are broken. When, for example, a mother and infant are separated or a horse is taken out of its herd, nature calls on powerful negative feelings to reestablish the bond. At least three kinds of feelings seem to be at work here. These feelings include separation anxiety, loneliness, and grief.

Separation Anxiety

Gus, a 4-year-old terrier mixed-breed dog, lived alone with Michael, a busy clothes salesman. When Gus was about 3½ years old, Michael noticed that the dog occasionally chewed things, such as shoes or rugs, when Michael was out. As Michael's business grew, Gus's chewing be-

Why Dogs Need Us

Ever wonder why dogs seem so eager for our affection and so miserable if they don't get it? Intentionally or not, we helped to create those needs ourselves, through the process of domestication, in which farm and house animals have been bred over time for specific physical and psychological traits. This is especially true of dogs, whose domestication has been going on for tens of thousands of years.

Through the process known scientifically as neotony, or the retention of infant characteristics into adulthood, the brain of today's adult domestic dog is, for all intents and purposes, wired like that of a puppy, giving dogs the psychological traits of enhanced playfulness, desire to please, and attachment to a parent figure. The result of this long-term genetic manipulation is that dogs have become greatly attached to humans, much like puppies to their mothers, literally *requiring* human companionship for their well-being.

It's often said that dogs show unconditional love, but it might be more accurate to say that dogs show unconditional *need*. When that need is unfilled, the dog must endure emotional distress. Fortunately, it's also one of the easiest and most fun of all dog needs to satisfy, since your efforts are immediately rewarded with their unmistakable show of appreciation. In all, the very traits that cause dogs to need our affection are the ones that endear them to us: their lovable, puppylike behavior.

---

came worse. Soon the dog was chewing not just the occasional shoe, but furniture legs, curtains, and whatever else he could get his teeth on.

Even when Michael's business hit a seasonal slow period, and Michael was home more of the time, Gus continued his destructive behavior whenever Michael left the house. By the time Michael brought Gus to me, he was at his wits' end. "I can't even leave for a short time," he told me. "If I'm gone for as much as an hour, Gus chews on the doors and windowsills. It's almost as if he's trying to escape from the house."

Robyn, a new client, was in a similar situation when she brought Scout, her 3-year-old male dachshund, to see me. "Scout's behavior has become intolerable," she told me. "Whenever I leave the house, he barks continuously. My neighbors are always complaining. Now he's started pulling the cushions off all the furniture and chewing on them."

A previous veterinarian had prescribed medication, which helped the problem only slightly. "He just seems to go crazy when I'm not around," Robyn told me in frustration. "But I can't spend every minute with him. What should I do, Doctor?"

Gus and Scout both showed the classic signs of separation anxiety, a severe combination of loneliness and fear that affects some pets when their primary bonded companion—almost always a human—is absent.

Gus and Scout both responded to treatment, although Scout didn't respond as completely as Gus. Using behavioral modification techniques along with some drug therapy and a lot of perseverance on Michael's part, he and I were able to move Gus back into his Comfort Zone. Unfortunately, as hard as Robyn and I tried, we could not achieve a complete resolution of Scout's distress. I would estimate that he improved by about 60 percent, which is to say that his painful feelings were reduced by that amount, and so was his unwanted behavior. We had moved him much closer to, but not into, his Comfort Zone.

Scientists believe that all social attachments, including love, probably originated with the mother-infant bond, which is of course essential for the survival of a helpless infant. A baby separated from its mother shows signs of feeling intense distress and cries, which in turn also seems to cause emotional distress in the mother. All human mothers can attest to the power of the emotional urge pushing them to protect and care for their crying infants. (For a vivid example of the power of these emotions, see "Scarlett's Story" on page 38.) The problem this creates for our modern

pets is that their very real emotional attachments to us have a flip side—
the unpleasant emotions they can feel when we aren't with them.

Loneliness

Loneliness is one of the most powerful emotional pains. An animal experiencing loneliness is way outside its Comfort Zone. This unpleasant
emotion—and its closely related feelings of isolation distress and separation anxiety—most likely originated to motivate social animals to
reconnect with their herd or group whenever they become separated. A
horse taken from the rest of the herd shows wide-eyed terror. If he is unable to rejoin his companions, his terror turns to apathy and despair. The
punishing power of isolation—solitary confinement—is one of the most
severe forms of punishment for humans, who are, after all, among nature's
most highly social animals. Prolonged isolation is known to cause even
the most hardened prisoners to lose their sanity.

Loneliness is so powerful that it can cause people and animals to seek
or continue in dysfunctional relationships. We've all known someone in
a bad relationship who refuses to end that relationship. The battered-wife
syndrome is the most visible example. Likewise, dogs will often remain
loyal to owners who neglect or even abuse them. For those stuck in such
a relationship, the pain of abuse is often easier to endure than the pain of
breaking the relationship. Later, we will see how The Pet Pleasure Principle explains this.

I will never forget Pebbles, a 4-year-old female Maltese. Pebbles was
owned by James, a rock musician who professed to love his dog, but for
all practical purposes had abandoned her. Lucinda, who was James'
housekeeper, brought Pebbles in to see me and recounted her story.

"The owner is a very successful man," she told me, "but he's gone all
day and most evenings, and he's on the road a lot. This poor dog is alone

all of the time, even on weekends. The only time she ever sees her master is when he's asleep."

I looked down at Pebbles and saw only a healthy young Maltese who, nevertheless, seemed rather subdued for her age. "She comes from a championship line," Lucinda assured me. "James told me he went to the best Maltese breeder in Southern California to get Pebbles."

The strange thing is that the dog and man seemed to care for each other a great deal. "When they're together," Lucinda told me, "Pebbles licks him and wags constantly. And she always sleeps in his bed, even when he's away. James is always buying things for Pebbles, everything imaginable. Beds, collars, toys of all kinds, fancy shampoos, colognes, doggy breath drops, food supplements. Every time James goes on the road, he brings home another souvenir for the dog."

The problem that brought Pebbles to my office was that she had begun barking when she was alone—sometimes 24 hours a day. The neighbors were complaining—even threatening to have the dog impounded. "I don't know what to do," Lucinda concluded tearfully. "She's such a good dog. I can't bear the thought of her being unhappy."

Pebbles' story is not at all uncommon. Although her master spared no expense to buy her "things," in reality he was leaving her most important emotional need unfulfilled. In a typical reaction, the young Maltese repaid her master's emotional neglect with continuing affection and loyalty. After examining Pebbles and finding her to be healthy, I mused on her problem. I was certain that James would never deliberately harm Pebbles. Instead, like many pet owners, he simply wasn't aware of all of a dog's needs—especially the emotional needs. And because James was basically well intentioned, I felt secure in suggesting a solution to Lucinda: to persuade James to offer Pebbles for adoption by someone who would fully care for her and meet all of her emotional needs.

A few weeks after Lucinda brought Pebbles to my office she called me, her voice bubbling with excitement. "I did what you suggested, Doctor," she told me. "When I told James what you said about Pebbles' loneliness, he was shocked. He agreed that Pebbles would have a much happier life in a better home. And then . . ." she paused a moment, before imparting a great secret, "I told him that my children and I would love to have Pebbles. He agreed, and she's been with us ever since!"

As Lucinda described Pebbles' delighted play with her children, I smiled. The little Maltese had stopped barking when alone and had become simply a relaxed, happy dog, living well within her Comfort Zone.

Pebbles is an excellent example of a dog who receives all the material things in life but not the one thing she deeply needs and wants: social companionship. To many, Pebbles would seem to be the epitome of a pampered pet. But as long as she lived with James, this little bundle of white fur endured terrible emotional pain.

Grief

Grief, experienced as a result of the loss of a bonded companion, is one of the most painful emotions, both for people and, seemingly, for animals. Elephant biologist Cynthia Moss writes of the elephant who, 15 months after having lost her mother, still regularly returned to the spot where she died to gently feel and turn her mother's skull. Such poignant stories have been reported many times by elephant observers. Dolphin trainer Karen Pryor tells the sad story of two dolphin companions: When one suddenly died, the other refused to eat and just swam slowly in circles with her eyes clenched tightly shut until she eventually died.

In my own veterinary practice, I have seen the devastation of grief time and again. Freddie, an 8-year-old Lhasa apso, had lived his entire life in the company of his caregivers, William and Laurie, and his littermate,

Barney. The two dogs were inseparable, accompanying each other everywhere, including on trips to the vet when only one of them needed to come.

When the dogs were nearly 8 years old, Barney developed an incurable illness and unexpectedly passed away one day when William and Laurie were at work. About 6 months later, William brought Freddie in to see me. "Ever since he lost Barney, he just mopes around," William told me. "He stopped eating completely when Barney died, although he's eating some now."

After examining Freddie and running some tests, it appeared to me that Freddie's problem was grief and depression from the loss of his companion. Sometimes in cases like this, the use of antidepressant medication can help, but William was adamant that natural means be tried first. "We're seeing small improvements," he told me. "We just wanted to make sure that there was nothing physically wrong with him."

I agreed to this approach, urging William and his wife to shower Freddie with love and attention. This prescription for TLC worked, and Freddie eventually returned to his old energetic self.

 ## Will Work for Hugs

A September 2000 news report from the Thailand Associated Press illustrates that social animals like Macaque monkeys view the emotional reward of social interaction to be as desirable as a tasty treat: Fruit growers in Thailand began using Macaque monkeys to harvest their coconuts, tamarinds, and mangos because of a shortage of human workers. The growers found that the monkeys were hard working when rewarded with a banana. But the furry creatures would work just as hard for a hug!

THE OTHER EMOTIONS THAT HURT: ANGER AND FRUSTRATION

Bosco, an active little terrier mutt, was the center of attention for his humans, Ray and Clara, until the fateful day that Clara brought home a new baby from the hospital. Overnight, there was a new center of attention in the house. Worse, Clara and Ray were so busy with their new responsibilities as parents that they no longer had time for Bosco. They still provided food and water, saw that his bedding was clean, and let him in and out of the house to answer the calls of nature, but there were no more games of tug-of-war or fetch, no more long grooming sessions—very little attention at all, except what was strictly necessary.

In just a few weeks, Bosco changed from a happy-go-lucky, friendly little pooch to a sullen, irritable, and angry dog who snapped at or bit anyone who came near him. When Clara brought Bosco in for a checkup, she readily admitted that she and Ray had been neglecting the dog, but with both working full time and a new baby, there simply wasn't time to give Bosco the attention he was used to. "I wish I could explain it to him," Clara lamented. "Now every time I try to pay him any attention, he snaps at me, exactly as if he were having a temper tantrum."

As I examined Bosco to make sure he wasn't suffering from any physical problem, the formerly friendly little pooch growled and glared at me. After the exam was over, I told Clara that her tantrum analogy was on the mark. "Bosco is a very angry little dog," I told her. "You're right that he doesn't understand what has happened, and he's responding with anger to a situation he finds intolerable. If you really can't make more time for him, I advise you to find a new home for him where he'll get the attention he craves."

Luckily for Bosco, Clara's sister, a dog lover, was looking for another

(continued on page 78)

CORY'S STORY

Although dogs are better known for their loyalty and strong bonds of attachment, I've also seen devastating grief among my cat patients. When I first saw Cory, a female domestic shorthair cat, I remember being struck by her ordinariness. She was simply an elderly cat with no distinctive features. Her coat was a light gray with some darker stripes, and she looked like thousands of other cats roaming the streets. But she was anything but ordinary. As I would come to learn, Cory was a very special cat, a cat whose love and loyalty reached beyond the grave.

Cory was 16 years old when her lifelong human companion—Anna, a 65-year-old woman—died. The woman had made no provisions for Cory's care in the event of her death, and consequently, Cory was simply left in Anna's apartment. Fortunately, she was found hiding in the closet by Eric, the apartment manager, who, having no pets of his own, took her into his home.

Eric, who brought Cory in to me, explained that in the 3 months he had cared for Cory, he had been unable to console or befriend her. "When her mistress was alive, she was confident and affectionate," he told me. "When I dropped by, she'd be sitting on Anna's lap and purring." He paused. "She's different now," he added. "She cries all the time, with the saddest meow you ever heard. She hides most of the day and usually doesn't use the litter box. If I didn't carry her food in to her, I'm sure she wouldn't eat. I'm hoping it's something physical that you can fix, but deep down, I think she just misses the old woman too much." It was clear to me that Eric had done everything he could in trying to give Cory love, affection, and a happy new home.

My examination of Cory revealed some gum disease and slightly shrunken kidneys, not unusual in a cat that age, but nothing that would account for all of Cory's symptoms. Blood tests showed no physical abnormalities. I suggested that Eric try her on an especially tasty diet for older cats, but after another month, the situation hadn't changed. As Cory lay on the examining table, passively looking up at us, Eric and I discussed her situation. "She's not any better," Eric told me sadly. "She's still avoiding me and urinating all over the apartment. I still have to coax her to eat. Frankly," he added, "I don't think she likes me."

I protested that it was more likely that Eric's first assessment was correct, and that at her age, Cory was simply unable to adjust to the death of her lifelong companion. We briefly discussed antidepressant medications, but the reality is that medication is always tricky with an elderly cat, and especially one that hides and refuses contact. The very act of giving medicine could be emotionally traumatizing to a cat like Cory and make her even more scared and withdrawn.

"She's a sweet cat," Eric said with a sigh, "But I hate to see her suffering like this."

I'm sorry to say that this story had an unhappy ending. All signs suggested that Cory was suffering from grief and depression due to the loss of her human companion and was now inconsolable. After further discussion, both Eric and I felt that Cory's chances for recovery and being ever again able to enjoy life in her Comfort Zone were very small and that euthanasia was the kindest option.

Luckily for cats and cat lovers, most stories like this have a happier ending—the cat will bond with his new owners. Cory's deep and seemingly permanent emotional scars were probably due to her age. With Eric's approval, I saved Cory's green collar with her name tag still attached. It hangs in my office not only in memory of a very special cat, but also of the immense power of emotions to affect animals' lives—for the better and the worse.

dog after her canine companion of 15 years passed away. "Bosco is so much happier with my sister," Clara told me a few weeks later. "Ray and I both felt sad to see him go, but he obviously needs much more attention than we can give him at this point in our lives."

ANIMAL ANGER

As Bosco's all-too-common story indicates, anger is not confined just to grumpy humans. It is a common emotional experience in animals and is expressed in a variety of ways. Hippopotamuses are well known for their quick anger when humans disturb their group. In fact, hippo attacks result in more human deaths in Africa every year than deaths caused by lions. Angry dolphins can also be dangerous, and, according to marine biologist Carol J. Howard, they slap their tails, sending up great sprays of water, and emit an impressive array of sounds—squawks, blats, and "raspberries."

Anger in animals has two main causes. One occurs when the animal is blocked in some way from achieving a goal, which leads to frustration and then to anger. The goal may be to get to food, to escape an undesirable situation, or simply to reach a desired destination. The blockage is most frequently a physical barrier, such as a glass window, but it can also be an emotional thwarting, such as a trainer withholding an expected reward after the animal has performed a particular behavior (the cause of anger in Howard's dolphins), or withholding of customary affection, as occurred with poor Bosco.

The second main cause of anger is harm or the threat of harm, through aggression or challenge from other another animal or human. To the animal's mind, harm may take the form of physical contact (such as touching a painful spot on a cat or dog), theft (such as trying to steal a dog's food while he's eating), or invading the animal's territory (the cause for the hippos' anger).

When our pets experience anger, it can be a destructive emotion, both to mental health and, as we will see in a later chapter, physical health as well. For one last look at anger, let's turn to a cat named Blue Eyes. A dominant male Siamese, Blue Eyes usually lorded it over his housemate, Queenie, a smaller, subordinate female. Usually Blue Eyes got first pick of toys, food, and attention. Occasionally, however, he went too far, as when he tried to take Queenie's favorite little fur mouse away from her. On those occasions, he was met by hissing, growling, swatting, and angry chasing, which usually ended with Blue Eyes cowering on top of the toilet tank while Queenie stood below him, back arched and tail switching, hissing furiously.

Getting Frustrated

Frustration is an unpleasant emotion that can trigger anger. Frustration, like all of the unpleasant emotions, moves your pet out of her Comfort Zone, so it's important to do your best to minimize it. As we saw in our look at anger, frustration results when your pet is prevented from reaching some goal. It probably arose in evolution to provide the motivation to overcome barriers to such important goals as mating or eating. Examples of frustration are the feelings of a chained dog being teased and provoked by some heartless person; an indoor cat who can't get to the birds right outside the window; and a caged dog who tries to get out of his cage by biting at the cage wires and digging at the cage floor. If frustration occurs for extended periods and at high levels, an animal may lapse into feelings of helplessness and depression.

EMOTIONAL SCARS

We all know that a bad cut, a burn, or broken bone can leave permanent visible reminders, and "Samson's Story" on page 81 shows that unpleasant emotional experiences can also leave permanent traces. These long-term reminders are emotional scars, and they show all appearances of being as devastating to animals as they are for people. In fact, the scars from emotional sufferings often last longer and cause more pain over a lifetime than physical scars, placing the animal in a recurrent or even perpetual state of discomfort (on the right of the Comfort/Discomfort Scale, and out of her Comfort Zone). In many cases, like Samson's, the animal has no way to move himself back into his Comfort Zone.

POST-TRAUMATIC STRESS

I'm sure you've heard of Post-Traumatic Stress Disorder (PTSD). This psychological disturbance in humans is a type of emotional scar, caused by such traumatic events as combat, sexual abuse, crime, and natural disasters. Humans suffering from PTSD generally fear and avoid whatever caused the trauma for months and sometimes years after the event, often experiencing recurrent emotional episodes that can be severely distressing. They may also have difficulty sleeping and have frequent nightmares.

In my practice, I see a number of psychological problems in animals that closely resemble PTSD in humans. There are a number of common fears that can badly upset a pet even years after the original trauma occurred. Among these are:

- Fear of people who have particular traits, such as sex, size, age group, race, or hair color, that evoke memories of someone who abused them earlier in their life

- Fear of motor vehicles or even of the street after a traumatic episode in or otherwise connected to cars or trucks. I have seen this fear with many of my patients. One was Angel, a little Italian Greyhound who, along with her owner, was hit by a car that ran a red light, putting them both in the hospital with broken legs. Monroe, a small mixed-breed dog, was in the car when his owner was broadsided, causing the car to roll over.

- Fear of other animals with which there has been a traumatic encounter. Buster, a sweet little dog who was brought to our hospital

SAMSON'S STORY

Samson, a 6-year-old male golden retriever, was the beloved canine companion of the Jimmerson family. Like all retrievers, he was devoted to his "people" and liked nothing better than to hang out with them and fetch a tennis ball for whoever would throw it. During the 1994 earthquake centered in Northridge, California, in a matter of a few short seconds Samson's life changed irrevocably. The dog was upstairs at the time, and in his panic to escape the terrifying shaking, he fell down a flight of stairs and had a seizure at the bottom.

From that day onward, Mr. Jimmerson told me, Samson has been a different dog. He was now terrified of the slightest shaking—as when a large truck rumbled by—and even the faintest noises. "For example," Mr. Jimmerson said, "he even trembles with fear just hearing the sound of a penny drop on the ground."

No longer the happy-go-lucky family companion, Samson was too on edge even to retrieve balls for more than a minute or two. With my help, the Jimmersons tried everything they could to ease Samson's fears, including giving him anti-anxiety medications, but nothing worked. For me as a veterinarian, this sort of case is very frustrating. Samson's discomfort was no different from that of a dog experiencing persistent physical pain. In both cases, the dog is desperate to be free of the unpleasant feelings. In both cases also, medicines may only be partially effective in alleviating the emotional pain, leaving the dog in some degree of ongoing emotional discomfort. For Samson, a terrifying trauma had created deep and apparently permanent painful emotional scars.

by someone who witnessed him being used as bait to train dogs used for fighting, went on to live a secure life with his rescuer, but remained terrified of other dogs throughout his life.

❖ Fear of loud noises as a result of being severely frightened by thunder, firecrackers, or other sounds

Fortunately, most of these emotional scars are not as constant or incapacitating as Samson's. All of the animals mentioned above recovered from their fears to at least some degree. (For more on treating fears in animals, see Chapter 6, "Ain't Misbehavin'.")

Why should unpleasant events have such long-term consequences? Once again it appears that the evolutionary process provides us with the answer. When the ancestors of our modern dogs and cats encountered such terrifying situations as an attack by a predator or a natural disaster, only those who acted quickly to save their own lives survived, while the slower ones perished. This resulted in greater survival of those animals with brains best able to form enduring memories of danger. For these animals, when something similar happened in the future, their fear memories would immediately motivate the animals to take action.

Here's how it works. A raccoon is out searching for food and comes across a bright orange flower with an unusual smell. He is sniffing the flower when a massive bear appears out of nowhere, emitting a deafening roar. Terrified, the raccoon runs as fast as his legs will take him until he spots a small hole in a rock formation and scampers into it. His chest heaves, and his little heart beats a mile a minute for some time until he realizes he is safe. He doesn't know it, but this intense emotional experience has just changed his brain in a big—and potentially lifesaving—way. His brain has formed an emotional memory not only of the bear itself, but also the landscape around him when the bear appeared. Now he will also become afraid when encountering the orange flower, its unusual smell, and the type of ground he was standing on. By including things associated with bears, the raccoon's fear will keep him away from areas where he is likely to encounter another bear—and it will quite possibly save his life. This sort of stored fear is called a *conditioned fear.*

The problem for modern animals like poor Samson is that the emotional scars of conditioned fears are often inappropriate or excessive for modern life. These fears are often attached to people and situations that are, in fact, harmless. A terrifying memory of the ground shaking underfoot might have served to save Samson's ancestors from walking on unsteady ground that might give way—like a cliff edge—but for a domestic dog kept as a pet, such a fear instilled by a very rare earthquake will now be activated many times a day by the vibrations of modern trucks.

EMOTIONAL STARVATION

In a popular episode of the classic sitcom *Seinfeld,* the character Elaine is kept awake by a little dog that yaps all night long because he is alone in a nearby apartment. In a typical human reaction, Elaine becomes very angry at this "mangy mutt," and in one of the rare misguided attempts at humor in an otherwise ingeniously written show, she kidnaps the dog and dumps him on the outskirts of town. (He later finds his way home.)

Now consider how shocking—and unfunny—Elaine's reaction would be if the dog had been deprived of food and were barking because he was hungry. In that case, the dog would be starving for food. In the scene they showed, the dog was starving for social companionship. In both cases, the dog is hurting and crying out for relief.

The word "starving" may seem extreme, but just as the body needs to take in water and nutrients to maintain physical health, recent scientific research shows that, to remain healthy, the *mind* also has certain requirements. For most higher social animals, including humans, the mind appears to require a certain amount of social companionship. For nonsocial as well as social animals, research strongly suggests there is a need for a steady intake of mental stimulation. If there isn't enough food to meet the body's needs, the unpleasant feeling of hunger results. If there isn't enough social companionship or mental stimulation to meet the mind's needs, the unpleasant feelings of loneliness or boredom result.

When a dog or cat doesn't get enough of a specific emotional need, such as companionship, the animal experiences an unpleasant feeling— a hunger—that motivates him to fill that emotional need. As we previously saw, an unmet emotional need results in a persistence of the unpleasant feeling—in essence, a feeling of starvation. This is what we can correctly call emotional starvation.

As with all other matters involving feelings, the unpleasantness of emotional starvation makes evolutionary sense. If the body needs nutrition to maintain physical health, then feelings of hunger motivate the animal to find food. The feelings become stronger and more unpleasant the longer the deprivation lasts. A similar process seems to operate for the mind. If a dog's mind needs stimulation to maintain mental health, then the unpleasant feeling of boredom motivates the dog to find stimulation to nourish his brain. One research study indicates that mental input and food input both caused similar mechanisms in the brain to evolve, to assure that animals would do their best to pursue and acquire them.

An Emotional Rescue

Here's another real-life story that shows what I mean. Lex and Gordo, both adult male black Labs, lived together in the backyard of the Porters, a professional couple with no children. It is hard to understand why Mr. and Mrs. Porter acquired the dogs, because they showed little if any interest in them. Although they provided regular food and water and had a shelter for the dogs, the Porters did not permit Luke and Gordo inside the house and rarely spent any time outside with them.

Lois, a neighbor of the Porters who is one of my clients, became concerned about the dogs and mentioned the situation to me. "Mrs. Porter told me she has an allergy to dogs," Lois explained. "She says the two dogs have each other for company, so they don't need anything else." Lois also told me that the dogs barked loudly whenever they saw any people in the yards next door. "They stop as soon as you come over to the fence and pet them," Lois told me. "What really worries me is that both the dogs cram their heads through the slats whenever they see me. It's almost like they hadn't eaten in days and were trying to get to food. You can tell they're trying as hard as they can to be near people—just to be petted."

Lex and Gordo provide an excellent example of the social needs of dogs. As in the story of Pebbles earlier in this chapter, Lex and Gordo received the basic needs of food, water, and shelter, but their emotional needs were unfulfuilled. Even with seemingly adequate canine companionship, their Labrador retrievers were literally starving for human companionship. At last report, Lois tells me that the Porters were looking into doggie daycare and hiring a dogwalker. When Lex and Gordo finally get the human companionship they are longong for, they will once again be able to enjoy life in their Comfort Zone.

In this chapter, we have seen how the important emotional pain of fear, boredom, and loneliness can impact our pets' lives and prevent them from living in their Comfort Zone. In the next chapter, I'll explore how these emotions and other unpleasant feelings contribute to the condition we commonly call stress, and I'll show you the two most important ways to de-stress your pet by empowering him. I'll also explain how to provide your pet with the ultimate de-stressing tool, a Safe Haven.

Cats Need Our Love, Too

Cats may be more at risk than dogs for emotional starvation from insufficient social companionship. After all, even many scientists regard cats as asocial animals who do not require or desire social companionship. However, experience and research show that this is very often not true for domestic cats, as all cat lovers know from their own observations. While some cats may appear to be happy in solitude, most others seem to show distinct pleasure from companionship with people and appear to be visibly distressed when they don't receive it.

Unfortunately, because of the widespread misconception about the solitary nature of cats, they are often treated as "latchkey" pets—pets that can fend for themselves, requiring little attention or care. Just put food and water down and take off for work—or for the weekend—and the cat will happily content himself. You can see this situation all the time: Just walk through an apartment complex and observe all the cats sitting in the windows and staring out at what's going on outside.

Likewise, cats often experience emotional starvation through lack of stimulation. The phrase "curiosity killed the cat" didn't come out of thin air. Cats like novelty. They need to explore. Place an empty box on the floor, and the cat jumps in. Leave a cupboard door open, and the cat hops in. Open the blinds, and the cat jumps up on the windowsill to peer out. For the cat, the feelings of exploring something new are emotionally rewarding. But the same old boring environment with nothing to do and no companionship can be emotionally punishing.

Chapter 5

ALL STRESSED OUT

ON MY EXAMINATION TABLE, Tabitha could not have been a calmer, more relaxed cat. It was hard to imagine that she was the same cat who, just a few months earlier, had made national news for her harrowing experience.

Carol Ann Timmel, an aspiring actress, had adopted Tabitha, a brown-and-orange tabby with a beautiful white belly, as a kitten, and for years, they'd shared their lives in a small apartment in New York City. When Carol Ann moved to California, she took Tabitha by airplane, but because of the airline regulations, Tabitha had to ride in the cargo hold rather than in the cabin with Carol Ann. During the flight, somehow the door on Tabitha's carrier opened. When the plane landed, and the baggage handlers loudly entered the cargo area, one of the handlers spotted Tabitha as she fled the commotion, back into the body of the plane.

The men looked for the cat, but were unable to locate her. By the time the airline notified Carol Ann that Tabitha was lost on the plane, it was already on its way back to New York with Tabitha aboard—somewhere. Over the course of the next 2 weeks, the plane traveled to Miami, Puerto Rico, and Los Angeles. Regular procedures and maintenance—loading and unloading baggage, fueling, testing of engines, mechanical repairs—continued normally. All were loud and undoubtedly upsetting for a lost cat. Despite Carol Ann's protests, Tabitha remained on board day after day as the plane continued to fly.

By now, Tabitha's story had become national news. Carol Ann filed suit in court to force the airline to permit a search, and, not wishing to suffer a public relations disaster, the airline finally relented and allowed Carol Ann to search the plane. After calling out her cat's name, Carol Ann was rewarded with a weak "meow" from overhead. Finally, after 13 days, 26 flights, and more than 30,000 air miles, Carol Ann pushed through a ceiling panel and found Tabitha. The cat had gone without food the whole time, probably obtained water from the condensation on the water pipes, and had endured stress few of us could imagine. But was it really stress she experienced? Or was it fear? Or both?

WHAT IS STRESS?

Stress is a word we all use frequently without thinking. If asked, most people would say that stress is something unpleasant or upsetting. Some consider stress and fear to be the same thing; others identify stress with any pressured situation. Instead of specifying exactly which unpleasant emotion—fear, anxiety, loneliness, separation anxiety, anger, frustration, boredom, or helplessness—is troubling a person or animal, we simply say that the individual is "stressed."

What's the difference, you might ask? Does it really matter whether you say your pet is suffering from separation anxiety or is stressed? The surprising answer is that it can make a great deal of difference. One of the most important reasons for being precise about an animal's problem is that certain drugs and psychotherapies are effective at alleviating specific unpleasant emotional states associated with stress. The drugs include Valium for anxiety, Prozac for depression, and Clomicalm for separation anxiety. If we simply lump all feelings together and call them "stress," we can't possibly choose the correct medication or treatment. If your dog gets "stressed" whenever he has to take a car trip, I can't treat him effectively unless I know whether the cause of his discomfort is nausea from carsickness, separation anxiety from leaving his companion dog, fear of cars, or anxiety about visiting the vet.

A second reason that it's important to specify what we mean by "stress" is that stress is associated not only with differing emotional feelings but also with such very different physically generated feelings as pain, nausea, extreme temperatures, and a distended bladder. A generalized anti-stress medicine would be unlikely to help any one of these conditions. From the animal's point of view, the only important element in each of these stressful situations is the feeling itself.

As a veterinarian, I apply very different treatments to relieve stress for a cat that is bored, a dog with separation anxiety, a physically abused dog, an emotionally abused dog, a lonely dog, or a cat that has been hit by a car. In every case, removing the sources of stress means removing the sources of unpleasant feelings. Effective treatment of stress is possible only when I know precisely (or as precisely as possible) what is creating the problem—the "stressor," *and* what unpleasant emotion it is eliciting.

A stressor is anything that causes an unpleasant feeling—or the feeling itself, as in, "Pain is a stressor." *Distress,* on the other hand, is what is experienced when stress reaches a level that disturbs, troubles, or hurts. Distress is the unpleasant feeling of anguish that occurs when there is no immediate or effective way to lessen or escape from upsetting emotions and return to the Comfort Zone.

SCHOTZI'S STORY

A good example of the way stress works is illustrated by Schotzi, a male Maltese dog who has been my patient since he was a pup. When Schotzi was 2 years old, Rochelle, his owner, changed jobs. In her previous job at a day-care center, she was able to take Schotzi to work with her every day, but her new position as office manager of a law office forced her to leave the dog at home. After this lifestyle change occurred, Schotzi began un-provoked snapping. One day, he bit Rochelle's finger for no reason. "He even growls when I pet him," she said tearfully after bringing him in for a checkup. It didn't take long for me to see Schotzi's new, unpleasant dispo-sition in action. While I was preparing to examine him, he lunged and bit the pants leg of our receptionist as she walked by.

After a series of tests showed nothing physically wrong, I concluded that Schotzi was probably exhibiting displaced aggression. As I explained to Rochelle, this rather common response serves as an outlet for frustra-tion when an animal is unable to relieve unpleasant stress-related feelings. Thus, an indoor cat that sees a strange cat outside the window may attack his cat or human companion instead of the real target of his agitation.

THE GOOD SIDE OF STRESS

You have probably heard about the "stress response," which is one of the ways that the body maintains balance and efficiency. This is actually a series of physiological responses coordinated by the body's autonomic nervous system, which is outside an animal's conscious control. The stress response includes such physical adjustments as increased heart rate, increased amounts of the hormone adrenaline (which helps your pet adapt to rapidly changing situations), and other defense mechanisms. Each of these mechanisms helps your pet respond to challenges and stay in or return to her Comfort Zone.

Before deciding how to treat Schotzi, Rochelle and I discussed the events that led up to her companion's aggressive behavior. "I know he's lonely without me," Rochelle said. "But I think there's more to it." We eventually worked out that the actual emotions affecting Schotzi were probably a combination of loneliness, boredom, and separation anxiety. I prescribed anti-anxiety medication to help calm Schotzi and then recommended that Rochelle find a way to get him some regular companionship.

A few weeks later, Rochelle called to let me know that Schotzi had returned to his old self. "I thought carefully about what you said and realized that the answer was obvious," she told me. "He needed company during the day. I started taking him to visit my mother on the way to work. She has a dachshund that Schotzi loves, and the two of them play together all day. Ever since I started taking him to his play dates, he's been much calmer and more his old affectionate self."

To me, Schotzi's case is a perfect demonstration that stress is not an entity in itself but a part of one or more unpleasant emotions. In other words, the "stress" that Schotzi experienced in Rochelle's absence was actually the combined emotions of loneliness and boredom.

Some stress is good—even necessary. Stress helps animals thrive in a complicated world. When a cat, for example, is challenged by good events, such as encountering a potential mate, or unpleasant events, such as disease, natural disasters, and psychological trauma, her body mobilizes the stress response. You can think of the stress response as a way to boost emotional and behavioral reactions to significant events. For example, imagine a house cat lying in the sun. If she begins to feel too warm, she'll simply relocate to a shadier area. If, however, the heat is more severe—say, from an approaching fire—she will still want to escape the heat, but now her quest is more urgent. Her body will automatically release adrenaline to prepare her for sudden physical action, and the unpleasant feelings of fear and even pain will spur her to make her escape.

Too much of the stress response for too long, however, can lead to physical or emotional damage, because the stress mechanisms are intended for short-term use. Long-term or very intensive stress responses can weaken the body and make it more susceptible to a wide variety of disorders. From my point of view as a veterinarian, my objective is to minimize unpleasant feelings while allowing the stress response to continue to serve its protective function.

Now let's look back at Tabitha, the flying feline. What did she actually experience during her lengthy ordeal? Was it stress or fear?

To me, the answer is that it was both. Fear was the *emotion* she experienced, and stress—the specific physical reactions she also experienced— was *part of* that fear. And this is the key. Research indicates that the feeling of "being stressed" comes from the underlying unpleasant emotion, such as anxiety or boredom, not from the body's physiological changes. When we try to help a cat like Tabitha with her discomfort, we need first of all to alleviate her fear, and when we have done that, she will also be relieved of stress. In other words, her so-called stress vanishes when we help her overcome the unpleasant emotion. Finding herself safe in Carol's arms relieved Tabitha's fear, and as it did, her stress—and the physical reactions that were a part of the stress—disappeared.

The lesson for you as a pet owner is to realize that, whenever your pet seems stressed, the way to help him is to identify and ease the unpleasant feelings he is experiencing. These unpleasant feelings are most often emotional, but they may also include such unpleasant physical discomforts as pain, an overdistended urinary bladder, hunger, and exposure to extreme cold.

WHAT YOU CAN DO

When your pet gets stressed, it isn't always obvious which feelings or emotions are operating. For example, if your dog suffers behavioral problems when you leave him alone at home, is he experiencing fear, boredom, loneliness, or separation anxiety? You can't ask him, so how do you figure out what's wrong?

The lazy way out of this is to simply say that Boris is stressed, but that won't help you ease his discomfort, nor will it help your vet figure out what's wrong with Boris. It's far more helpful to make a list of possible emotional upsets your pet may be experiencing. It can also be helpful to prepare a timeline, either on paper or mentally, of changes and events that have occurred lately that might be affecting Boris. Is there a new pet in the house? Has a noisy dog moved in next door? Have members of the household been arguing? Has Boris been left alone more than usual?

Here's an example of how this can work. Farina, a sweet 13-year-old Russian blue cat, had a history of periodic bouts of asthma. Farina's human companion, Anna Marie, was well aware that these episodes were often brought on by upsetting events, and she asked me to prescribe anti-anxiety medication in preparation for a move to a new house. Farina did well during the move, but shortly after the cat and her companion had settled into the house, Farina had another attack of asthma.

Anna Marie and I assumed that this attack had been triggered by the move, but when Farina's troubles continued, Anna Marie investigated the house's history. "I spoke to the woman who owned the house before," she told me. "It turns out she had three dogs and four cats. Do you suppose Farina could be responding to their smells?"

I congratulated Anna Marie on her detective work, and advised her to give the entire house a thorough cleaning to get rid of the odors. We also put Farina on anti-anxiety medications to give her a chance to adjust to what must have been overwhelming smells and a perceived threat from seven unknown animals. After a few weeks, her bouts of asthma ended, and Anna Marie reported that her beloved pet had settled nicely into her new home.

To understand stress in your pet, always keep in mind that

❖ Every list of "causes of stress" can essentially be viewed as a list of "causes of unpleasant feelings."

❖ Every list of "stress reducers" is essentially a list of "unpleasant feeling reducers."

❖ Every list of "signs of stress" (such as trembling, hiding, not eating, overeating, excessive sleeping, pacing, destructiveness, lethargy, inappropriate urination) may be seen as a list of "signs of unpleasant feelings."

HOW PETS CAN COPE

Nature provides your pet (and you) with three major ways to deal with unpleasant feelings.

1. **Adaptation** enables your pet to accommodate herself to a changed environment that is causing unpleasant emotions. A good example is an outdoor cat who is converted to an indoor cat. Anyone who has been around a cat in this situation knows that she may express her displeasure frequently and loudly, howling to get out and trying to escape whenever a door is opened. Many cats eventually adapt, learning to enjoy looking out the window and finding sources of entertainment and stimulation indoors. These cats lead their lives differently, but comfortably, indoors.

2. **Habituation** is a type of learning that occurs when an animal is repeatedly challenged by the same event. This mechanism allows your pet to reduce the unpleasant responses to a repeated event. For example,

a dog may frantically bark at the doorbell, perceiving a threat outside. Eventually, he may learn that the doorbell itself presents no threat and will simply ignore it when it rings. (Habituation is one of the psychological methods used to relieve both animals and humans of phobias.)

3. **Coping** is the most versatile method of dealing with unpleasant emotions. Coping is all about control. Animals that feel they have control over unpleasant events and feelings are far better able to deal with any sort of unpleasant experiences than those who feel they have no way to affect their situation. For example, to cope with the unpleasant emotion of fear, an animal may run away from whatever he perceives as a threat. If he is unable for any reason to escape, his fear will grow in intensity, moving him further and further from his Comfort Zone.

AT THE CONTROLS

Yogi was a 16-year-old female Sheltie who belonged to the Andersons, longtime clients of mine. As she grew older, Yogi developed arthritis in both her front legs that eventually became so severe and deforming that she could no longer stand. Eventually this little dog was confined to lying in her bed and other places in the house.

Was Yogi stressed? Was she unhappy? Listen to Mrs. Anderson: "Yogi's favorite thing was always walks. So now we take her on 'walks' in a little red wagon. She has a special bark she uses when she wants to go on a walk. She has a different bark for when she's hungry. She seems as alert and happy as she was when she could still get around on her own."

Yogi's severe disability had stripped her of all normal methods of control over her environment. Like a human paraplegic, Yogi had become dependent upon others for virtually everything. Yet Yogi had not lost all control in her life. On the contrary, the arrangement that her owners worked out with her allowed her to give commands, and thereby to assert some control over the things she found most important in her life. This sense of control obviously provided her with a key factor for her emotional well-being.

Control is the single most important tool for coping with and lessening the discomfort of unpleasant emotions and other feelings. In nature, animals usually have a great deal of control over all aspects of their lives. When they're hungry, they can seek food; when their bladders are full, they can urinate whenever and wherever they like; when they're alone, they can look for company; when they're frightened, they can flee. All of these actions are means of exerting control over unpleasant events and the feelings they produce.

For all animals, the intensity and psychological impact of feelings such as fear, anxiety, pain, and many others are greatly reduced when the animal has control over the situation. The animal knows he can modify or turn off the unpleasantness any time he chooses to. Because control is so effective at lessening the discomfort of unpleasant feelings, it is one of the most important factors in your pet's effort to get back into his Comfort Zone whenever he is outside of it. On the other hand, taking control away from your pet (or not giving it to him) removes one of his most effective means of protecting himself from discomfort and imposes a huge obstacle to his ability to get himself back into his Comfort Zone.

A dog who is kept on a short chain in the backyard, for example, has lost control over many aspects of his own physical comfort. He can't move from the hot sun into the shade, get in out of the rain, or relieve himself at a distance from where he's chained. It's far better, if the dog must be kept outside, to allow him to roam freely within a fenced yard, with a well-made doghouse or other shelter for him to retreat to. This setup restores control, allowing the dog to return to his Comfort Zone when the elements have moved him outside of it.

How Control Makes Us Feel Good

For people, a sense of control is one of the strongest predictors of positive feelings of well-being. The same seems to be true of animals. Experiments show that in the laboratory, animals who can make changes in their living conditions—such as building nests in an otherwise bare cage—appear much more active and content than animals with no such control.

Many animals seem to enjoy a sense of control for its own sake. When white-footed mice were given control over the lighting of their cage, they appeared to engage in a true power struggle with the experimenters. If the experimenters made the lights bright, the mice dimmed them to darkness. If the scientists made the room dark, the mice turned the lights up to bright. The mice chose to exert control, even if it meant having the lights at levels they did not ordinarily prefer. This experiment shows that control matters so much to animals that it often outweighs other desires. If you've ever had a litter of puppies or kittens, you have probably observed this dynamic yourself: When you put the kittens or puppies in their box, they inevitably want out. When you bring them out of the box, they are just as likely to want to return—on their own.

When animals lose control of their lives, especially in circumstances that last for a long time or are extremely unpleasant, they can lapse into a state of helplessness and hopelessness similar to human depression. (This sort of "learned helplessness" is often used in experiments as a model for human depression.) Animals in this state can have great difficulty coping with life's tasks and challenges, even the most routine, such as competing for food.

GOOBY'S STORY

I saw the importance of control nearly every day when I went outside with my Balinese cat, Gooby. Gooby was an indoor cat, but he was well behaved and went on walks with me around the neighborhood. He walked wherever he liked, and I followed along.

Most days I started out by sitting in the yard, reading and writing while Gooby and my other cat lounged near me. Gooby, who was always eager to go out on his walks, made repeated attempts to run by me, scurry down the steps to the sidewalk, and begin his walk. When I blocked his escape and told him we would go on a walk shortly, Gooby sulked and began howling in that guttural voice that Siamese cat owners know so well. As soon as I gave in to his howling and prepared for the walk, Gooby immediately stopped crying.

But here is the interesting thing: Often, when he ran down the few steps from the yard to the front sidewalk, he just stopped, plopped down, and laid there on the sidewalk. This is exactly what he had been doing a minute before, 15 feet away, in the yard—with the same smells, the same sounds, the same sunshine, the same breeze blowing in his face. Just moments before, he had been very unhappy; now, doing the exact same

EMPOWERING YOUR PET

I hope I've persuaded you how important it is to give your pet as great a sense of control over her own life as possible. How to do this will depend on your pet's personality and specific situation. I recommend examining her life for potential unpleasant situations and emotions, then thinking about how you might help her to change these. Two of the most important ways to do this are to allow her choices and to respond when she makes requests.

Choice is one of the most meaningful means of control, allowing your thing (lying down and gazing around), he looked totally content. If I picked this contented creature up and brought him back to the yard, he immediately started up with his howl to go on another "walk."

I can see only one thing different between my yard and the public sidewalk just a few steps away: When Gooby was off our property, he had control. Whether he actually exerted the control is irrelevant; he knew he could get up and walk anywhere he chose. He called the shots. I am convinced that it is not the sidewalk itself but his sense of control that he howled for and took such apparent delight in.

I thought Gooby's desire for control was rather unusual until I started telling his story in the talks I give around the country. When I finish speaking, audience members almost always approach to tell me that they thought their cat (or dog) was the only one who did that. I frequently hear about cats who howl or pace to go outside, but then once outside just lie down on the patio; dogs who want to be let off their leashes, but once released stay right next to their master; even pet mice who want access to another compartment of their cage, but once allowed who access stay in their original compartment. Every owner reached the same conclusion: "He just seems to want the control, even when he doesn't take advantage of it."

pet to lessen or avoid unpleasant circumstances. For example, a pet door can let your pet choose whether to be inside or outside. If that is not possible, then providing several places for your cat or dog to look outside and observe the world is often sufficient. If your pet spends a great deal of time indoors alone, giving him a wide variety of toys or leaving the TV tuned to a nature channel will allow him some choice in ways to fill his time.

Always bear in mind that if your pet feels she has some ability to lessen or avoid unpleasant feelings, she'll cope much better with these feelings. Bitsy, a tortoiseshell Oriental shorthair cat, enjoys chewing on dog toys. Her owner makes sure Bitsy always has several such toys available to play with whenever she is frustrated or bored. "When I'm too busy to play with Bitsy, she goes off by herself and has a good 'chew,'" her owner told me.

All these techniques will help your pet stave off unpleasant emotions linked to stress, but the single most important thing you can do to help your pet cope is to provide him with a Safe Haven (see page 101).

Making Their Needs Known

Your dog can't speak English, but chances are that he can make his needs and desires known. Pay attention to his signals and, when appropriate, try to act on them. For example, many dogs let you know by body language as well as vocally when they want to go outside or on a walk, when they want to play, and when they are hungry (for some dogs, alas, this can be 24/7). When you respond to these requests, your dog feels a sense of control over his life and thus remains in his Comfort Zone.

Cats also signal their desires through pawing, meowing, or body language, and your job as a caregiver is to be alert to these signals. Bitsy, the tortoiseshell mentioned earlier, waits until her mistress is up and making coffee, then jumps up expectantly on the kitchen stool to await her daily treat (a commercial anti-hairball treat). "When I'm a little slow getting it for her, she reminds me with a loud meow," Bitsy's companion told me.

Putting on the Brakes

I do not advocate giving your pet total control over her life. Like teenagers, pets do not always make wise choices. Thus, allowing your pet to choose how much to eat could lead to obesity. (Though some cats do very well on a free-feeding schedule.) When deciding how much control to give your pet, carefully assess her circumstances and personality: Some pets can handle a lot more freedom than others.

Allowing a pet control can also be problematic for dogs with dominant personalities. They may respond to increased ability to control by attempting to acquire an excessive amount of control, manifested as dominance and aggression. For this type of dog, control must be rigidly structured. For example, make the dog earn the right to exert any control by first obeying a command from you.

A SAFE HAVEN: THE ULTIMATE COPING TOOL

As Hurricane Andrew swept through the Miami Metrozoo, a number of the barriers to the animal enclosures fell before the colossal force of the winds. With fences and walls destroyed, many of the zoo animals could

 The Importance of Hope

Hope is the emotional state that keeps us going, even in the face of adversity. An individual has hope when she has any level of expectation, even small, that a good event will occur. When that expectation is no longer there, hope is lost, creating the mental state of hopelessness, an emotionally devastating condition that can lead to despair and depression in animals as well as in humans.

For all living beings, the key element that sustains hope—and prevents hopelessness—is control. When a person or pet has a degree of control over the events in his life, he maintains hope. Conversely, when all control is lost (when everything in life is dictated by forces outside his control), then the animal has no chance or hope to change his situation in any meaningful way.

Assuring that your pet has some sense of control over her life will help ensure that she never becomes hopeless. For more information on ways to empower your pet's life, see Chapter 7, "The Best Quality of Life."

easily have escaped their exhibit spaces. When zoo officials were able to survey the devastation, however, they made an interesting discovery. A large number of the animals—many still visibly upset from the horrifying event—had remained in their damaged enclosures. In the most frightening of circumstances, these animals clearly preferred the security of their Safe Havens over freedom.

Likewise, after a severe thunderstorm or earthquake, most cat owners know exactly where to find their pets—under the bed or inside the closet. During a terrifying event, the frightened felines will always seek the one place that restores a sense of security to their world: their Safe Havens.

In the long course of the evolution of the animal mind, the idea of the Safe Haven slowly became a part of the psychological makeup of all higher animals, including humans. For us, a private den, home office or study, workshop or craft room—a safe place from which to retreat from the world's vicissitudes—can provide great peace of mind. This psychological need is served for some by bomb shelters and cyclone cellars.

The latest research in animal psychology provides extensive support for the idea that a dependable and secure place to retreat from the tribulations of life is *the* single most important element of mental health and comfort. A Safe Haven provides a sense of stability and security. It empowers your pet to face fears, difficulties, and adversity with much greater confidence.

In zoos and animals shelters, animal caretakers have found that providing a place to hide markedly reduces the fear and anxiety of captive animals. A great example is the children's petting zoo at Zoo Atlanta. Zookeepers noticed that pygmy sheep and goats seemed to experience unpleasant emotions when they were always available for young visitors to interact with. Some of these beleaguered animals began trying to avoid human contact or even behaved aggressively to the young zoo-goers.

Rules for Respecting Your Pet's Safe Haven

For your pet's hiding place to really be a Safe Haven—to keep him relaxed and free from unpleasant feelings—you and your family must follow certain rules.

1. The first and most important rule for respecting your pet's Safe Haven is: *Nothing bad happens here.* This is her protected sanctuary. She needs to trust that she is safe here from all threats and unhappy experiences. The Safe Haven must always be associated with a lessening—never an increasing—of unpleasant feelings and emotional stress. If you need to remove your pet from her haven, always do so gently and lovingly. *Never* reprimand or punish her here.

2. While inside his Safe Haven, your pet must experience less fear and anxiety. If you're shouting at your pet when he runs into his Safe Haven, you must stop immediately.

3. The Safe Haven must be readily accessible—and always available—to your pet, allowing a reliable way for him to remove himself from upsetting stimulation and events. A haven in a room that is sometimes shut or locked will not work because it is not always available.

4. When your pet retreats to her Safe Haven, be alert for what the cause of her flight might be. If you can identify a cause, such as family squabbling or wild children, try to stop or tone down the upsetting stimulus.

5. Bear in mind that many pets sleep and spend a lot of their free time in their Safe Havens, so using it doesn't always indicate that something is disturbing your pet. It is important, though, to always keep a protective eye out when your pet is in his Safe Haven. Maybe he's feeling sick or hiding from a threat you don't know about.

Keep in mind that even a Safe Haven won't lessen unpleasant feelings of boredom or loneliness. The only way to remedy these conditions is by providing your pet with mental stimulation and/or companionship.

Providing the sheep and goats with a private shelter to retreat to immediately reduced the undesirable behavior. The researchers concluded that allowing the animals control over the amount of their interaction with humans allowed them to remain comfortable with the contact that did occur. Other studies have shown that measures of the stress response drop when animals are provided a safe place to hide. The Safe Haven provides the animal with the ultimate sense of control: the knowledge that no matter what happens, he has a place to go where he will be safe. Because of this knowledge, any unpleasant feelings, such as fear and anxiety, are lessened, because he knows he can turn them off or diminish their intensity any time he chooses.

For your pet, having a Safe Haven means that common causes of emotional distress, such as loud noises, strange people, thunderstorms, abuse, torment from children or other animals, and disturbing smells, can all be handled. If the haven is sufficiently secure, it puts your pet in control.

ESCAPING FROM BULLIES

For cats and dogs in multi-pet households, a Safe Haven may be even more important. It's not unusual for one pet to bully another, or for one or more pets to simply have difficulty getting along. When this happens, the bullied animal may live in perpetual fear and anxiety and may eventually spend all his time trying to hide. If a pet is being picked on by other animals in the house, having a private Safe Haven to retreat to is critical to emotional security and self-confidence.

Angelica's story is a perfect example. Angelica was a beautiful long-haired marmalade cat who had lived happily with her owners, Matt and Joseph, for 3 years. One day, Joseph brought home a beagle, Pablo, whose owner, a coworker, was unable to keep him. Pablo was delighted with his new feline companion, as he'd had two cats to play with in his previous home. Angelica, however, was not so charmed. Although Pablo posed no threat to her, he constantly badgered her to play. Angelica misunderstood and became nervous and fearful, always looking around for the dog when she wished to walk on the floor and spending much of her time on the fireplace mantle, hissing at the friendly beagle below.

Matt and Joseph wanted the animals to get along, so they hit on an idea based on the Safe Haven: They bought a baby gate and placed it across the door of the guest room. Angelica could easily slip through the slats and retreat to a corner of the room out of sight, but Pablo could not enter. As a result, Angelica knew she could hide any time she wanted. After 2 weeks, she was far more relaxed and began playing with the beagle—but only when *she* wanted to.

On the other hand, having no Safe Haven can lead to severe emotional problems. This is perhaps most clearly seen in the cat or dog who has been shuffled from foster home to foster home. The poor creature has no Safe Haven and can't develop a sense of security. He remains nervous, frightened, and easily traumatized. This unfortunate pet will regain strength and stability only when he gains a secure and dependable Safe Haven.

CREATING A SAFE HAVEN FOR YOUR PET

Safe Havens come in many forms. Depending on the layout of your house or apartment, it may be a corner of the closet, under the bed, a crate, a box, a perch on top of a high bookshelf, a doghouse—any place that your cat or dog can call his own.

The best Safe Havens are those that are chosen by the pets themselves. Instinct is usually the best guide to personal safety. When you get a new pet, make sure that there are a number of places she can choose from to make her Safe Haven. If you usually leave the bedroom door open, under

BENNY'S STORY

An especially poignant story of the value of a Safe Haven concerns Benny, a 3-year-old male mixed-breed cat with brown, black, and white stripes. Benny shared his life with Tammy, who was a college student. Because Tammy lived in a rural area that seemed relatively safe for cats, she allowed Benny to go outdoors. Benny showed every sign of enjoying being outside, even crying for Tammy to let him out when snow was on the ground. Every time Tammy opened her front door, Benny immediately bounded outside, his nose twitching as he tested the air. When Tammy came home from school at the end of the day, she inevitably found Benny waiting on the front porch for her.

When Tammy was at home, reading or relaxing outside on her front porch, Benny often joined her. Sometimes, she saw him dash up onto the porch, seemingly to escape some real or imagined threat that spooked him. "Benny definitely sees the porch as his haven," she told me during one of Benny's annual checkups. "He seems to feel safe and secure there."

Sadly, Benny's life ended one cool October day. Tammy came home from school and found Benny curled up on the front porch just outside her front door. He was not breathing. She rushed him to our clinic, but he had died. The wounds on Benny's body told me he had been hit by a car. As Tammy and I discussed the situation, we realized that Benny must have been struck by a car on the one road at the end of Tammy's long driveway, and even with his severe injuries had made his way back home. Benny had spent his last moments seeking out his Safe Haven—the safest place he knew. Tammy was understandably devastated by Benny's death, but she received some comfort in knowing that Benny had died in a place that provided him with the most emotional comfort possible.

the bed is always a good option. Others include a covered basket, a crate, or an open closet in a spare room. Your pet may already have a Safe Haven—think about where she retreats to after being upset or frightened. When a rumbling garbage truck arrives, and the workmen bang the trash cans around, or when a group of loud people arrive, at the front door, where does your pet disappear to? It will be the place where he feels safest. Once you have identified your pet's Safe Haven, you can fortify it to maximize its protective qualities.

To fortify your pet's Safe Haven, put yourself in your pet's position. If you were hiding in this place, what would make you feel more secure? It's usually a good idea to make a partial enclosure more fully enclosed. For instance, you could add walls to a cubbyhole, or drape blankets or towels to add curtain-like visual barriers. Your pet will appreciate your doing what you can to make the inside of the haven as dark as possible. If your cat has chosen a spot on top of a bookcase, consider placing an attractive box or basket there for the cat to hide in. (Make sure it is well secured so that it can't fall off when your cat leaps in.)

The ideal Safe Haven excludes all upsetting sounds, smells, and sights. However, it's unrealistic to expect a pet's Safe Haven to be fully soundproof or free from all disturbing stimuli.

What matters most is that your pet learns that he is safe while inside his sanctuary. He may still hear loud noises, he may still smell the scent of a bully animal, but he knows he will not be harmed as long as he is inside his own Safe Haven.

When you have more than one pet, the issue of a Safe Haven is a little more complicated, especially if two or more of the pets don't get along. As with Angelica, whose story is described on page 104, it's important to make sure that a "bully" animal is not able to enter the bullied animal's Safe Haven. To bully-proof your pet's Safe Haven, you'll need some sort of physical barrier, such as a very small entrance or a baby gate. If a smaller pet is seeking escape or protection from a larger one, and the animals are different enough in size, construct a little house with a small doorway that will allow only the smaller pet to enter. If the Safe Haven belongs to a cat, sometimes placing the Safe Haven too high for other pets to reach will work. (Joseph and Matt could have helped Angelica by placing a wicker box or basket for her to hide in on the mantle.) In some cases, you'll have to train the bully animal to make sure he knows that his companion's Safe Haven is strictly off limits.

Making a Safe Haven available is the single most important thing you can do to help your pet enjoy peace of mind and stay in his or her Comfort Zone. In the next chapter, we'll look at how The Pet Pleasure Principle can make your relationship with your pet even better by getting her to stop doing the things you don't want her to do and start doing the things that you'd like her to do.

Chapter 6

AIN'T MISBEHAVIN'

IT WAS A VERY BUSY DAY at the animal hospital when Jeremy called to discuss what he called a "behavior problem" with Duke, his 2-year-old male golden retriever. As Jeremy described it, in the past few months, Duke had begun to bark almost constantly. It didn't matter whether Jeremy was home or not. The final straw was that Duke was now digging holes in the backyard. Jeremy was frustrated and, I sensed, a little angry. "I've tried everything I can to get him to stop barking and digging," he told me, "but nothing works. I just don't understand it. Duke's never misbehaved like this before."

Before I had a chance to continue the conversation and get more information, I was paged to the waiting room "stat" for an incoming emergency. I quickly said goodbye to Jeremy and told him that I would call later that day. As the day drew to a close, I decided that rather than call, I would stop by Jeremy's house on my way home to see Duke's living situation for myself.

When I knocked on Jeremy's door and got no response, I cursed myself for not calling first. But before I got too far into my thought, I heard barking from behind the house. Almost instantly Duke appeared at the fence that stretched across the driveway at the side of the house. He was barking loudly and excitedly.

As I made my way over to greet him, a slim, dark-haired young woman ran out of the house across the street, calling out, "It's okay, Duke, I'm coming!" This is odd, I thought.

By the time she reached us, Duke had jammed his head through the narrow opening between the gateposts, straining to extend his neck toward the woman. She began to pet him vigorously, and I then noticed that she had a leash in her hand. Perplexed, I introduced myself as Duke's vet, and the woman reciprocated by telling me her name was Wendy. I asked her if she was caring for Duke. She rolled her eyes upward and, with a strong sarcastic tone, replied, "Yeah, I guess *that's* the understatement of the year."

I must have looked perplexed, because she went on to say, "Duke is the loneliest dog we've ever known. Jeremy—Mr. Bigshot movie producer—never gives him any attention. Not only is he gone 15 hours a day, he's often out of town for months on end to oversee the shooting of his movies. And whether he's home or not, he keeps Duke outside all hours of the day and night. We've never seen him walking Duke, or, for that matter, playing or spending any time with him."

I shook my head in shock and sympathy for Duke. Before I could say anything, she went on, "Whenever Duke sees anybody walking by—even if the person is on the other side of the street—he forces his head through this gate and whimpers just to get the passerby to pet him. It's become too much for us to take."

"Us?" I asked.

Wendy nodded. "A bunch of us in the neighborhood formed a group to help Duke out. We asked Jeremy if he would mind if we took Duke on walks. He said he didn't care. Nice, huh? So we take turns coming over to walk him. Duke gets so excited he bounces around like he's bursting with joy. He's really a loving dog," she added. "Any one of us in our group would happily adopt him, but we've asked Jeremy several times, and he always says no."

I stood for a moment, taking in the young woman's distressing report. "Jeremy has told me Duke barks constantly and digs holes in the yard," I said.

"Well, no kidding," Wendy shot back. "If you were him, wouldn't you be crying for attention and trying to dig your way out?"

I thanked Wendy for her concern for Duke and asked if she would mind if I called her occasionally to see how Duke was doing. She happily gave me her number, and I left.

Here was an interesting situation, I thought. A dog's behavior is seen as misbehavior by one person and as perfectly understandable behavior by others.

I knew what I had to do. When I reached Jeremy by phone the next day, I quickly got to the point. After a very short discussion, it was clear that Jeremy would not be able to give Duke the attention he needed, so I told him that Duke needed to be in a different home. Period. Once I had explained Duke's emotional needs, Jeremy agreed, and I made a happy phone call to Wendy. Duke is now in a loving home getting all the companionship, attention, walks, and playtime he could possibly want.

Oh, and he no longer barks or digs.

The main point of Duke's story is that Jeremy had called me to solve a problem of "misbehavior." Do you think Duke was misbehaving? In this chapter, we'll take a much closer look at the answer to this question.

When your cat or dog continues to do something you don't like despite your attempts to stop it, he is often doing so because of an emotional or physical discomfort. When this happens, whatever he is doing—desirable or not—is simply his attempt to relieve that discomfort and move toward pleasure on the Pleasure/Discomfort Scale. In other words, when your pet sometimes does things you don't like, she ain't misbehavin'.

Luckily for you and your pet, The Pet Pleasure Principle not only explains why our pets do the things they do, it also clearly gives us the guide we need to change the behaviors we don't like. In fact, it provides a basic blueprint to change pet behavior for virtually *any* reason. For example, it's important for dogs' safety and socialization for them to learn to obey standard commands. You may want your dog—or even your cat—to be able to perform tricks. And you will certainly want your pet to avoid digging up your planter, biting, scratching, threatening with displays of aggression, barking excessively, urinating in the wrong places, or engaging in destructive behavior, such as shredding mattresses or clawing furniture. (I'll tell you how The Pet Pleasure Principle works in each of these cases a bit later in the chapter, starting on page 113.)

Another example of this principle at work is the case of Max. Max is a large, 3-year-old mixed-breed dog who becomes extremely upset when his owner is away. His behavior at these times includes loud howling, attempts to escape from the house by chewing through doors, and urinating and defecating on the floor.

Is Max a "bad dog?" Not at all. If we examine his behavior in relation to The Pet Pleasure Principle, the reasons for his actions become quite clear. We know that any animal who is on the discomfort side of the Pleasure/Discomfort Scale will try to move himself toward pleasure, to get out of discomfort and back into his Comfort Zone. In Max's case, the discomfort is due to separation anxiety. As if he were trying to relieve the pain of a slipped disk in his back, Max will do anything he can to relieve his emotional pain. His howling may be an attempt to call his owner back, his chewing the woodwork and digging are most likely an attempt to escape, and the urination and defecation are the physiological results of extreme anxiety (remember times when you've been very nervous and had to visit the bathroom?).

Once we understand Max's dilemma, it becomes very clear what needs to be done to change his behavior: We need to find a way to move Max back into his Comfort Zone. It's that straightforward. When a pet's behavior is due to emotional discomfort, this is the absolute best, most logical, most effective, kindest, and most correct method of changing that behavior. It's the same thing you would do if the unwanted behavior were due to physical discomfort.

USING THE PET PLEASURE PRINCIPLE TO CHANGE BEHAVIOR

There are volumes written on how to change your pet's behavior, and though they may not spell it out, their techniques are all based in one way or another on The Pet Pleasure Principle: An animal will always behave in the way that brings him the greatest overall pleasure. In terms of the Pleasure/Discomfort Scale, the behavior your pet will virtually always choose to perform is the one that he perceives as putting him closest to the pleasure end of the scale. Therefore, to change undesirable behavior, you need to make a more acceptable behavior result in greater perceived pleasure for your pet. If you can do that, your cat or dog should choose the new behavior fairly quickly.

There are four basic methods to change your pet's behavior using The Pet Pleasure Principle: eliminate discomfort, give your pet something more pleasurable to do, make the undesirable behavior less rewarding than a desirable behavior, and use counterconditioning. Let's look at each method.

Method #1: Eliminate Your Pet's Discomfort

If the motivation for your pet's behavior is to lessen an unpleasant feeling, then eliminating your pet's discomfort is always the best solution. Whenever you can, find a way to ease your pet's unpleasant emotional or physical feelings. Often, this alone will be enough to change undesirable behavior.

If you remember Max's separation anxiety, you can see how his owner could relieve his discomfort using one of several options.

* Use behavioral modification techniques, sometimes with the help of medications, to help him regain his emotional well-being and confidence when he is alone.

* Offer Max things to do when his owner is away, such as providing interactive toys and hiding food treats that he can hunt for, to lessen the emotional discomfort of boredom.

* Provide him with companionship, either through doggy day care or by having a dog-walker spend time with him, to help ease his distress from loneliness and boredom.

Each of these techniques is designed to move Max toward pleasure on the Pleasure/Discomfort Scale—back into his Comfort Zone. Once he is back there, he'll no longer have the need to try to do it himself.

Method #2: Give Your Pet Something More Pleasurable to Do

Another way to change your pet's undesirable behavior is to give her something more enjoyable to do. This means finding a way to make another behavior (including doing nothing at all) pay off with a bigger reward. This can be accomplished by offering a behavioral option that is naturally more pleasurable, or rewarding an alternate behavior to make it more pleasurable that what she is currently doing. The latter

# The Unseen Rewards

Animals view the world in different ways than we do. They smell things we can't smell; they see things we don't see. And very often, they are rewarded in ways that we don't perceive.

Recall the imaginary situation at the beginning of Chapter 4, where Bogie the puppy can't be housetrained because you inadvertently keep rewarding him with your attention for piddling on the carpet. Your attention is one of the most common unseen rewards.

Other rewards can often be difficult for humans to even guess at. For example, when a dog is digging in the garden, it may not be out of boredom but because he likes the smell of the different things he digs up. A cat who sprays his urine in the house may be doing it not because of any emotional upsets but because he may receive a pleasurable feeling from exerting his territorial claim (like the sense of pride you might get by beating your opponent in a game of tennis or golf). Or he could have a physical problem like a urinary tract infection.

Always be aware that if your pet is performing some behavior that makes no sense to you, the behavior may be providing him with an unseen reward that is bringing him pleasure or lessening a discomfort—either one moving him toward pleasure on the Pleasure/Discomfort Scale.

---

technique is the main principle of virtually all animal training today. For example:

- ❖ If your dogs jumps up on people, he'll often stop if you lavish him with attention and praise for staying down. For your dog, this increases the pleasure of the alternate, more acceptable behavior.

- ❖ If your dog chews on your shoes, buy a tasty chew toy or treat that he would find more pleasurable to chew on. This solution should soon have him choosing the new treats over your shoes. (Of course, finding the right attractive item may require some effort on your part, and in some cases, you may simply be unable to find something he likes better. In that case, you'll simply have to be more vigilant about keeping your shoes shut in the closet. In addition, be sure to avoid chew toys made of materials or fabrics that closely resemble the objects you don't want chewed, because it can be hard for dogs to distinguish the allowable chewie from the disallowed).

❖ Cats who claw the furniture often find other scratching surfaces more pleasurable. Try to find a scratching post made of material that she likes better, like sisal rope (this also may require some searching on your part). Boosting the pleasure even more with a little catnip rubbed onto the post will often solve the scratching problem. (For more information on unwanted scratching, see page 140.)

Any time the behavior you want your pet to do moves him closer to pleasure on the Pleasure/Discomfort Scale than what you *don't* want him to do, it should become his preferred behavior.

METHOD #3: REMOVE THE REWARD

Make the current behavior result in no increase in pleasure or in less pleasure. To reduce the pleasure your pet receives from his undesirable behavior, remove the reward the current behavior provides, or make the consequences of the behavior unpleasant enough that the behavior isn't worth it (punishment). If you remove the reward, the behavior no longer brings an increase of pleasure, removing the motive for the behavior.

Consider the common example of a dog who begs at the dinner table. This behavior is almost always the result of someone rewarding the dog repeatedly (or maybe even just once) by giving her a bit of tasty "people" food. Clearly, to stop this behavior the reward must be removed—which means no treats from the dinner table, ever. Over a period of time with no reward, the dog will learn that her behavior no longer brings about an increase in pleasure, eliminating her motivation to continue begging.

(Warning: All it takes to keep the begging going is for someone to occasionally sneak a treat to the dog.)

A more effective technique in changing a pet's behavior than simply removing the reward is making an undesired behavior result in a move toward discomfort on the scale. An alternative behavior, such as doing nothing or doing something more acceptable, will then give your pet the greater pleasure. This technique works by having something unpleasant happen when the pet performs the undesired behavior.

For example, if your cat gets into cabinets where he might damage expensive objects or come in contact with dangerous chemicals, try putting a load of Ping-Pong balls inside the cabinet door. The next time your cat opens the door, the balls will clatter out, startling the cat and scaring him away. A cat may learn his lesson the first time he is startled, but in some cases, it could take several repetitions before he makes the connection between his behavior and the unpleasant result. From that point on, the cat will realize that *not* trying to get into the cabinet will result in greater pleasure.

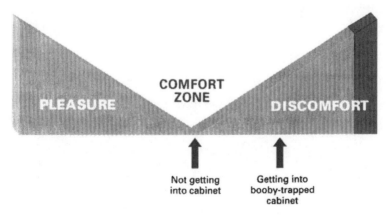

As this diagram shows, the result of the behavioral option you regard as more desirable (staying out of the cabinet) now moves the cat further toward pleasure than the undesirable behavior (getting into the cabinet).

In a similar situation, if your cat constantly gets up on the counter, covering the counter with aluminum foil or sticky paper makes the jumping up unpleasant, so that *not* jumping on the counter becomes more pleasant than jumping up.

It's important to note that making the consequences unpleasant is inappropriate when the reason for your pet's actions is to lessen discomfort. You should *never* increase the trauma of a pet who is already enduring emotional or physical discomfort. (For the one important exception to this rule, see "Is Punishment Ever a Good Idea?" on page 129.)

Thus, when a dog is barking because he is in physical or emotional pain, shouting at him will only make him suffer more. When a pet's behavior is an attempt to relieve discomfort, your foremost objective is to help your pet get the relief he seeks.

Competing Rewards

A slightly more complicated behavior problem involves pets who chew on bandages that protect healing wounds. If your dog chews at his bandage, applying a bitter-tasting ointment will make the chewing unpleasant. As long as the unpleasantness of the taste outweighs the positive reward your dog gets from chewing, then *not* chewing will move him further toward pleasure on the Pleasure/Discomfort Scale. The reason this technique often fails is that the motivation to lick comes from the dog's desire to lessen the discomfort of the healing wound (or the bandage itself). This motivation is sometimes so powerful that the bitter taste is not enough to outweigh it. In the dog's eyes, chewing, even with the nasty taste, will move him further toward pleasure on the scale than not chewing.

It's easy to sympathize with the poor dog. If you have a terrible itch

MELISSA'S STORY

I heard an amusing example of behavior retraining from Sandra, a friend of mine who had an adventurous 6-month-old kitten named Melissa. Though Melissa was being raised as an indoor-only cat, she continually tried to get out through the front door, which was only a few yards from a moderately busy street. "I tried everything I could think of to keep her away from the door," Sandra told me. "But she seemed drawn to it. And she was so quick, I knew that sooner or later she would succeed in getting out."

And get out she did: One afternoon, while Sandra struggled to bring several bags of groceries indoors, Melissa managed to scamper out the partially open door—just as a large delivery truck drove by and backfired. "Melissa turned around like a shot," Sandra told me. "She headed for the back of the house and spent the next several hours under the bed. And she has never again tried to get out the front door!"

While it's not possible to arrange for a timely truck backfire, it is sometimes possible to put the same principle into effect yourself. Mabel, a longtime client of mine, told me how her mixed-breed dog, Buster, woke her up in the morning by standing on his hind legs and placing his front paws on her stomach while she lay in bed. She didn't usually mind being awakened, but lately he had begun to wake Mabel earlier and earlier in the morning. Not wanting to yell at Buster, she hit upon a solution. Knowing how much Buster disliked having his nails trimmed, Mabel placed a nail trimmer on her nightstand. The next morning when Buster placed his front paws on her, she reached for the trimmers and calmly began trimming his toenails. She told me that it only took two times before Buster decided to not wake her up so early anymore.

The principle for stopping a pet from engaging in dangerous, destructive, or otherwise undesired behaviors is the same: Make doing something else, including simply refraining from doing the undesirable behavior, result in a better payoff.

in the middle of your back, and it hurts to bend your arm into a position to scratch the itch, you'll accept the pain to get at the itch—up to a point. If the pain became intense enough, you would choose to forgo scratching. In humans, this is the way the justice and penal systems operate—the unpleasantness of fines and imprisonment (the "cost") raises the level of discomfort so high that not performing the forbidden behavior, or doing something else, results in a greater net pleasure than doing it. Punishment is nothing more or less than making a behavior result in—or risk resulting in—a move toward discomfort on the Pleasure/ Discomfort Scale.

Begging for Attention

Attention-getting behavior is another good example of your pet doing things you don't like in order to get a reward. In this case, the reward is your attention, even if it's negative attention like fussing at him. This behavior is not unlike that of a teenager who misbehaves just so his parents will at least give him *some* attention (see "The Unseen Rewards" on page 115).

Does your dog bark or nose you to encourage you to interact with him? Perhaps your cat walks back and forth across the keyboard when you're at the computer. These are common attention-getting behaviors in pets. Luckily, you can often handle them with two strategies.

1. First, make sure your pet receives plenty of attention at other times (so his emotional needs may not be so intense at inconvenient times).

2. Second, stop responding to all of your pet's pleas for attention, and teach him a different way to signal his desires. For a dog, this might involve lavishly praising him for sitting alertly nearby. For a cat, praise and a treat for a less disruptive way of seeking attention may eventually do the trick. Once your pet realizes that the new behavior, rather than what he's currently doing, results in the reward, he will be more likely to perform the new behavior. For an

example of extreme attention-getting behavior, see "Mookie's Story" on page 122.

Method #4: Counterconditioning

Still another way to encourage your pet to change his behavior is to make an unpleasant behavior more pleasant. When you want your pet to do something he doesn't want to do (such as take a pill or sit still for a nail trim), you can often form an association in his mind between the undesirable outcome (the discomfort) and a pleasurable one. This technique, called counterconditioning, is intended to change the meaning of a thing or event from unpleasant to pleasant. It is the principle behind a number of behavioral modification techniques. For example, when the veterinarian gives your dog a treat every time she comes into the animal hospital, the aim is to get the dog to associate the pleasant treat with the unpleasant trip, thus changing her perception of visiting the vet to something with a good, rather than bad, outcome.

When my own cat, Gooby, developed kidney failure, I had to give him several pills a day. He hated it and was soon running away from me every time I approached him, convinced that I was about to give him another pill. Knowing that he loved his harness walks outside, I developed a routine whereby I would give him a pill and then immediately put his harness on and take him outside. It took less than a week for him to become perfectly willing to take his pill. A bad thing soon came to mean a good thing, and he wanted the good thing.

If your cat will not get into his carrier because it has become associated with unpleasant trips to the vet, counterconditioning can often be used to change his perception of the carrier. To develop a more pleasant association with the carrier, try using play, attention, and tasty food treats. Playing with your cat while he is near the carrier, then offering him tasty

(continued on page 124)

MOOKIE'S STORY

When I first met Mookie, I remember thinking that there could be no stronger love than she felt for Michael. I was awed at how this 11-year-old, jet black female Labrador mix clung to her master, never taking her eyes from him, never letting the distance between them exceed a few feet before she again quickly closed the gap. Here, it seemed to me, was the epitome of canine love.

But Michael didn't see Mookie's devotion in such heartwarming terms. The clinginess, in fact, was why he had brought Mookie to me. The story he told me both explained Mookie's extreme devotion and showed how emotional pain can devastate a pet's confidence and emotional well-being.

"Mookie spent her first 9 years with a devoted and gentle old man," Michael told me. "The man was a widower, and I'm told he and Mookie were inseparable. They spent their days taking walks in the park and running errands in the car. The old man was retired, so he was able to devote himself full-time to Mookie. When he left her alone, it was never for long, but one morning he left to run an errand and never returned. Sadly, he was killed in a tragic car crash."

Looking at Mookie's sweet, intelligent face, I could imagine how devastated she must have been at losing her lifelong companion.

Michael ruffled the dog's shiny black fur and continued. "Luckily for Mookie, a friend of the old fellow found her the next day and turned her over to a rescue organization. They placed her in a foster home with 15 other dogs. Then every Saturday, they took her to the adoption fair in a parking lot near my home."

Michael continued, telling me how week after week, he saw her in one of the cages, a sweet-looking black dog with gray around her muzzle. "Something about her caught my eye," he told me. "She was so pretty, I was sure someone would adopt her, but I guess she was too old. I began stopping and petting her, and it was like I'd offered water to an animal dying of thirst. Some kind of bond formed between us—after a couple more weeks of no one showing an interest in her, I just had to adopt her myself, even though I already had two dogs."

I nodded. I could tell by the way he had stooped down to gently stroke Mookie as we continued to talk that he cared deeply for her. And now I could see the root of Michael's problem—and the beginning of a solution. "No wonder she is so dependent on you," I said. "Your analogy of an animal dying of thirst is a good one. Until she met you, Mookie was thirsting for human companionship."

"It's only been 2 weeks," Michael said, "but ever since I brought her home, she's always plastered right by me, even when I go to the bathroom. When she's not touching me, she's looking at me.

"I'm no dog psychiatrist," he went on, "but she seems to have a really extreme need for human companionship. Maybe she feels insecure. I've really grown to love Mookie, and I can't bear seeing her live this way."

I told Michael that he was almost certainly right on all counts. "Mookie has been suffering," I told him. "Losing her companion was a terrible blow, and it was made worse by the months in a foster home with 15 dogs and little human companionship. For all her years, she had been the only dog, with lots of love and attention for her and her alone. She's in pain— very much the way a dog with a broken leg would be in pain."

"I understand," Michael said, "But I'm not retired. I don't have time to spend every second with her."

"You don't need to do that," I told him. "What Mookie needs most is the feeling that she has a caring human companion to form a stable, dependable bond with. I expect that as she learns you are there to stay, she will become less clingy. But because of her history, she will probably always need extra attention."

"I guess I can handle that," Michael said. "But how long will it take?"

I told Michael there was no way of predicting how long it would take for Mookie to regain her confidence. I prescribed an anti-anxiety medication to help in the meantime, and Michael agreed to give Mookie extra attention on his own timetable. When he called a few weeks later, he reported that the program seemed to be working. "She's still a lot needier than the other dogs," he told me. "But she seems to be okay when I leave her, and she's not following me around every second like she was. In fact, she's even starting to enjoy playing with the other dogs."

treats inside the carrier, will help to change the carrier from a bad thing to a good thing in your cat's mind.

Here's another favorite story of how a negative association was changed into a positive one: Pepper, a spirited black-and-white male Labrador mix, became hyperexcited and barked madly when the mail carrier walked up the driveway. Pepper behaved as if he actually wanted to get at the carrier and tear him to pieces. The carrier astutely noted what was happening and began to bring a dog biscuit every day, which he tossed through the fence to Pepper. Soon Pepper began to bark less, and eventually the letter carrier was able to hand the biscuit directly to him.

After a few weeks, at mail delivery time, Pepper kept an eagle eye on the driveway. As soon as he sighted the mail carrier, he began to excitedly run in circles, whimpering with delight. When he got his biscuit, Pepper now happily sat as the mailman petted him. Those little biscuits had changed the meaning of the mail carrier's arrival from one of threat to one of pleasant feelings.

Double the Incentive

Sometimes, it's possible to "supermotivate" your pet to change by both rewarding the preferred behavior *and* discouraging undesirable behavior. For example, if your dog constantly jumps up on visitors, a verbal reprimand each time he does it will discourage him because your disapproval and unhappiness are enough to increase his discomfort. But you'll get the best results if you offer him a treat each time he greets visitors in a less objectionable way. The result of this double-edged approach is that the undesirable behavior (jumping on visitors) is now *much* less appealing to your dog than the desirable behavior (greeting visitors with a friendly wag). As a result, your dog is much more likely to choose the new behavior.

Each of these four methods uses The Pet Pleasure Principle. When you successfully apply this principle, the behavior you want your pet to perform gives him greater pleasure than other behavioral choices. As a result, he will be more highly motivated to stop doing things you don't want him to do and start doing things you do want.

Bear in mind that The Pet Pleasure Principle, along with the four methods by which it is applied, is a general principle. In correcting undesirable behavior, The Pet Pleasure Principle and its methods are applied in the form of specific behavior-modification techniques—techniques that must be performed correctly. I will discuss a few of the more common techniques later in this chapter, but to make sure you use the techniques that are most appropriate for your own pet and your unique situation, you should consult with a certified trainer or animal behaviorist. Information on finding a certified behaviorist or trainer, as well as other sources of detailed behavioral modification techniques, are included in "Appendix" on page 280.

TECHNOLOGY TO THE RESCUE?

Ads for a number of new technological gadgets promise to make pets behave the way you want them to. Before using any of these devices, it's a good idea to examine them from the perspective of The Pet Pleasure Principle. For example, electronic shock collars are supposed to stop "unwanted barking" by giving dogs an unpleasant shock each time they bark. These collars may stop the barking, but be aware that they have the potential to increase your dog's overall discomfort, since he's probably barking because he is trying to relieve an existing emotional discomfort. If adding the unpleasantness of the collar's shock moves him even further toward discomfort on the Pleasure/Discomfort Scale, he not only receives

When Is a Treat a Treat?

Your pet's "value" system is based on The Pet Pleasure Principle. His interest in something depends on the amount of pleasure it either gives him or takes away from him. Thus, when rewarding your dog or cat with a treat, make sure that it's a *really* good treat (from your pet's perspective, of course).

Many things can work as treats. Even simple praise is hugely rewarding for most dogs. But if you're using a food reward, be sure that the treat is truly tasty. While most dogs (and many cats) welcome a snack at any time, a piece of the same old kibble may not be rewarding enough to motivate a change in behavior.

What really rings most pets' chimes, and is therefore most likely to help change behavior, is a special, delicious treat, such as a commercial treat or a piece of cheese.

---

no relief from his current discomfort, but now he has an extra discomfort heaped on top of that. Imagine having a terrible itch on your arm, and every time you reach to scratch it, you receive a painful shock. How would *you* feel?

More humane are anti-bark collars that make use of a mildly unpleasant yet distracting odor, such as citronella. However, using the collar still attempts to change behavior without regard for the dog's underlying motivation for barking (such as loneliness). Suppressing barking without relieving the dog's discomfort not only leaves him out of his Comfort Zone but makes him even more uncomfortable.

Consider a dog like Duke, whom you met at the beginning of this chapter. He is left alone all day in the fenced yard with no human company. He barks constantly because of the distress of his unmet emotional need for companionship. Now consider his owner, Jeremy, responding to this by taking him to the vet to be surgically debarked. The barking problem is solved, but the dog's problem isn't. His suffering continues. The owner got what he wanted, but who's paying the price?

THE ELECTRIC FENCE

Invisible electric "fences" consist of wires placed underground or under carpeting that provide an electrical shock in your dog's collar when he crosses over the wire. These devices operate on The Pet Pleasure Principle in that they make the undesired action—crossing the line—less pleasant than the desired action, which is staying inside the fence barrier. However, The Pet Pleasure Principle itself shows why these devices may at times fail. Your dog will no doubt stay on the desired side of the "fence" as long as there's no rewarding reason to cross the line, simply because it's more pleasant not to suffer a shock than to suffer one.

However, if your dog sees a big enough reward outside his fenced area (say, a cat, and he *loves* chasing cats), he may perceive the pleasure of crossing the fence as outweighing the unpleasantness of a shock. If so, you can bet he'll choose to pursue that option—the one that feels best to him. As long as the move toward pleasure on the Pleasure/Discomfort Scale (cat chasing) is greater than the move toward discomfort (electric shock), the net result is a gain in pleasure.

This is the very type of calculation Michel Cabanac observed rats making when they weighed tasty food against the frigid cold they had to endure to get to a treat (see page 44). We humans make calculations like this all the time. If a person has to walk a block in the sunshine to get a delicious café mocha with whipped cream, she'll see the pleasure as clearly outweighing the effort of walking. But if the coffee shop is 16 blocks away, and there is an icy sleet with 45-mile-per-hour winds, the pleasure of the coffee would be strongly outweighed by the unpleasantness of the effort to get it. Exactly like Cabanac's rats.

Please note, by the way, that the shock collar and the electric fence, though both operating on The Pet Pleasure Principle, are very different techniques from your dog's point of view. Shock collars are used primarily in situations where the dog is already experiencing some kind of dis-

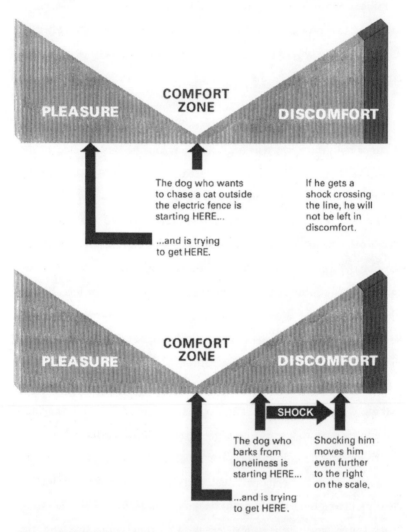

COMFORT ZONE

PLEASURE

DISCOMFORT

The dog who wants to chase a cat outside the electric fence is starting HERE...

If he gets a shock crossing the line, he will not be left in discomfort.

...and is trying to get HERE.

COMFORT ZONE

PLEASURE

DISCOMFORT

SHOCK

The dog who barks from loneliness is starting HERE...

Shocking him moves him even further to the right on the scale.

...and is trying to get HERE.

Even though both shock collars and electric fences use an electric shock to deter inappropriate behavior, the fence is much kinder to your pet, as this diagram shows.

comfort and is trying to move back into his Comfort Zone. By moving the dog even further toward discomfort, the shock collar hurts an already hurting dog even more. The electric fence, in contrast, is very different because the dog is usually already in his Comfort Zone, and his goal is to gain pleasure. In this case, the shock may or may not deter him from crossing the invisible fence line, but it also doesn't leave him in discomfort.

IS PUNISHMENT EVER A GOOD IDEA?

There is a common belief among animal trainers today that physical punishment is wrong—that "you should never hit your dog." I wholeheartedly agree. But this belief also implies a potentially dangerous and harmful notion: that nonphysical punishment—emotional punishment—is therefore acceptable.

I'm sure you can immediately sense that something is wrong with this view. *All* unpleasant feelings are unpleasant to an animal. They all work the same way: to motivate the animal to do what needs to be done to lessen the discomfort. Animal trainers may claim that they use no physical punishment, but if they use, say, isolation as a punishment, the animal may feel just as bad as if he'd been beaten.

This is not to say that punishment of any kind is always inappropriate or cruel, but that emotional punishments can be every bit as severe and painful to animals as physical punishment. The most important message here is that any punishment of a behavior caused by attempts to relieve distress adds still more unpleasant feelings and increases the distress.

Very frequently, when I see a dog for some itchy condition—fleas, allergies, skin mites—the dog's owner says something like, "He scratches all the time, and it drives us crazy. But all I have to do is yell 'stop it!' and he does." The owner usually sounds proud, as if to let me know that he's been right on top of things and doing his job. But he hasn't. As I proceed to explain, the dog is just trying to relieve his discomfort.

Anything done to an animal that causes unpleasant feelings is acceptable only if the ultimate outcome is an increase in overall pleasure. A typical example is an unpleasant medical treatment that will result in the pet's greater overall health.

A few years ago, I removed a benign fatty tumor from the flank of Kyra, a rather hyperactive female tortoiseshell cat who lived with one of my longtime clients. Kyra began to scratch and bite at the stitches as soon as she awoke from anesthesia. Kyra was, of course, only trying to alleviate the discomfort caused by the stitches and return to her Comfort Zone.

Can All Behavior Be Changed?

Though The Pet Pleasure Principle is the most useful tool we have for changing your pet's behavior, the truth is that not all behavior can be changed. Some unwanted behavior is simply too highly motivated to be changed by offering a more pleasurable option. For example, if your dog is suffering from extreme itchiness or pain, she may lick or bite at the affected area until it is raw. Because the initial discomfort is so intense, there is no alternative option that will be preferable to her and no reasonably administered deterrent that would move her further toward pleasure on the Pleasure/Discomfort Scale. (This is a situation when you and the vet need to find a medical solution to her problem—fast.)

Some instinctive behaviors, such as territorial marking or some forms of aggression, also may not be readily amenable to change, though they can often be prevented (by having your pet neutered, for example). For all undesirable behaviors, you should consult your vet to see if the problem has a physical cause. If it doesn't, consult with a certified trainer, an animal behaviorist, or your vet for a behavioral modification plan tailored to your pet's situation.

However, ripping out the stitches would prevent the wound from healing properly, if at all, with the ultimate outcome being an even greater shift out of her Comfort Zone. The only solution to prevent that from happening was to place a large plastic ("Elizabethan") collar around Kyra's neck until the incision had healed. The collar prevented Kyra from trying to relieve her own discomfort, leaving her outside her Comfort Zone, and the collar itself added to her discomfort. But the wound healed quickly, resulting in an overall increase in her pleasure.

DRUG THERAPY

When its use is warranted, drug therapy can be an important and beneficial part of a veterinarian's behavior-modification arsenal. Veterinarians prescribe psychotropic drugs (drugs that affect mood and feelings) for emotional pain in the same way aspirin is used for physical pain: to lessen the intensity of unpleasant feelings. From the perspective of The Pet Pleasure Principle, the drugs take a dog or cat and move him out of discomfort into his Comfort Zone. If drug therapy can get him entirely into his Comfort Zone, he feels good and no longer has a need to attempt to relieve his own discomfort.

Of the specific medications used to help pets, the two most common types are those used to relieve anxiety and depression. Whenever I prescribe psychotropic drugs, I have two aims in mind:

1. **Most important:** to relieve the pet's emotional distress and move her back into her Comfort Zone. This often resolves the problem by itself. When it doesn't, it relieves enough emotional distress to make behavior-modification techniques more effective.

2. **Secondary but related:** to help improve behavior problems that have been caused by the pet's discomfort.

In other words, if I am treating a pet for an undesirable behavior, my *principle* aim is to alleviate any unpleasant feelings that may be motivating her to perform that behavior. I look at stopping the unwanted behavior as the beneficial by-product of achieving my first goal. For every degree that I can lessen a pet's emotional distress (usually through a combination of medication and behavior-modification techniques), the motivation for the behavior is lessened by the same degree. The emotional components of some undesirable behaviors, such as territorial marking, certain forms of aggression, and furniture scratching in cats, are not well understood at present, so we are still very much in a learning phase with the use of drugs in these cases.

How Drugs Work

About 2 years ago, Jillian, a well-dressed young woman in her mid-20s, brought Knobby in to see me. Knobby, a male Bengal cat with stunning stripes just like those on a true tiger, was 5 years old. Jillian explained to me that for several months, Knobby had been showing very unusual behavior. He urinated throughout the house; howled loudly and constantly ("You can hear him from down the street," Jillian told me); aggressively attacked Jillian's other cat, Snickers, whom Jillian was now feeling very sorry for; and constantly followed Jillian around, persistently clawing at the door if Jillian went into a room and closed the door behind her.

After digesting this list of symptoms, I asked Jill how she would describe Knobby's overall emotional state. "That's easy," she replied. "Agitated." We talked at length about Jillian's house, events, surroundings, and everything else that might have had an emotional impact on Knobby, but nothing stood out as a possible cause of his psychological state.

I ran some tests on Knobby and found no organic disease to explain his condition. "I'm afraid we don't know the cause of Knobby's problems," I told Jillian at our next meeting. "But he's obviously in emotional distress, and I'd like to try to ease his discomfort with some medication." Jillian readily agreed, and I prescribed an antidepressant that also has antianxiety effects.

I called Jillian a few weeks later. She was elated. "Doctor Mac, Knobby is so much better! He's not attacking Snickers anymore, he's no longer so needy, and I haven't found any recent urine spots in the house. He seems as relaxed and secure as he was before all this happened." I was thrilled to hear Jillian's report. Over the next 2 years, I saw Knobby occasionally for routine checkups. On one of these occasions, Jillian told me that she had tried several times to slowly decrease the dose of medication as I had advised. "It doesn't work," she concluded. "Every time I cut it back below a certain level, he goes right back to his agitation."

On her most recent visit, I admired Knobby's sleek tiger-striped fur and lordly demeanor. "He seems to be feeling fine," I told Jillian. "How has his emotional state been?"

"As long as he's on his medication, he's great," she responded. "I can't tell you how good he feels. He's so much more relaxed, and so much happier. I mean *so* much happier."

Knobby's story has two morals: first, that medication can be a powerful tool to relieve emotional discomfort; and second, that it can sometimes help animals feel better even when the exact causes of their emotional distress—or the exact emotions involved—are unknown.

Sometimes medication can help without completely resolving emotional distress. Jep, a Border collie–mix, belonged to Karyn, an artisan who frequently traveled to jewelry shows. This was a problem because

Jep was afraid of cars and trucks. Karyn had adopted Jep as an adult dog and didn't know his history, but "I think he must have had a bad experience when he was younger," Karyn told me. "He acts like he's terrified of the van. Maybe he was in an accident once." I agreed that Karyn's assessment was likely and explained how Karyn could try to desensitize Jep by taking him on short trips and combining the trips with treats. "It's no good, Doc," Karyn told me a few weeks later. "As soon as I open the van door, he starts whining and trembling."

I told Karyn to continue to make her trips as pleasant for the dog as possible and also had her put Jep on anti-anxiety medication for a day before longer trips. Karyn reported back that Jep still didn't like to travel, but he was much calmer and no longer trembled and cried when she put him in the van.

An important limitation of the benefits of psychotropic drugs is that some animals "suffer in silence." For many animals, the outward signs of emotional distress may not be evident, or they may be too subtle to recognize. This is the same problem we often have in detecting physical pain in animals—we can't know it's there if the animal doesn't show any signs of pain. Sadly, those pets who endure their emotional distress "silently" often go without the treatment that could help them feel better.

DESENSITIZATION

Desensitization is another way to help pets return to their Comfort Zone when they have a fear of something specific, such as cars, house visitors, and other animals. As the name implies, this is a process whereby the pet is gradually desensitized to—that is, becomes used to—unpleasant situations or events so that they are no longer perceived as threatening. Desensitization should *always* be done under the supervision of a certified trainer or animal behaviorist because if it is done incorrectly, it could actually worsen your pet's fear. The process usually involves exposing the pet to the feared object or event, starting with a very small or distant exposure and very gradually increasing the exposure. The pet is rewarded for remaining calm as the intensity of the exposure gradually increases. The objective is to have the pet feel calm and relaxed when fully exposed to the once-fearful stimulus.

How Your Pet Views Your Car

In humans, a phobia is a fear that is out of proportion to the actual danger or risks of the thing feared, such as an intense fear of riding in elevators. Dogs and cats who are afraid of riding in cars do not have clinical phobias like this. Rather, their fear is reasonable, since not only have many of these pets formed a negative association with the car, but there is nothing in the animals' evolutionary past to have prepared them to deal with an experience of rumbling and vibrating while moving at speeds far in excess of anything their ancestors ever encountered. To these cats and dogs, the car is a strange, unfamiliar box on wheels that often carries them to bad places like the vet or boarding facilities.

You can keep your dog from forming a negative association with your car by taking her all sorts of places with you from puppyhood on, so she associates the car with exciting adventures and rewards as well as vet trips. I've never seen a dog who regularly rides to the dog park be afraid of riding in the car! As for cats, it's unusual for a cat to love riding in a car, but if you expose your cat to short car rides from early kittenhood, you can often get her to at least tolerate (if not enjoy) the experience.

Desensitization is often used in conjunction with counterconditioning (for the added effect of changing the meaning of a stimulus from unpleasant to pleasant). As we saw with Jep, whose story is described on page 133, desensitization is sometimes used for dogs and cats who are fearful about riding in cars. The process starts with a very low level of exposure, such as merely sitting in the parked car for a minute (and being given a tasty treat), then works up to sitting in the car while it starts, then later short trips up and down the driveway, and so on until the pet is relaxed during the whole ride.

GRADUAL ACCLIMATIZATION

Another way to use desensitization is exemplified by the case of Senna, an aging male Siamese who developed an illness that required daily pills. Suzanne, Senna's companion, explained to me that Senna had a bad experience with pills when he was younger and ever since had acted terrified and fought to get away whenever she needed to dose him. Suzanne was very doubtful that she would be able to pill her cat on such a regular basis.

Because there was not an urgent need to start the pills right away, I set up a plan for Suzanne: "For a week or so, I want you to hold Senna in your lap, and use your fingers to gently touch his face and lips. When he's comfortable with that, use your fingers to touch the gums under Senna's upper lip. Then use your fingers to gently open his mouth just a tiny bit, and after a few days of that, open it a little wider." Suzanne was dubious, but agreed to do as I asked. Within just a few weeks, Suzanne reported that Senna seemed comfortable with these "mouth manipulations," so I started her on the final phase of the program, which was to begin with a tiny fraction of a pill placed on the back of Senna's tongue. Gradually,

Suzanne increased the size of his dose until Senna was getting a full tablet once a day. Just what the doctor ordered.

"I can't believe this," Suzanne told me a couple of weeks later. "I did as you said—and he doesn't act scared or try to get away. Sometimes he even purrs while he's getting his pill."

Not all pets will respond to desensitization as effectively as Senna, but his reaction shows how something that once was a source of unpleasant emotions can become a neutral and nonthreatening part of a pet's life.

THE PET PLEASURE PRINCIPLE IN ACTION

Now, let's take a look at four of the most common undesirable behaviors: overeating, destructive behavior (including scratching, chewing, and digging), inappropriate elimination, and making too much noise. Each may have several possible causes—but the bottom line is that it is safe to assume that your cat or dog is doing what she's doing in order to move toward pleasure on the Pleasure/Discomfort Scale. And in each case, the basic rule used to stop the behavior is to make doing something else (including doing nothing) more pleasurable or less uncomfortable for your pet than the undesirable behavior. Keep in mind that this can be done by

- ❖ Alleviating any discomfort that is motivating the behavior
- ❖ Offering an option that is more pleasurable
- ❖ Removing the reward so that the undesirable behavior does not increase your pet's pleasure or comfort, and/or finding a way to make the undesirable behavior increase your pet's discomfort
- ❖ Counterconditioning and desensitization

Note: This section is *not* intended to be a comprehensive guide to solving behavioral problems in your pets. Please refer to "Appendix" on page 280 or consult with a trainer or animal behaviorist if your pet has a serious or persistent behavior problem.

OVEREATING

You don't need scientific research to tell you that eating a favorite food makes you feel better when you're blue. Not surprisingly, the same seems to be true for your pet. Researchers at the University of California, San Francisco, recently reported that rats exposed to chronic stress ate more comfort food than rats not experiencing stress. The researchers found that the excess food decreased stress-related hormone levels, suggesting that the consumption of comfort food was an attempt to reduce anxiety.

Recent studies have shown that obesity in pet animals is on the rise. I firmly believe that this can be explained in a large part by this concept of comfort food; eating is a way to offset anxiety or other unpleasant emotions. If a dog or cat is fearful, anxious, lonely, or bored and he's unable to obtain relief in other ways, he may eat to relieve the discomfort. If the unpleasant emotional experience continues, the eating will also continue.

Amy, a busy elder-law attorney, brought in her white long-haired cat, Mee-ow, for a routine checkup. I was surprised to see that Mee-ow had gained several pounds since his last visit. In fact, Mee-ow was now a feline lard bucket—nearly 20 pounds on a medium-size cat's frame. I knew that Mee-ow was left alone while Amy worked, but, as Amy explained, that was now many more hours a day. "My law practice has grown," she told me, "and I often work till late at night. When I come home, Mee-ow's food dish is empty, and he cries for treats." She paused, then shook her head shamefacedly. "Eating's all he's got, Dr. McMillan. I can't say no to this one pleasure."

I hear this "it's his one pleasure" a *lot* when I see obese animals in my examination room. In Amy's case, I could see that she was well aware of the emotional deprivation her pet was experiencing. I explained that the excess weight could cause or aggravate health problems that could shorten Mee-ow's life. "And your cat's excess weight is almost certainly telling you something else," I continued. "It seems pretty clear to me that Mee-ow is a very unhappy cat. I believe that he's bored and lonely, and he is eating because it makes him feel better. If I'm right, he won't stop overeating until we can find a way to provide for his emotional needs."

I told Amy that we needed to gradually cut back on Mee-ow's calorie intake. "But the most important thing to do is provide him with plenty of play and social interaction. In short, we need to spice up his life." By Amy's smile, I could tell she liked what she was hearing. I continued, "We need Mee-ow to have an emotionally fulfilled life—a life he can call fun—so that he won't have to seek his comfort in food."

"I'll do everything I can," Amy promised. "I'll try to spend less time at work, and I'll play with poor Mee-ow more when I'm home. It's the least he deserves for all the love he's given me."

Amy called a few weeks later to say that the new program was working. She was spending extra time with her cat. She had also adopted another, younger cat. "They bonded right away," she told me excitedly. "The kitten has Mee-ow chasing him all over the house." While not all cats respond as favorably to a newcomer added to the household, Mee-ow seemed to love it. When I next saw Mee-ow, he was much closer to his normal weight of 12 pounds and seemed much more content. With Amy's renewed attention and a young, energetic companion to provide activity and company, he was now in the satisfying center of his Comfort Zone. And without relying on comfort food to get him there.

DESTRUCTIVE BEHAVIOR

Throughout this book, I've told you about the many cats and dogs among my patients who have been treated for such destructive behaviors as chewing furniture, clothing, and even woodwork. There are a number of reasons for destructive behavior, but the thing to bear in mind is that—as with virtually all behaviors—these behaviors are an attempt by your pet to move toward pleasure and away from discomfort on the Pleasure/ Discomfort Scale. As we now know, if the purpose of the behavior is to lessen a discomfort, the first line of treatment is to remove the source of the discomfort.

Scratching

Cats have an instinctive need to shed their claws as they grow out, thereby unsheathing the new, razor-sharp claws. As everyone knows, this instinct shows itself in cats, especially indoor-only cats, by clawing furniture, carpets, stereo speakers, and draperies. We can't be sure whether the motivation for this is a discomfort they feel in their paws, a pleasurable sensation they feel when doing it, or both.

Regardless of which feeling(s) may be involved, all methods of eliminating unwanted scratching are based on The Pet Pleasure Principle. You *must* provide your cat with an alternative scratching surface that gives him more pleasure while scratching than the divan, rug, or stereo speakers. Put some thought into your choice: Many people give their cats carpet-covered scratching posts, then are enraged when the cat can't tell the difference between the carpeted post and the carpeted floor. And if you put a flimsy post up, and it falls on the cat when he's trying to use it, you can bet he won't go near it again! Instead, give your cat a sturdy scratching post that's big and tall enough to let him stretch out. Make sure it has a surface that a cat can really sink his claws into, such as sisal rope, rough bark, or corrugated cardboard.

To make sure the new scratching post will be more attractive to your cat, you need to go beyond simply providing a better-feeling surface. You also need to boost the pleasure of the new clawing surface through such means as praising the cat when he uses the new surface and making the new location a place where fun things happen. For example, place treats or toys on or around the new scratching surface, rub some catnip (if your cat responds to it) into the material of the post, and play games with your cat in the area.

As you may already be thinking, The Pet Pleasure Principle has a further use here. It is also helpful to make the carpet or sofa *less* pleasant to use. Covering the area temporarily with a sticky or crinkly surface (such as aluminum foil) or building a tower of plastic cups that will tumble as soon as she begins to scratch are just two examples. By heightening the pleasure of using the new scratching surface and lessening the pleasure of using the current surface, the cat should soon learn that the new area brings more—hopefully *much* more—pleasure than the old one.

Chewing

Chewing on fabric or shoes (or, say, your hand) is natural behavior for kittens and puppies, who learn about their new world by using their mouths (like human infants use their little hands to grab things) and then go through a normal teething period as their baby teeth are falling out. Providing these youngsters with their own, more satisfying chew toys— such as nylon bones, heavy rubber play items, and thick rope toys for puppies; and shearling "mice" for kittens—may be enough to draw a pet away from valuable clothing items.

Some adult cats, most notably Siamese, never seem to outgrow the desire to chew on fabric, especially wool. Often, the only solution is to make the chewed items or surfaces unavailable to the cat. Sometimes the cat will respond favorably to being given his own special chew rag.

(Note: Don't try this if your pet actually *eats* the material, because this could cause intestinal blockages.)

As a deterrent—making the chewing result in a move toward discomfort on the Pleasure/Discomfort Scale—commercial pet-repellant sprays may be effective. These sprays make the fabric taste so bad that chewing becomes more unpleasant than the alternative, not chewing.

Digging

The Pet Pleasure Principle can also help you determine when to prevent a pet from performing unwanted or dangerous behavior without causing the pet further distress. For example, there appear to be at least three common motivational forces behind digging. Possibly due to an evolutionary history of digging to find prey, the activity just seems to be fun for many dogs. In addition, we believe that some dogs dig because of a lack of mental stimulation. And of course, there is often the desire to escape confinement, such as a fenced yard.

Which of these motivations is the cause of a dog's digging determines the outcome of blocking the behavior with, say, a wooden plank placed over the digging spot. If a dog is digging because he is bored, preventing digging will prevent him from moving into his Comfort Zone, thus leaving him in discomfort. But if he's digging just for the fun of digging, blocking his behavior will not leave him in discomfort because he is already in his Comfort Zone.

For a dog who is bored or lonely, it's essential to relieve those feelings

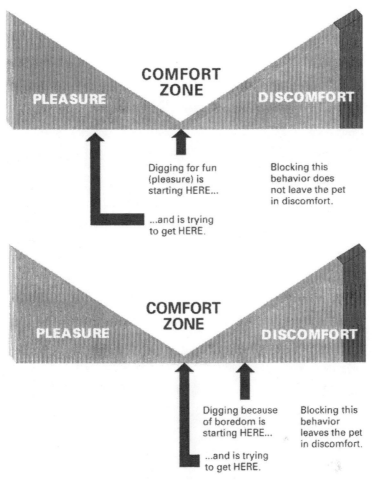

COMFORT
ZONE

PLEASURE   DISCOMFORT

Digging for fun
(pleasure) is
starting HERE...

Blocking this
behavior does
not leave the pet
in discomfort.

...and is trying
to get HERE.

COMFORT
ZONE

PLEASURE   DISCOMFORT

Digging because
of boredom is
starting HERE...

Blocking this
behavior
leaves the pet
in discomfort.

...and is trying
to get HERE.

This diagram shows two possible causes for a dog's digging: fun and
boredom. If your dog is digging because he's bored, you can get him to stop
by providing more interesting things for him to do. If it's just for fun, you can
simply block his access to the digging area.

by providing him with stimulation and companionship. A dog who digs
because he simply enjoys digging would not be harmed or left in discomfort if his behavior is blocked. This dog was already in his Comfort Zone.

Of course, knowing this doesn't mean it's *good* to block a fun behavior.
The best solution is to arrange things so that the behavior is no longer

destructive. For example, you might provide the dog with his own area in the yard where he may dig to his heart's content. Yella, a golden retriever, had his own sand area, where he would "dig" a swimming pool that his owner filled for him on especially hot days.

Always bear in mind that the discomforts of boredom and loneliness are probably among the most common reasons for destructive behaviors. Anxieties and fear are some others. In such cases, even though the behavior caused by these discomforts may appear willful or naughty, your pet is trying only to return to his or her Comfort Zone.

INAPPROPRIATE ELIMINATION

Inappropriate elimination is very common in cats and dogs; unfortunately, we don't understand what feelings motivate this behavior in many cases. Much of what I have to say about it is speculation.

For a wide variety of reasons, otherwise well-behaved dogs and cats may begin to urinate or have bowel movements in the house or other areas where they are not supposed to "go." Aside from the obvious physical disorders that make the pet unable to hold his eliminations (such as urinary incontinence or severe diarrhea) or create a discomfort that he is trying to relieve (such as cystitis or lower bowel diseases), mental factors can also be a cause. For example, cognitive dysfunction syndrome, a disorder resembling Alzheimer's disease in humans, can impair an animal's ability to control his eliminations.

There are also the emotional causes. We know that anxiety and other emotional upsets are often associated with cats urinating outside of their litter boxes, so it seems likely that feelings underlie this feline behavior. But exactly which feelings is unclear. Does urinating outside of the box relieve anxiety? If so, how? Might it be a general expression of unhappiness, like a person who chews his fingernails when nervous?

Or does the cat feel some sort of pleasure when urinating on carpets? We often see cats select specific targets when urinating outside of their box, such as on pieces of their owner's clothing, behind the sofa, or in the owner's bed. What feeling would motivate a cat to urinate in such specific areas?

There are other clues to the role of feelings in this behavior. One is seen in cats that have a painful bladder disorder and experience the pain while trying to urinate in the box. The learning process that can change the meaning of a neutral or unpleasant object to a pleasant one can also cause the opposite to happen. In these cats, because the pain becomes associated with the box and litter, the cats seem to forge an association between the formerly neutral box and the unpleasant pain. As a result, they avoid the box and urinate in other places. The other clue to feelings in these conditions is the simple fact that anti-anxiety medicines often stop the behavior, suggesting that the relief of anxiety is the motivation for at least some cats' inappropriate urinations.

Although our understanding of the role of feelings in unusual elimination behaviors is limited, our approach to them still uses The Pet Pleasure Principle. The foremost objective is to identify and alleviate any discomforts—to return the pet to her Comfort Zone. As always, this includes discomforts caused by physical (health) problems *and* those of emotional origin. If health problems such as a urinary tract infection are ruled out by your veterinarian, then you need to analyze your home for any causes of anxiety, loneliness, boredom, separation anxiety, or other emotional distress.

Bear in mind as you embark on your detective work that many sources of anxiety may be evident to your cat or dog but not to you. Their sensitive noses pick up much more than a human nose, so smells of other animals outside could create great anxiety without your notice.

(continued on page 148)

Why Your Pet Ain't Misbehavin'

This chart gives you an at-a-glance overview of the painful emotional feelings responsible for your pet's undesirable behavior, and what you should and shouldn't do about it.

Emotional Pain*	Frequent Signs (including undesirable behaviors)	Possible Causes
Loneliness	Vocalizing (meowing, barking, howling); jumping, nudging, or pawing humans; destructive behavior (chewing clothing, furniture); possibly overeating	Isolation; inadequate social interaction and companionship
Boredom	Vocalizing; passivity; excessive sleep; nudging for play, bringing toys to owner; repetitive behaviors; possibly overeating, pacing	Inadequate mental stimulation; monotonous, unchanging environment
Fear and anxiety	Hiding; timidity; inappropriate elimination; unexplained aggression; possibly overeating	Change of owner, household schedule, or residence; new person or animal in house; threats and attacks from other "bully" animal in house; abuse; many other threatening and frightening situations or events
Separation distress	Vocalizing (may be extreme and prolonged); trembling; loss of bladder or bowel control; diarrhea; severe destructive behavior; attempts to escape; hiding; decreased appetite	Separation from bonded human companion (occasionally may occur when separated from animal companion)
Anger	Aggressive or destructive behavior	Frustration; aggression or challenge from other animal or human
Depression and grief	Listlessness; decreased appetite	Loss of companion (animal or human); unrelieved unpleasant feelings and experiences (such as loneliness, living with an abusive person)

* All of these forms of emotional pain are commonly referred to as "emotional stress" (see Chapter 5).
** Not all listed responses may be appropriate for your pet. You should always obtain the proper diagnosis and treatment of your pet's undesirable behavior by consulting a qualified trainer or animal behaviorist.

Proper Responses** (to ease emotional pain and help the pet move into his Comfort Zone)	Improper Responses (that do not ease emotional pain or make it worse, leaving the pet unable to reach his Comfort Zone)
Social enrichment; increased human companionship; increased compatible animal companionship (may be counterproductive for some animals)	Punishment; shock collars; devocalization (such as surgical debarking); social isolation; neglect (doing nothing)
Environmental enrichment: variety, novelty, fun; new and engaging activities; play; interactive toys; compatible animal companionship	Punishment; neglect
Identify and remove the source of emotional distress; desensitization; drug treatment; provide opportunities to cope (such as a Safe Haven; see page 101)	Punishment; neglect
Restore contact with human companion; desensitization; counterconditioning; drug treatment; increased activities for pet when left alone; increased social interaction	Punishment; neglect
Identify and remove the source of threat or frustration; counterconditioning	Punishment
Restore contact with lost companion, if possible; give increased attention; provide a new social contact; activity, fun; drug treatment	Punishment

Other possible causes include the gain or loss of a significant other, another pet, a new baby, or house construction next door. In the case of litter-box problems, perfumed litter, infrequent cleaning, a too-small box, or one placed in a busy area could all lead to avoidance issues.

MAKING TOO MUCH NOISE

Any pet who cries, barks, whines, or meows excessively is usually trying to tell you something. Until proven otherwise, you should presume that the message is "I'm hurting, and I need your help." The hurt could be in just about any type and form, physical or emotional, including hunger, boredom, nausea, back pain, loneliness, anxiety, excessively full bladder, or fear.

If you have ever visited the local animal shelter, you've seen this communication in its most dramatic—and heartrending—display. The simple presence of a human being in the animal holding area sends the dogs into a deafening cacophony of howling and barking. The effort of these dogs to produce the loudest sound they possibly can is clear. If you had an electronic dog translator, you would be overwhelmed with one plea: "I'm hurting from loneliness, and I need your help! Take me home with you!"

As with every other "undesirable" behavior, the first responsibility of the pet's caregiver is to find the cause of any discomfort and eliminate it. Because hurts come in all varieties, if you can't immediately determine the cause, you should always take your pet to your veterinarian to make sure there isn't an underlying physical reason for his distress.

As we saw in the case of poor Duke at the beginning of this chapter, when the neighbor's dog keeps you awake all night with his barking, you now know what he's almost certainly trying to say. Ignoring barking or meowing without trying to remove the cause of the pet's discomfort will leave her with no way to return to her Comfort Zone. That's why she's crying out for help.

SIT! STAY! GOOD DOG!

The Pet Pleasure Principle is not only the foundation for changing inappropriate behavior, it is the guide for teaching appropriate and necessary behavior. Whether you are training your dog to obey standard commands (heel, sit, stay) or getting your cat to be still while you give her a pill, applying specific techniques that use The Pet Pleasure Principle is the key to success. Creating a new mode of behavior is just a matter of making that desirable behavior the most pleasurable option for your pet to select.

There are many effective styles of dog (and cat) training, and all of them make use of The Pet Pleasure Principle in some form. It's easy to see this in standard training methods, because the reward for desirable behavior is obvious—a tasty food treat, petting and praise, or a fun activity—and the punishment for undesirable behavior is equally recognizable (disapproval).

One of the biggest recent advancements in animal training is "clicker training," which is a wonderful example of The Pet Pleasure Principle in action. Originally developed for use with dolphins and other marine mammals, clicker training is a teaching method that uses a toy clicker combined with positive reinforcement.

Punishment plays no part in clicker training. When the trainer first begins to teach a pet using clicker training, the pet first learns to associate the sound of the clicker with a desirable treat (usually food). After several repetitions, an association is forged between the treat and the click, much like the association a cat forms between the sound of the electric can opener and food.

Clicker training creates and molds, rather than stops, behavior. For example, a dog that goes crazy barking when the mailman approaches is not yelled at for barking, but instead clicked (rewarded) for staying calm and quiet. (He is then given a treat.)

Pets who are being clicker-trained come to learn that the meaning of the click is "Something good is coming." The clicker grabs the animal's attention at the moment he is performing the desirable behavior. He is rewarded immediately afterward. With repetition, the pet learns to associate the sound of the clicker and the desirable behavior with the reward. Eventually, you can stop using the clicker and the food treat, and praise your pet as a continued reward. For more information on clicker training, see page 285.

In the next chapter, we'll take a look at your pet's quality of life. We'll see what it is, how to measure it, and, most important, how to make sure it is the best you can provide for your beloved companion.

Chapter 7

THE BEST QUALITY OF LIFE

WHEN LOUIE, a 1-year-old male Jack Russell terrier, came into my office, he was a literal bundle of energy, practically bouncing off walls and giving friendly licks to everyone in sight. He seemed so happy and outgoing that just seeing him made me smile. However, I soon learned that Louie had been born with hydrocephalus, a congenital neurological disorder that impairs the normal drainage of spinal fluid from the brain, causing the fluid to accumulate and press against the brain tissue. As a result of the increased fluid pressure, the gray matter of the brain thins and does not function properly.

Louie's owner, a physical therapist named Denise, told me that ever since she had adopted Louie as a young puppy, he'd showed abnormal behavior. "He's very slow to learn things," she explained. "It took me twice as long as with other dogs to paper-train him, and even now he still has frequent accidents inside. He also seems to have trouble seeing. I just want to make sure there's nothing physically wrong that we can correct."

I ordered a series of brain scans and found that the thickness of Louie's cortical brain layers—the part of the brain involved with thinking— measured only one-fifth the normal thickness. When I reported this news to Denise, she looked stunned at first, then shrugged and scratched the little terrier on the head. "Well, I guess this just confirms that he's never going to be mentally sharp," she said after a moment. "But as you can see, Doctor, you don't have to be smart to be happy."

Gazing down at the spirited young dog, I had to agree that Louie indeed seemed very happy. He was never going to win any prizes for intelligence and probably would never learn anything beyond maybe one or two of the most basic commands, but Louie obviously felt that things were just fine. In other words, looking at Louie's life from his—not my—point of view, his mental disabilities were actually not disabilities at all and therefore didn't detract from his cheerful nature. As we will see, little Louie, with his severe congenital malformation, had a very good quality of life.

THE ULTIMATE GUIDE

My job as a veterinarian, and your job as your pet's primary caregiver, is to give your pet the best quality of life possible. But how do we do this? No puppy or kitten comes with an owner's manual, and the veterinary medical profession has until recently been silent on this topic. In fact, despite the fact that health-care scientists have been studying quality of life in people for the past 30 years, and that animal lovers and veterinarians have been using the phrase frequently in reference to their pet animals for almost as long, not one scientific paper had ever appeared on quality of life in a veterinary medical journal. This inexplicable void led me to write the first paper on animal quality of life, which was published in the *Journal of the American Veterinary Medical Association*. But that was in 2000, so a serious look at quality of life in animals is still recent.

It would be very difficult to find an animal lover who didn't believe that quality of life is the single most important aspect of pet care. I believe that quality of life, more than any other concept, should serve as the ultimate guide for *all* animal care, ranging from pet care to zoos, circuses, marine mammal aquariums, farms, research laboratories, and magic acts in Las Vegas. Quality of life should also be the deciding factor in issues from animal mistreatment and comfort to health-care decisions in companion animals, including the ultimate question of euthanasia.

IT'S ALL ABOUT FEELINGS

What exactly is quality of life? Despite the intuitive sense we all have that we know what quality of life is, it has been a surprisingly difficult term for scientists to define. In general, quality of life is the overall view of how life is going, weighing in the enjoyments, difficulties, rewards, and failures. Like happiness, quality of life involves an evaluation of life as a whole—it reflects a general level of life satisfaction. A good quality of life is a pervasive sense over time that all is well: Life itself, not just this moment in time, is good.

Your cat or dog (just like you and me) experiences pleasant and unpleasant feelings virtually all the time, moment by moment. The best theory at the present time holds that it is the ratio of time your pet spends experiencing pleasant feelings versus unpleasant feelings that is the main factor in determining her quality of life.

The important point here is that *feelings* play the central role in quality of life; and it appears that it is *only* through feelings that anything influences quality of life. If something doesn't elicit a feeling—pleasant or unpleasant—it's not relevant to quality of life. Thus, an "ugly" scar, a missing toe, or coming from a championship blood line don't affect a cat's or dog's quality of life because these things don't cause him to experience good or bad feelings. Louie's lack of mental acuity didn't affect his quality of life because, from his view of his life, it didn't have any influence on his feelings. On the other hand, for a cat to be able to chase butterflies, a dog to get lots of car rides where he can stick his head out the window, or for the same pets to suffer an illness or have an uncaring owner—these *would* influence quality of life, because they all affect the way the animal feels.

Even something that we humans might consider a serious physical handicap may have no effect on a pet's quality of life. Bailey, a 3-year-old male Siamese cat, developed an infection in his right front paw when he was a kitten. His mother chewed the paw off (likely an instinctive attempt to remove the threat to his life), leaving only a stump at the shoulder. The mother cat's human caregiver, Nathalie, had no hesitation in keeping Bailey as a companion cat. "I admit he looks a little funny," Nathalie told me during one of Bailey's routine checkups. "And at first, I was worried he wouldn't be able to keep up with the other cats. But he can jump and run and play as well as any of them. Bailey doesn't seem to realize that there is anything 'wrong' with him."

Obviously, Bailey's very good quality of life isn't in the least affected by his handicap.

You can think of quality of life as being represented by a balance scale. On one side of the scale are pleasant feelings. On the other side of the scale are unpleasant feelings. In animals, quality of life can be viewed as the balance of feelings on the two sides of the scale. If something tips the scale—in either direction—it affects quality of life. If it doesn't tip the scales even slightly, it doesn't elicit or affect any feelings and therefore has no effect on quality of life.

Sometimes one very major feeling, such as an intense unpleasant

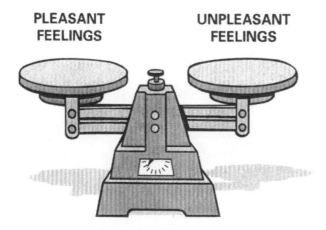

PLEASANT FEELINGS

UNPLEASANT FEELINGS

The balance between pleasant and unpleasant feelings determines your pet's quality of life.

feeling of pain or loneliness, tips the scales heavily toward the unpleasant side. In this case, the small pleasures remaining in life can't offset that one unpleasant feeling. Likewise, a large pleasure, such as frequent trips to the dog park, can outweigh the soreness of an arthritic knee. If a dog has sufficient large and small pleasures in his life, they may be able to counterbalance even a major illness, helping to maintain a relatively good quality of life. When thinking about quality-of-life issues for your pet, remember that

* Animals experience pleasant or unpleasant feelings virtually constantly
* Quality of life is determined by the balance of pleasant versus unpleasant feelings
* It is only through feelings that anything influences quality of life
* Any factor that doesn't elicit or alter a feeling has no effect on quality of life

Tipping the Scales

In Chapter 2, we saw how unpleasant feelings command more attention than pleasant feelings because they arise in response to threats and dangers and are therefore more urgent and important to survival than pleasant feelings. In addition, unpleasant feelings are so effective at refocusing the mind's attention that some unpleasant feelings, such as those elicited by urgent threats to life, virtually shout "Pay attention to me!" and allow very little room for pleasant feelings to compete.

Not surprisingly, then, unpleasant feelings seem to have a much larger effect on quality of life than pleasant feelings. If your pet is in great pain or starving for oxygen because of a lung problem, her quality of life will not be good, no matter how many toys and treats she has or how much attention you pay to her. Likewise, if she is suffering from unrelenting loneliness or grief, the "little pleasures" in life will not be able to counterbalance the very great emotional hurt weighing on the "unpleasant feelings" side of the scale.

If your pet develops a chronic, progressive illness, medical treatment, including pain medication, can often keep the balance of her quality of life weighed toward pleasant feelings. However, as the disease progresses, the scales will ultimately begin to tip toward unpleasant feelings. For more on the progression of disease and its impact on quality of life, see Chapter 11, "A Peaceful End."

An Individual Matter

Quality of life isn't as straightforward as it sometimes seems. It is a common reaction when seeing a person confined to a wheelchair or maneuvering with a white cane to assume that his quality of life is diminished. The truth is that you have no way of knowing how that person would judge his quality of life. His quality of life is determined by *his* view of his life, not your view. What you are really saying is that you yourself would not want that life. The same is true for our pets: A condition such as blindness or loss of a limb that we think would cause a poor quality of life may not affect our cat's or dog's quality of life in the same way, or maybe not at all.

In people as well as animals, quality of life is determined by the nature of the individual's experiences as well as her preferences and needs. All of these are influenced by the person's or animal's unique genetic makeup. For example, while one human may value social companionship over physical health, another may have the opposite values.

We see the same sorts of individual differences among cats and dogs. A good example is the value of human companionship to dogs. In situations where a dog is deprived of human companionship, one dog may be stoically unaffected, while another could become emotionally debilitated. The same is true of pain tolerance. Little Nip, a lovable dachshund, yelped and cried as if he were being tortured whenever he had his toenails clipped. Little Nip's sheltie companion, Lola, on the other hand, would sit still for uncomfortable procedures such as removal of stitches without flinching or whimpering.

Our pets each have different personalities, needs, desires, and sources of joy (have you seen the array of cat toys in the pet stores?). Terri, a client of mine for many years, has two cats—Murphy and Charlie. Terri has a pet door installed in her house, so her cats can go in and out as they please, but Murphy is the only one who goes out. In fact, whenever Murphy is confined inside he howls, paces, and leaps from window to window. Charlie, however, doesn't care if he's confined inside. In fact, he probably doesn't even know when it happens. Murphy and Charlie provide an excellent example of how the effects of various factors on quality of life can differ drastically between animals: Indoor confinement greatly affects Murphy's quality of life but has no effect on Charlie's.

This feature of quality of life—that it is influenced in very individualized ways from animal to animal—certainly makes our interactions with animals more interesting, but it is also a big reason why accurately measuring quality of life in animals is so challenging. Consider, for example, a ranking of quality-of-life items for cats. How would you rank the ability to go outdoors? For cats like Murphy, having access to the outdoors would rank very highly, but for cats like Charlie, having access to the outdoors wouldn't even be ranked—going outdoors is meaningless to their quality of life.

We can see, then, that the central element of quality of life—and happiness—is that it comes from within. It is how the individual, using his own life preferences, assesses the overall "goodness" or "badness" of his life. Because of this, the only way to measure quality of life is from the standpoint of the individual animal. Let's look one more time at Louie, the brain-damaged dog I told you about earlier. Mental impairments like Louie's are not something anyone would choose to have. But a slow-witted pet may still have an excellent quality of life—because that quality is determined by what he thinks of his own life, not what others think. Louie obviously feels his own life is terrific. If Louie, or any other animal or person with mental deficiencies judges his life to be good, then it is.

THE FORMULA FOR A GOOD QUALITY OF LIFE

It used to be believed that as long as a cat or dog was well fed, healthy, and sheltered from the elements, he had a good quality of life. But think about this in your own terms. If food, shelter, and health were all you had, would you consider yourself happy, or even content? Remember—you have enough to eat, but not necessarily the foods you like best. You have a roof over your head, but it's nothing special, and there's no climate control. You are healthy enough—you aren't sick—but you have no companionship. You have no television, no music, and no books or magazines to read. You're bored. You have nothing to look forward to. In other words, you have all the basic physical requirements for life, but there's nothing to enjoy, and there's certainly nothing you could call *fun.* Is this a high quality of life?

Let's compare two dogs. Both dogs have equal levels of physical comfort. That's all the first dog has—food, water, and shelter. The other dog has, in addition, a rich array of joys, such as frequent trips to the dog park with his family, lots of playing fetch with the Frisbee, a lot of people to interact with, and a variety of delicious foods to eat. Can there be any question as to which dog has the greater happiness? Obviously, it's the dog with the greater pleasures. As psychologists James Averill and Thomas More write in their essay *Happiness,* "A life without its share of elementary pleasures could hardly be regarded as happy."

Good quality of life = comfort + pleasure

What is the basic formula for a good quality of life in animals? Comfort and pleasure.

We can see how this formula ideally matches the quality-of-life scale we just looked at. When a pet is in a state of comfort, she experiences no (or very few) discomforts, so there is nothing weighing down the 'unpleasant feelings' side of the scales. But if that pet has comfort and nothing else, there is also nothing weighing down the 'pleasant feelings'

Too Much of a Good Thing?

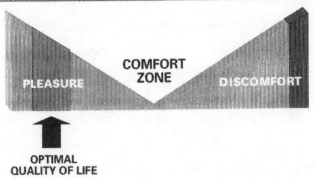

The point of optimal pleasure. At this point, pets experience the best quality of life.

Optimal quality of life occurs at the point where a pet has comfort and a meaningful amount of pleasure, as this diagram shows. But you will notice that I didn't place optimal quality of life all the way to the left of the scale, at the point of maximal pleasure. This is because, during the long course of evolution, the "ultrapleasures" so common in today's world were rarely—if ever—available.

For example, sweet taste was associated with ripe fruit, which assured the intake of good nutrition. The innate desire for the pleasure of sweet taste, however, leads our pets (and us!) to crave today's refined sweets that do nothing to contribute to our well-being and may in fact harm it. The same is true for fat, which we encounter in french fries, ice cream, and potato chips. For carnivores like your cat and dog, fat was available only when they successfully killed prey. With the constant fight for survival in nature, it was very unlikely that there would be an excess of fat to eat.

If doughnuts and cookies had been widely available during the course of evolution, you may be sure that our brains would have developed mental safeguards for self-control to assure that we didn't overeat these very tasty foods. As it is, however, for our pets as well as for ourselves, it is easy to overdo sweets and fats, proving that, in today's world, maximal pleasures do not necessarily lead to the best quality of life.

side of the scales. The scales balance relatively equally, giving an animal with a comfortable life a satisfactory, but not high, quality of life. Now envision what happens to the scales when a life of comfort is enriched with pleasures. The scales tip more and more toward the pleasurable side, giving the animal a much higher quality of life.

AT YOUR PLEASURE

As with most quality-of-life issues, pleasure is a very individual matter. For example, many pets love to be petted and scratched. Some, however, seem indifferent to petting or even avoid contact. A few animals seem to crave petting as their greatest pleasure in life. Pyewacket, a male orange Tabby cat who was the hospital cat in our veterinary clinic when I first started practice, had a truly insatiable desire to be scratched and petted. He would instantly pester any of us who sat down at a desk by forcefully ramming his head into our arms and hands. If that didn't get him the petting he wanted, or if we scratched him and then stopped, Pye would plop down on his side next to any hand he could get near and, reaching with both of his front paws, grab hold of the nearby person's hand and pull it onto the top of his head, as if he were putting on a hat. If we scratched him and then had to leave the room, he would chase after us until we sat down somewhere else, and the coercion to pet him would begin again.

Other animals may have particular cravings for certain types of play. Some dogs may enjoy chasing a ball, playing tug-of-war with a rope, or playing hide-and-seek, while some cats might like chasing a feather toy, batting a ball around, or pouncing on one another. All pets likewise have individual tastes in food treats. Among my patients, I've seen dogs that go crazy for various fruits like bananas and apples, others whose ultimate treats are carrots and broccoli, and still others who would kill for popcorn. And all cat lovers know how the legendary feline finicky nature

MAGGIE'S STORY

One sunny afternoon, Gregg Marx was out in the fresh air of Hollywood, walking his two dogs, Maggie and Kylie. Gregg had adopted the two mixed-breed dogs from the animal shelter a few months earlier and had formed a strong bond with them both in a short time. On the walk, the three of them suddenly and unexpectedly encountered another dog running loose. Spooked, Maggie and Kylie both took off with such force that Gregg lost his grip on their leashes. Gregg ran after the dogs, soon catching up with Kylie. He looked down Fairfax Avenue and saw Maggie running off, too scared even to respond to his shouts of her name. As he watched her, she was gone.

Gregg was distraught. He searched the area for the next 8 hours, but had to give up when it got dark. Over the next several days, Gregg alerted every animal shelter in L.A. and even called the city Animal Control to see if Maggie had been picked up dead. She was nowhere. Gregg placed photo ads in the L.A. *Times* and posted lost-dog signs that advertised a reward.

As the days turned into weeks, Gregg steadily increased the reward—what had started as a $500 reward was now $5,000. He began to lose hope of ever seeing Maggie again. Finally, after a number of crank (and even some cruel) calls and some false alarms, Gregg received a call from a woman who had seen Maggie's picture in the newspaper. She thought it

results in a wide range of preferred treats, from yogurt to tuna to store-bought tidbits. If you experiment, your pet will let you know what foods and activities she enjoys most. But have patience—it sometimes takes a bit of effort to find (or invent!) the things that give your pet thrills.

Pleasure for your pet consists of anything that she considers agreeable and desirable. For most pets, it would include the broad categories of play, social companionship, mental stimulation, and delicious foods. Pay attention to your pet's individual wants and desires, and try to satisfy looked like the dirty, skinny, scroungy dog who had been living under her house for several weeks.

Forcing himself not to let his hopes get too high, Gregg jumped into his car and raced over to the address the woman had given him. When he arrived, she led him to an opening that went under the house. Using a flashlight, Gregg crawled into the opening and made his way another 20 feet on his belly before spotting a frightened dog cowering in a dark corner. "Maggie?" Gregg murmured.

The dog's head cocked slightly, then raised up to get a clearer look. Gregg saw the dog's eyes open wide, and it seemed that the moment of recognition hit them both at the same time. Gregg quickly crawled from under the house, and Maggie followed him out into the light of day.

Once outside, Maggie, skinny and weak from 7 weeks on her own, jumped up on her rear legs and placed her paws on Gregg's shoulders. As she bounced up and down on her hind legs, Maggie whimpered loudly. She licked Gregg's face continuously, pausing only long enough to whimper even louder, as if she were excitedly "talking" to Gregg. "As if," Gregg later told me, "she was trying to tell me the whole story of what happened to her." She was so vocal and animated, Gregg said, that he couldn't calm her down. This was a reunion where both Gregg and Maggie were experiencing the greatest of animal pleasures: pure joy.

them as much as you can. The more time your pet spends on the pleasure side of the Pleasure/Discomfort Scale, the better her quality of life will be.

ANIMAL HAPPINESS

No more vivid picture of animal happiness exists than at the dog park tucked into a valley in the Santa Monica mountains near my home. As I sit on the bench at the park's edge, I watch as dogs of every shape, size, color, and age run around with seemingly boundless energy. On one day, I counted 75 dogs of all breeds, including basset hounds, chocolate Labs, golden retrievers, dachshunds, Dalmatians, boxers, poodles, and myriad mixed breeds, all energetically involved in every activity you can imagine a dog enjoying. These dogs sniff each other, bark out messages to one another, and hold their tails high with the clear message: "I'm friendly— just coming over to check you out."

Some dogs play fetch with balls, sticks, and Frisbees. Others dig holes, roll around on the ground, chase each other, race to get to a thrown ball, play-fight, and carry big sticks around in their mouths. This is a scene of utter joy and pleasure, and nothing is more obvious than that these animals are happy.

So what exactly is this thing called happiness? There are two ways to define the term: enjoyment of pleasures of the moment, such as dogs in the dog park experience when they are playing with their companions; and a long-term mood, the view that life as a whole is good and pleasant. As we saw earlier, for a good quality of life, a pet's experience should include plenty of these pleasures of the moment, adding up to a long-term sense that life is good.

In humans, a wide variety of activities and events elicit the experience of happiness. Discovery, creativity, accomplishment, play, competition, exercise, eating and drinking, companionship, and reunion with familiar people, animals, or objects, all can create feelings of joy. Very similar activities and events seem to produce the same feelings in animals.

Is there a difference between happiness level and quality of life? In people, psychologists sometimes use the two terms interchangeably, and at our current level of understanding, this appears to be the best and most accurate way to view the concepts in animals. Because quality of life and happiness are so similar, what works for increasing one turns out to work for increasing the other. If you were to make a list of ways to increase happiness in animals and a list of ways to increase quality of life, at our current level of understanding, you would end up with identical lists.

THE HAPPINESS SET POINT

Billy, a 4-year-old male Beagle, the pet of a charmingly sweet client of mine named Nora, is a happy dog. He doesn't just wag his tail, he wags the whole back end of his body. He doesn't just get excited, he wiggles around as if he can't control his joy. Billy is happy when he meets a new person; he's happy when he encounters another dog. He's happy going to the dog park; he's happy going to the vet. He's happy getting a tasty treat, getting an injection, getting grimy in the dirt, and getting a bath. He's just plain happy. He simply has, like many people, what we would rightly call a happy disposition.

Billy presents an interesting view of animal happiness. If Billy were asked to evaluate his life as a whole, what would his response be? From his behavior, we could safely surmise that he would evaluate it favorably. Billy does have deviations from his happy mood. Nora has described to me his occasional downs (it's pretty hard for him to have any ups!); some of these down moods have resulted from the illnesses I have treated him for. But Nora reports that, within a short time, Billy is always back to his happy self.

Scientists believe that many animals share a trait that assures that no event—either good or bad—will have a permanent mental impact. The survival advantage of this trait is that we (and other animals) can adapt to

(continued on page 168)

The Pursuit of Happiness

As we saw earlier, for animals (and humans too), emotions operate at virtually all times, giving us feelings of pleasantness or unpleasantness on a constant basis. Scientists who study happiness in humans have found that the frequency and duration of pleasantness, as opposed to its intensity, is the factor most closely associated with overall happiness level.

Psychologists generally believe that to be able to experience happiness about one's life overall, the individual must be able to form a view and assessment of his or her overall life. Yet many scientists still believe that animals live only in the present, unable to form a concept of their life as a whole. Based on both scientific and anecdotal evidence, my own feeling is that animals *do* experience long-term positive moods like happiness.

The psychological condition known as "learned helplessness" appears to involve an evaluative interpretation of life overall. An animal can be reduced to a state of helplessness and hopelessness by being put in an unpleasant situation from which there is no escape or chance of lessening the unpleasantness. Under these circumstances, the animal has no control over its situation. In the laboratory, this is often done by using electric shocks; in pets, this kind of situation can occur in a household where a pet is being physically abused. An animal in a state of helplessness becomes completely passive, showing no interest in former pleasures and ultimately making no further attempts to escape from the discomfort. Such an animal seems to be assessing his life as so hopeless that there is no reason to make any attempt at improvement. It is as if the animal were saying, "I can't do anything to change my situation, so I'm not even going to try." If such an *unpleasurable* mental state can incorporate a broad life view, then it is safe to presume that a pleasurable mental state, like happiness, would do so also.

Going one step further, can an animal strive for a better life? We know that many animals (including, in varying ways, humans) form dominance relationships, in which social status is ranked. Once called "pecking orders," from early studies in chickens, such rankings are now termed dominance hierarchies. Dominance hierarchies exist in most species of birds and mammals. These systems give a structure to animal societies, and greatly minimize confusion, social instability, and violent confrontations.

There are distinct advantages to having dominant status. For example, dominant animals generally get the best food and resting spots as well as higher-quality mates. They are also freer to move about, show greater resistance to disease, and control the attention of group members. By achieving dominant status, an animal clearly acquires a much higher quality of life. The most common way for a subordinate animal to move up within the group is to challenge the dominant individual to a contest, usually a "fight" employing ritualized displays of strength.

The key question is: What, in the challenger's mind, is the goal of such a challenge? After all, the challenger will not instantly have access to all the good things the dominant animal had enjoyed. According to Marc Bekoff, a professor of animal behavior at the University of Colorado, it appears that there is often no known immediate reward to the challenge. And if there is truly no immediate reward, then this phenomenon—challenge within the dominance hierarchy—appears to offer evidence that animals have the ability to evaluate their life as a whole and take action to achieve a better overall life.

Another indication that animals view their life as a whole can be seen in certain situations where an animal's life has changed significantly. Marine biologist Carol Howard, in her book *Dolphin Chronicles*, recounts the story of two dolphins that were captured, studied extensively in captivity, and then freed back into the ocean. The things that had pleased the dolphins in captivity—such as being rubbed by a person or playing with toys—were of little interest once the dolphins were again living in the wild. Although the pleasures of captivity had been important when the dolphins were confined, once freed, their life overall was now presumably much more satisfying. This would be like a lonely person who enjoys watching television, but, when surrounded by new friends, activities, and a much more fulfilling life, finds himself much less interested in couch-potato pursuits.

changes in the environment without becoming either emotionally incapacitated by traumatic events or complacent or reckless over events of good fortune. Being able to rebound emotionally from the good as well as the bad assures that we can effectively respond to the next challenge in life.

Lottery winners interviewed a year later generally report that the "high" of winning has faded away. Likewise, studies of people seriously injured in car accidents have found that less than a month after they suffered paralyzing spinal cord injuries, happiness was again these people's prevailing emotion.

As psychologist David Myers puts it, "Every desirable experience—passionate love, a spiritual high, the pleasure of a new possession, the exhilaration of success—is transitory." This psychological trait, in which deviations from one's base level of happiness are temporary, has been called by psychologist David Lykken the "happiness set point." Happiness levels in people appear to be very similar to the household thermostat, relatively fixed at one setting and always tending to return to that setting when outside forces act to change it.

The Happiness Set Point in Pets

From studies and observations in animals, it appears that they have a happiness set point, too. A study of dogs whose hind legs had become paralyzed showed that their mental attitude, as judged by their owners, was as good 3 months after as before the paralysis in 85 percent of the animals.

A dramatic example of emotional resilience in the face of adversity comes from Essex, England, where a male Jack Russell terrier who came to be named Ben had been homelessly wandering the rough streets of the town. When he was cruelly blinded by being stabbed in both of his eyes with sharpened sticks, the poor dog seemed doomed to a lonely and shortened life. As fate would have it, help for Ben came in the form of a friend—another homeless Jack Russell, later named Bill. The much smaller Bill became Ben's guide as they struggled to survive. They developed a partnership based on touch—Bill led and Ben followed as they looked out for one another.

After several months on the streets, the hapless pair—scrawny from lack of adequate food—were rescued and brought to the local pound, where they received food and loving attention. The veterinarians found that the injuries that Ben had suffered at the hands of an unknown assailant were so severe that his eyes had to be surgically removed. But Ben not only bounced back from the surgery, his life improved from that point on.

More than 5,000 calls came in from people wishing to adopt Ben and Bill. The clinic gave them to the care of Lady Yvonne Becher of Brighton, in Sussex. When I recently spoke to Lady Becher, she told me about Ben's life over the past year since she adopted the two dogs. The two of them, she said, are still inseparable. "Ben is so happy. He loves playing ball. He not only plays tug-of-war with Bill and our other Jack Russell terrier, but he usually wins. He never acts as if he's disabled in any way." Then she added, "I can't imagine him being any happier than he is." While no one can know Ben's happiness level before his tragedy, his exceedingly high level of happiness now certainly suggests a complete emotional recovery from his horrible trauma.

As we saw in Chapter 4, the loss of a companion can cause extreme grief in animals. But, as in people, these emotional lows also appear to fade with time. Jasper, an 8-year-old orange tiger-striped male cat, was the companion of Albert Griffith, an elderly retired banker who lived alone except for his beloved pet. I first met Jasper one Friday afternoon when the local police brought him in. The neighbors had called them when they realized no one had seen Mr. Griffith for several days. When the police entered Mr. Griffith's apartment, they found

Happiness Boosters

Happiness booster	How it affects quality of life	How to use it to enhance happiness and quality of life
A Safe Haven	Provides security, a place to escape from unpleasant situation, a sense of control. "Nothing bad happens here."	Make sure a Safe Haven is always available and that its sanctity is never violated by other pets or yourself.
A sense of control	Control over stress-inducing feelings reduces the impact of the unpleasant feelings. A perception of no control leads to helplessness, a very unpleasant emotion. No control over unpleasant events increases their harmful impact.	Offer opportunities for choice (such as whether to go in or out, which food to eat today). Allow pet to make requests (such as signaling when to go for a walk, play, or get petted) and honor the requests whenever possible. Provide a Safe Haven and plenty of toys and other diversions.
Social relationships	Social companionship promotes pleasant feelings (for social animals). Social deprivation and isolation lead to loneliness and related unpleasant feelings.	Provide abundant social interaction and companionship with compatible animals and humans.

him lifeless on the floor. Jasper was sitting next to him, as if expecting his master to arise any minute. Sadly, the authorities determined that Mr. Griffith had been deceased for at least 96 hours. Poor Jasper had been waiting for days for his beloved companion to wake up and care for him.

Mental stimulation	Insufficient stimulation produces the intense discomfort of boredom. Stimulation promotes pleasant feelings.	Offer novelty, variety, activities, play, fun, challenges, exploration, outings, and games.
Good health	Discomforts of illness and injury directly and indirectly cause unpleasant feelings. Illness, injury, and disability interfere with enjoyment of pleasures.	Provide high-quality veterinary care. Alleviate all discomforts associated with illness to the greatest degree possible. Restore lost functions of disabilities to promote pleasures (for example, provide a cart for a paralyzed dog). For mental health disorders, discuss with your veterinarian the use of psychotropic medication to ease unpleasant feelings.
Good food	Inadequate food intake promotes unpleasant feelings of hunger. Too much food leads to obesity and associated discomforts (such as diseases, painful joints). Sufficient high-quality, tasty food is pleasurable.	Feed high-quality, tasty foods in appropriate amounts. Offer treats in moderation.

We kept Jasper in our hospital until a new home could be found for him. For weeks, he lay virtually motionless and was unresponsive to our attempts to befriend him. He scarcely ate, and he lost a fair amount of weight. Finally, Jasper began to show some interest in life again. One of our nurses told me that she noticed the cat following her movements with his eyes. The next day, Jasper stood up and walked unsteadily toward her, then eventually began to purr when she petted him. Although it took several more months for Jasper to fully recover emotionally, Anna, a charming client who loved cats, adopted him and reported a short time later that Jasper was fitting in well in her household. "He's definitely on his way to feeling good again," she told me.

HAPPINESS BOOSTERS

Happiness boosters are what I call those things that promote happiness—and therefore a higher quality of life—in your pet. They include all the sources of joy and pleasure we've talked about in previous chapters, the things that raise the level of emotional pleasantness and help your pet to perceive her life overall as being good: a Safe Haven, social companionship, mental stimulation, good health, good food, and a sense of control. Happiness boosters also include those things that lessen unpleasant feelings. It's not an accident that each of these happiness boosters is linked to the activities and interests that evolution has hardwired into your pet's mind to benefit her well-being.

PLAY AND HAPPINESS

Tandy, a very small calico cat, is as playful as a kitten despite her relatively advanced age of 14. "She'll play with anything," her human companion, Kathy, tells me. "A ball, a toy mouse, a pencil, a piece of string. She very often plays by herself, especially with tiny rabbit-fur mice, tossing them in the air and chasing them. She also likes to carry them around in her mouth, making strange jungle noises as she does."

According to Kathy, Tandy also plays well with others. "She and the other cat, Monster, like to chase each other down our long hall," she says. "They take turns, first one cat chasing, then the other. It sounds like a whole herd of cats, rather than two. Tandy also loves it when I play with her, and I try to do that at least once a day for 15 minutes or so. I usually drag one of her toys on a string or play 'keep away' with colored paper strips. Whatever it is, she acts as if she could keep it up for hours."

Although no one in the scientific community can say for sure, it's generally believed that the purpose of play is to develop skills—such as hunting and avoiding predators—that are useful in life as well as to promote social relationships. Marc Bekoff, whom I mentioned earlier, is one of the world's foremost authorities on animal play. He told me that his most recent research suggests that a major purpose of play is to establish the rules and guidelines that help mold the basic foundations of social conduct in life.

Play is important for many species of animals, including mammals, birds, and even turtles. Young foxes wrestle and play-fight; kangaroos engage in play bouts of boxing, wrestling, and kicking each other; ravens drop objects in flight, and then swoop down and catch them; kid goats play "king of the mountain," taking turns at defending the highest spot in the yard or pasture; and Japanese macaques have been observed making snowballs and rolling them around.

Just as in human play, play in animals appears to be very, very enjoyable. Studies have shown that laboratory animals will run mazes for the reward of a brief period of play. One study showed that dogs spend approximately 25 percent of their time using toys. As the story of Tandy shows, many pet animals continue to be playful throughout their lives. I'm sure you've noticed the eager anticipation with which your own cat or dog looks forward to play time. Birdie, my female mixed-breed cat, often drags her string toy up or down a full flight of stairs to me; when I reach for it, her pupils dilate wide as she anticipates the fun about to

Let the Cat Out . . . Or Keep Her In?

For best quality of life, should your cat be an indoor cat or an outdoor cat? Probably no other decision is so important to your cat's overall quality of life. Cats appear to get great enjoyment from exploring new scents and items in their environment. Yet the inside of a house can be unchanging, monotonous, and largely devoid of mental stimulation.

Many of my clients who have lived with cats in both situations—indoors only and those with access to the outdoors—have described the cats with outdoor access as much brighter, more energetic, and seemingly happier than indoor-only cats.

On the other hand, many indoor-only cats seem perfectly content, and they are certainly safer than outdoor cats. The outdoors may hold enticing things to explore, but it also contains unfriendly dogs (and in many areas, coyotes), automobiles, and other cats that may hurt them and spread disease. Cats with outdoor access also kill large numbers of songbirds, lizards, and small mammals such as chipmunks.

Whether to keep your cat in or let her out is not an easy decision and depends on a number of circumstances, including your living space. I have tried to create what I feel is the best of both worlds for my own two cats. Birdie and Boo are both allowed outside—but only when I am with them. Whenever I signal that it is time and then open the door, they enthusiastically bound outside. With all the smells, noises, and activity outside, they begin. When Gooby, my male Balinese cat, wanted to play, he would bring a crumpled-up piece of paper to me and drop it at my feet. I threw it, he fetched it and brought it back, and the routine would continue over and over.

Wolfie, an exuberant golden retriever, becomes visibly excited whenever members of his family (or visitors) take a yellow tennis ball out of a

---

seem to get a great deal of stimulation and satisfaction from exploring the great outdoors.

If your physical situation allows you to, I recommend offering your cat this sort of controlled access to the outdoors. I encourage my clients with cats, especially young cats, to slowly introduce their pet to wearing a harness (available at any pet store) and going on "walks" outside. The cat may walk with you on leash like a dog, but many cats are content to simply lounge near you, sniffing the air and batting at unfamiliar objects. This doesn't work for all pet cats, because some are simply too frightened, or there are too many dangers outside. But when it's a workable option, the cat's life can be a lot more stimulating and fun.

Another way to safely let your cat experience the pleasures of the outdoors is to buy or build a large screened enclosure for the backyard or an apartment terrace, which will allow your pet to sniff and explore without danger from dogs, coyotes, other cats, or cars.

If providing these types of outdoor access isn't feasible for your situation, you can enhance your indoor cat's quality of life by giving her a lot of play and stimulating things to do. Don't assume that two cats will keep each other entertained (most cats will engage in stimulating activity with each other for no more than a few minutes a day). The goal is to try your best to give your indoor cat an emotionally fulfilled, *fun* life.

---

box that is kept for his use. He begins yipping and dancing, his toenails clattering on the tile floors in anticipation of the imminent round of ball-retrieving. Brownie, a 14-year-old female chocolate-point Siamese cat, knows that when her caretakers turn off the TV at night they will head for the bedroom and a few minutes of playing with her before going to sleep. As soon as the TV snaps off, Brownie begins to mew in excitement, and follows closely on the heels of her humans as they prepare for bed, meowing occasionally as if to remind them not to forget to bring out her favorite woven string so she can play a fine game of chase before lights out.

ENGAGEMENT AND ACCOMPLISHMENT

In humans, one of the most important contributors to life satisfaction is active and challenging engagement (as opposed to passive observation) in the world. Surprisingly, active engagement appears to be important to animals, too. Research has shown that when white rats are provided with sensory stimulation (such as observing another cage filled with rats) but are prevented from interacting with the stimuli, they develop smaller brains than those rats who can freely interact with their environment.

In addition to active engagement in the world, many animals seem to have psychological needs that are something like goals or a drive for achievement in humans. While animals' goals are most likely not as complex as those in humans, compelling evidence supports the supposition that in animals, as well as in humans, successfully achieving goals is emotionally rewarding.

We've all heard of sheepdogs who seem to enjoy herding and will herd groups of small children or other pets in the house on their own initiative. Many dogs, especially retrievers, eagerly chase balls or Frisbees, and seem to enjoy successfully catching the thrown object in their mouths.

One of my clients has a cat, Anastasia, who, according to the client, "has a regular agenda that she follows. In the morning, she trails me through the house, sitting alertly nearby as I do my chores. One of my chores is to straighten the towels in the bathroom, and when I have finished, Anna does *her* chore, which is to snag each towel with her claws and pull it to the floor. She never plays with the towels or lies on them—apparently she sees it as her job to pull the towels down, and when she is through, she walks away with what I swear is an air of satisfaction."

I'm sure that you have experienced that sense of accomplishment or achievement from activities well performed, whether in sports or at work. In studies involving many different species of animal, it has been shown that animals seem to prefer to "work" for their food, even when they can get it for "free." When given the choice between obtaining food without any effort or performing some task in order to get food, many animals will choose to perform the task.

A revealing example of animals' desire to "work" comes from marine-mammal veterinarian James McBain, D.V.M., who recounts an incident involving seals at a small marine aquarium on Vancouver Island. The curator of the aquarium called Dr. McBain because many of the performing seals had not been eating for nearly 2 weeks. Oddly, all the seals appeared healthy, did not seem to be losing weight, and still performed well in the shows. The seals' pen was separated from the ocean by a single wall. On the theory that small fish may have somehow gotten into the pen and were being eaten by the seals, a diver was sent into the pool to check for fish.

After thoroughly checking out the seal pen, the diver surfaced with

(continued on page 180)

Quality of Life . . . Or Not?

As a veterinarian, I am often asked to help clients make decisions that affect the quality of life of their pets. Sometimes the decision is obvious, and sometimes it is not so clear. To understand better the factors that are weighed in quality-of-life decisions, imagine that you are a veterinarian consulting with patients about their pets. What opinion would you have given in each of these cases?

Sabrina, a pretty gray Tabby cat, developed total blindness due to a congenital condition at the age of 6 years. Her owner, Martha, was distraught, fearing that her cat would be miserable if she couldn't see. I reassured Martha that cats receive much of their information about the world through scent and hearing, and predicted that Sabrina would adjust well. Six months after Sabrina became blind, Martha called to tell me that my prediction had come true. "She can get around as well as any cat I've ever known," she told me. "If I didn't know better, I'd think she could see normally."

Perky, a 12-year-old long-haired dachshund, was the apple of his human companion's eye. The companion, Fredda, a retired schoolteacher, first brought Perky to me when the dog developed a severe slipped disc in his back. We performed surgery right away, but unfortunately, it was not successful, and Perky was left with paralysis in both of his hind legs. "That's all right," Fredda responded when I told her the unwelcome news. "For everything Perky's given me, I'll do whatever it takes to keep his life happy." As Perky recovered from the surgery, Fredda fashioned a kind of sling for his hindquarters that attached to a harness. Whenever Perky wanted to get around the house or go for a walk in the neighborhood, Fredda assisted him with use of the sling. The last time I saw Perky for a routine checkup, he seemed healthy and happy despite his handicap. In response to my question, Fredda smiled. "Perky's quality of life is wonderful," she said. "He doesn't act disabled in any way, and he seems as happy as he ever was."

Ellen, a waitress, recently moved to a new apartment with Sophia, her white domestic shorthair cat. She brought Sophia to me for an itchy skin problem and remarked that she and the cat were both "stressing out" from all the noise created by her new neighbors. Previously, Ellen and the cat had lived in a small cottage in the back of a large estate, where they had privacy, and Sophia had the run of the yard. Now Sophia was not only totally confined indoors, she also had to put up with strange and disruptive new sounds and smells. I sadly had to agree with Ellen that because of the emotional distress, Sophia's quality of life would probably not improve until Ellen could afford to move again to a new and more congenial place.

Tesse, a 13-year-old dachshund, was a bundle of miseries when her owner, Scott, brought her in. I could hear the black-and-tan dog's breathing because of a chronic nasal infection and watched as she walked gingerly, unable to see because of cataracts in both eyes. She also had a severe, itchy skin disease on her flanks that had not responded successfully to any treatments. "On top of everything else," Scott told me with a sigh, "she's been acting as if she has Alzheimer's disease. She can't remember when she's been fed and barks for food all the time. Oh, and she's also become incontinent, so I have to keep her in just one room. Frankly, Dr. Mac, I don't think her life is bringing her much pleasure anymore." I had to agree with Scott's assessment: Tesse's many ailments had become so severe that her quality of life was compromised, with not a great chance that it could be improved.

When I first saw Yasup, a 13-year-old female terrier mix, I almost laughed. Her short, wiry hair revealed very lumpy skin, caused, I was soon to learn, from numerous benign fatty tumors all over her body that ranged in size from that of an egg to one as large as a softball. The tumors didn't affect Yasup's health in any way, but gave her a decidedly odd appearance. "She's so bumpy and lumpy that the little boy on our street has started calling her 'lumpy dog' when we're on our walks," her human companion told me cheerfully, after learning that the lumps weren't dangerous. "Since she doesn't seem to mind, why should I?"

a surprising find. The pool did contain a few fish, "but more impor-
tantly," Dr. McBain relates, "there was a hole in the wall between the
pool and the ocean that was approximately 3 feet in diameter. The
opening in the pen was large enough for seals to come and go at their
leisure. The seals had been going out to the bay to feed but had not
missed a show in 2 weeks."

A Quality-of-Life Thermometer

As a veterinarian, I've often wished I had a quality-of-life thermometer
so that I could simply take a reading of the way the animal is seeing his
life. The problem is that it is difficult to measure quality of life when my
patients can't tell me how they feel. Human doctors have the same difficulty when dealing with infants, the mentally disabled, or the severely ill.
In those cases, doctors usually assess quality of life using information from
parents, spouses, partners, caregivers, siblings, and health-care providers.
We do something very similar with pets, relying on the subjective im-
pressions of the primary caregiver or caregivers—the people who know
the pet best.

The best way to assess your pet's quality of life is first to inventory
all sources of feelings—both pleasant and unpleasant. This would include health-related feelings as well as others. Be aware, though, that
not all health-related issues affect your pet the same way they might affect you.

In addition, it's not always possible to separate health- and non-
health-related feelings. One of my patients, McGee, an 8-year-old male
black cocker spaniel, developed a severe skin disease that caused his hair
to become matted and greasy and to give off a very unpleasant odor. His
owners, the Duffys, began to avoid contact with their dog and eventu-

ally relegated McGee to the backyard. Now, in addition to the itchy skin, poor McGee suffered from loneliness as a direct consequence of his health issue. (This story does have a happy ending: After several months of treatment, McGee's skin condition improved, and he was allowed back in the house.)

As with McGee, it's important when examining your pet's life for factors affecting her quality of life to include *all* sources of feelings.

THE QUALITY-OF-LIFE QUESTIONNAIRE

Although it's not a quality-of-life thermometer, the following questionnaire, which I use at my animal hospital, will help you get a good idea of your pet's quality of life. This and all future quality-of-life evaluation tools will go through a continual process of refinement and improvement as research teaches us more about animal minds.

The questionnaire is designed to determine your pet's quality of life by weighing the broad array of life factors that matter to animals. Please be aware that this questionnaire has not yet been scientifically validated to determine its accuracy, and therefore the results should be considered only estimates. As you go through the questions, keep in mind that every animal is an individual with different needs, desires, and preferences. The questionnaire should be completed by the member(s) of your family who knows your pet's personality and nature best. It can be helpful to repeat the questionnaire periodically, especially when your pet experiences medical problems, change, or disruption in his daily life. Comparing the follow-up score with previous scores can provide meaningful information about your pet's ongoing quality of life.

Pet Quality-of-Life Evaluation

1. List all the things during your pet's life that have given him pleasure, such as going on walks, interacting with people or animals, playing, being petted, eating, rolling in the grass, and exploring objects and places.

How many of these things is your pet currently getting meaningful pleasure from? _____ (1a)

How many of these things was your pet getting meaningful pleasure from when he was feeling his best, physically and emotionally? _____ (1b)

2. List all the activities and experiences during your pet's life that you feel he would regard as *fun*. Examples include playing games, chasing butterflies, playful pouncing on things or animals, digging holes, and running through the water at the beach. (Note that all of the things on this list give pleasure and thus would also have been on your list in Question #1. However, this list will be considerably shorter since there are many things that bring pleasure but are not generally considered *fun*, such as curling up on your lap, eating, getting a massage, and lying on cold surfaces.)

How many of these things is your pet currently experiencing as *fun*? _____ (2a)

How many of these things was your pet experiencing as fun when he was feeling his best, physically and emotionally? _____ (2b)

3. On a scale of 1 to 10, 1 being unbearably severe discomfort (extreme distress, suffering) and 10 being complete comfort (no discomforts), what do you judge your pet's comfort level to be? (For reference, a discomfort is any unpleasant feeling such as nausea, sickly feelings, difficulty breathing, pain, itchiness, hunger, fear, separation anxiety, general anxiety, loneliness, boredom, anger, and depression). _____

4. On a scale of 1 to 10, 1 being no enjoyment and 10 being the highest possible level of enjoyment, what do you consider to be your pet's current enjoyment of life? _____

5. Imagine that you are a pet animal of the same species as your pet and that you have the best quality of life you can imagine a member of this species having. On a scale of 1 to 10, 1 being extremely unwilling and 10 being extremely willing, how willing would you—as a pet animal—be to exchange your life for the life your pet is living? _____

CALCULATIONS

Add 1a + 2a = _____ (This is A)

Add 1b + 2b = _____ (This is B)

Now subtract: B – A = _____ (This is Y)

Add up answers for questions 3, 4, and 5 = _____ (This is X)

Finally, subtract: X – Y, and enter here to get your pet's Quality-of-Life Score (if Y is greater than X, then enter 0) = _____

SCORING INTERPRETATION

Note: This is a nonscientific interpretation of the quality-of-life score. This test has not been validated by scientific methods.

The highest score is 30, and the lowest is 0.

26–30	Very good to excellent quality of life.
21–25	Good quality of life.
16–20	Fair quality of life.
11–15	Low quality of life.
0–10	Poor quality of life.

It's the Feeling That Counts

In people, happiness consists of a cognitive component and an emotional component. The cognitive component involves how you *think* about your life, and the emotional component involves how you *feel* about your life. For example, when assessing your happiness level, you might report your cognitive assessment in such objective terms as "I've achieved most of my life's goals." The emotional component, in contrast, forms your life assessment on a gut-level, feeling basis, which you might express as, "I *feel* fulfilled."

Much scientific evidence supports the intuitive belief that your *thoughts* about your life cause you to *feel* happy or unhappy with your life. However, a great deal of scientific evidence also shows that this system works the other way around: Feelings influence your thoughts about life. If you're feeling good about how things are going, you think happier thoughts, while if you feel bad, you think more negative thoughts.

As for animals, all evidence points toward them having, like humans, the capacity for the emotional component. Where things get murky is determining whether there is a cognitive component in animal happiness. Do cats, dogs, and other mammals form *thoughts* about their lot in life? Or do they just *feel* it?

In people, happiness is an evaluation of life over a period of time, not the feeling of the moment. It is reasonable to believe that animals have a more limited cognitive evaluation than humans of their overall lives so, accordingly, they likely experience happiness more on the basis of current feelings than we humans do. For example, a person currently experiencing severe pain may still report her happiness level as high (because she knows that the pain is only temporary). A dog with the same degree of pain, on the other hand, may use that unpleasant feeling as the primary—or even sole—basis for his feelings about his level of happiness.

It's quite possible that because of limitations of cognition and language, an animal's experience of happiness may involve little (or none) of the cognitive element. Animal happiness may be *only* a feeling about how life is faring—being no more than an experience *felt* as "life is good."

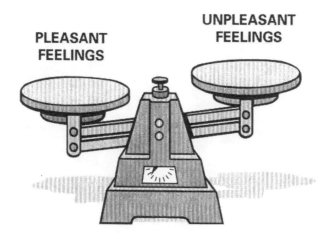

Tipping the scale toward pleasure.

"I promise to do everything in my power to keep your life in this balance until you take your very last breath."

Chapter 8

THE MIND/BODY CONNECTION

BEFORE I ENTERED VETERINARY COLLEGE, my coursework for my undergraduate degree in zoology involved several research studies observing animals in their natural environment. One of my projects focused on the population dynamics and behavior of the common field mouse. I would set out small box traps in a large grassy field, check the traps daily, record my catches, and release the mice unharmed.

Whenever I checked the traps, I found most to be empty, while the others each contained a single mouse—always staring at me with wide, frightened eyes. I made notations in my notebook and then gently set each tiny creature free. On one such trip, however, when I reached the last trap, it felt a little heavier than the others. As I opened the trap door, I peered in to see not just a single trembling furry mouse looking back at me, but also five tiny, hairless, pink infant mice lying on the bare metal floor of the trap. A mother mouse had given birth in the trap. I quickly released her and the babies into the tall grass. I realized that had I been even a few hours later in making my rounds, the mother and her infants would probably have perished.

Troubled that my study might have been the cause of this near-tragedy, I terminated the trapping part of the experiment right then. But I was immediately struck by the similarity of what had happened to this mother mouse and what happens in pregnant women, who can be triggered into premature labor when experiencing emotional stress.

This little pregnant mouse ventured from her nest to seek food, became entrapped in a fearful place, and went into labor as a result. Just as in a human being, emotions in that mouse's mind had apparently caused a powerful physical change in her body. This realization was the beginning of what would become one of the most important principles in my later career as an animal doctor.

IT'S ALL IN THE MIND

It has been well-known for a number of years that emotions and physical stress can trigger a wide array of illnesses and influence the outcome of countless diseases in humans. What is not so well-known is that most of the research investigating these mind/body effects has been conducted not on human beings, but on animals.

In literally thousands of papers buried in the scientific and medical journals on university library shelves, it has been confirmed again and again that the health of animals, like that of people, is profoundly linked to the workings of the mind. Through my own articles in medical journals and my lectures, I have conveyed this information to the veterinary medical profession, but it is still essentially unknown to most of the 152 million pet owners like you, who need it most.

Although a definitive cause-and-effect interaction between mind and body has not been proven in animals, the evidence appears overwhelming that animals' emotions do affect their bodily health. For example, studies have shown that loneliness is linked to immune deficiencies in monkeys, anger is associated with heart disease in dogs, and fear appears to trigger as fatal thyroid condition in rabbits. Stomach ulcers, high blood pressure, urinary disorders, and arthritis have all been shown to be connected to emotional distress in animals.

I've seen a whole gamut of mind/body effects on the health of my own animal patients. Examples include Aiko, a 10-year-old Siamese cat who developed diabetes after his human companion began a new job that left little time for him; Frannie, a 5-year-old female Scottie who was so terrified of thunderstorms that an especially severe storm caused her to develop signs of a bladder infection; and Boomer, a black Lab who came down with a rapidly progressive fatal disease right after his beloved human companion died of AIDS. It is a common experience in veterinary clinics like ours to see dogs react to the stress of medical examination the same way humans do—with elevated blood pressure readings, which can be mistaken for hypertension (chronic high blood pressure).

How the Mind/Body Connection Works

Believe it or not, it is only recently that scientists have found some of the key mechanisms by which body and mind are tied together: hormones and neuropeptides, chemical messengers that constantly relay signals back and forth between the mind, the immune system, and other bodily systems. This constant communication makes sense when you realize that nature designed the entire organism—nervous system and all the other cells of the body—to work together as a harmonious whole. When an animal is challenged by, say, an environmental threat, this complex information system ensures that the animal will respond as a whole unit.

Just as unhappy emotions and feelings are linked to illness in animals, happy emotions and positive feelings are linked to improved health and increased recovery from illness. Learning how to use your own pet's mind/body connection can help you make your pet's life not only the happiest it can be but the healthiest as well. For example, while we all know our pets love to be held and petted, the latest scientific findings suggest that petting and other compassionate human contact can have potent positive effects on pets' physical health. These benefits include slowing the progression of disease, lessening pain, improving survival from surgery, increasing reproductive success, boosting the immune system, and increasing resistance to cancer. (For more on the power of human touch, see page 198.)

HOW EMOTIONS CAN MAKE YOUR PET SICK

Sadly, I've seen numerous cases in my practice of pets whose fear or heartbreak literally made them ill. The story of Rico and Pablo is a good example of emotion-based illness. Rico and Pablo were two jet-black male cats. They had lived together as the closest of companions for their entire lives—all 16 years. Both had been exceptionally healthy up until the day that Pablo began to show problems passing urine. After running several tests and x-rays, I made the tragic discovery that Pablo had inoperable bladder cancer. With no treatment available, his discomfort quickly worsened, and Suzanne, Pablo's caring owner, and I made the painful decision that euthanasia was our most humane option.

Rico was never the same. According to Suzanne, he was simply inconsolable without his feline companion. He began meowing nonstop, 24 hours a day. Within a few weeks, Suzanne brought Rico to see me because his health had begun to deteriorate. He had lost weight and was experiencing lack of coordination. Tests revealed serious blood-cell abnormalities. It appeared that Rico's once-robust health was ravaged by his grief over losing Pablo. Within a week, Rico's illness had taken his life.

SHAWNEE'S STORY

Shawnee, a sleek 5-year-old black Labrador retriever, came into our clinic with a severe gastrointestinal upset. My first impression of Shawnee as she trembled in the examining room was of a thin and very nervous dog. "The poor thing has been throwing up for 2 days," Arline, the dog's distraught companion, told me. "She's had these problems in the past, but never so severe or continuous."

As I checked the dog out, I questioned Arline about the onset of Shawnee's problems. Arline told me that Shawnee had not eaten anything unusual and had not had access to any medications or other possible toxins.

"Has anything upsetting occurred around the household lately?" I asked. "Visitors, or anything else that might have upset Shawnee?"

Arline thought a moment, then nodded. "We have two teenagers," she said. "A few weeks ago, they started arguing and yelling at each other. It's just escalated. Now whenever they start up, Shawnee growls, then takes off for another room."

I nodded. "Would you say that Shawnee's problems began when the kids began arguing?" Again, Arline thought for a moment, then said, "I can't be sure, but I think the vomiting began right around that time."

Shawnee's gastrointestinal upsets were so closely connected to the emotionally upsetting events that it seemed quite likely her physical illness was being triggered by emotional factors. I advised Arline to enlist her teenagers in helping to calm the atmosphere for the dog and also prescribed a calming medication.

A few weeks later, Arline called to tell me that Shawnee was doing much better. "The kids wouldn't stop yelling for me," she told me ruefully. "But when I explained they were making the dog sick, they both immediately agreed to keep the arguing down, and so far, it's working."

Not all such cases have such a tragic outcome, but it is often the case that a physical illness in your pet is a sign that he is experiencing some type of emotional distress. I think of Timbo, a 12-year-old male minia- ture dachshund, whose human companions, Beverly and Richard, often took trips to Europe for 4 or 5 weeks. Beverly had told me that Timbo became anxious and often trembled when she and Richard began to pack for a trip. After a particularly lengthy trip was followed by another of shorter duration, Timbo's pet-sitter, Anita, called to tell me the dog had developed diarrhea. "They're due back tomorrow," she told me, "but I didn't want to take a chance."

In light of Timbo's history, I didn't treat him with anything at that time but asked Anita to have Beverly call me when she returned. Just as I ex- pected, the problem went away as soon as the little dog was reunited with his owners. Six months later, Beverly called: She and Richard were preparing for another trip, and Timbo had begun passing blood in his urine. It appeared obvious to me that Richard and Beverly's trips were the trigger for a variety of health problems for Timbo. This time, I treated him with antibiotics for a urinary tract infection and suggested anti- anxiety medications for Timbo when the couple prepared for future trips.

Rascal, a beautiful 4-year-old male black-and-white longhair cat, also had problems when his human companion, Brian, traveled. Unlike Timbo and most other pets, however, Rascal invariably became ill *after* Brian returned home. On one memorable occasion, a worried Brian brought Rascal in. His normally energetic and outgoing cat now was the picture of feline distress: His ears were back, his eyes were half shut, and he showed no interest in anything. "He's been like this ever since I got home," Brian told me. "He's been vomiting and having diarrhea, and I can't get him to eat anything."

My diagnosis was gastroenteritis, a condition that can be due to a common viral infection or eating the wrong food but is also seen commonly in animals (and people) with no obvious cause other than recent emotional upsets. I advised Brian to give Rascal extra attention and check back in a couple of days. Sure enough, when Brian called at the end of the week, he reported that the problems had disappeared and Rascal was his usual rambunctious, loveable self. On Brian's next trip out of town, he asked the pet-sitter to check for any health problems, but once again, the illness showed up only on Brian's return. As before, it appeared that the problems were set off by emotional factors. The next time Brian was scheduled to travel, I prescribed anti-anxiety medication for Rascal, and this time there was no problem upon Brian's return.

Rascal's case is by no means unique. Many of my patients have developed health problems when they experience fear or anxiety, and for many, these unpleasant emotions are triggered by seeing their human companions packing the family belongings in preparation for a move or an extended trip out of town. My own cat, Gooby, developed a urinary blockage just as I had finished packing the van to move from northern to southern California a few years ago. Once he had been treated, and the move was over, he was fine.

Other animals become sick when an unusual event occurs, or there is a change in the household routine. After the Sylmar–San Fernando earthquake in southern California in 1971, local animal hospitals reported an increase in the number of cats with urinary tract disease.

IGNORING THE POWER OF THE MIND

Scientific evidence of the link between mind and body began with the Russian scientist Pavlov's experiments with dogs, in which he trained the animals to associate food with the sound of a bell ringing. Soon the dogs would salivate in anticipation of eating when they heard the bell, whether or not food was present. This showed that a sound the dog's brain took in by hearing the bell was somehow being turned into a physical change in the body—in this case, the secretion of saliva from the salivary glands.

Similar experiments have shown that the immune system can be trained in the same way. For example, if a stimulus (such as the ringing of a bell) is paired with the injection of an immune-system stimulant, eventually the sound of the bell alone will cause the same immune response. This type of study established a connection between the brain (which perceives the bell sound) and the body's immune system.

Emotional sufferings—such as loneliness, fear, and boredom—appear to have a similar power to cause changes in the body, affecting blood pressure, immune response, digestion, and other bodily systems. Extensive research suggests that unpleasant emotions can actually alter the physical workings of the body so dramatically that death may result. Zookeepers have reported, for example, that young elephants, when taken from their social group, will sometimes die suddenly, in what is called "broken-heart syndrome."

Although precise measurements aren't possible, it now appears that psychological factors are among the most potent of all factors affecting bodily health—possibly even stronger than many physical influences. This means that it is essential for everyone who cares for animals to tend to the animal's mental and emotional health as well as the physical. It is the emotional and physical together—not one or the other—that comprise an animal's well-being.

Unfortunately, the training of physicians and veterinarians has historically been oriented toward physical answers. We have been trained to search for single causes, specific physical problems, and physical remedies. Our training has instructed us to separate physical problems from mental problems. The complex interrelationship of the patient's emotions, physiology, and environment has been virtually ignored, and sometimes this can harm our patients.

GETTING EMOTIONAL

Pet owners, too, have been encouraged by their veterinarians to focus mainly on the physical health of their pets. I'm sure you have been urged to keep your cat's or dog's vaccinations up to date as well as to feed your pet a healthy diet and take her to the veterinarian promptly if health problems appear. But chances are that no one has told you that to maintain good health, her mental and emotional well-being are just as important as—and possibly more important than—good food and medical care.

I think of Lisa, the image of a devoted pet owner. She was scrupulous about bringing Brittany, her gray female poodle mix, in for a yearly checkup and vaccinations and fed her pet the highest quality pet food money could buy. When Brittany was about 7 years old, she began to develop a problem with on-again, off-again vomiting. A thorough examination revealed no physical problems, so we decided to switch Brittany to a different type of food and keep an eye on her.

A few weeks later, Lisa brought Brittany back in. She was distraught. "She's been throwing up every few hours," she told me. "Please help her, Doctor."

Again, a physical examination revealed no abnormalities. I asked Lisa about changes or disruptions in her household. At first she hesitated, then in a rush she said, "Things have been terrible for weeks." She covered her face with her hands, then continued, "My husband has a bad temper, and he shouts at me, says terrible things. It's been getting worse, to the point where I'm thinking of leaving him." Again she paused. "He has never shouted at Brittany, but I'm sure she can tell how upset I've been."

I agreed with Lisa that Brittany was almost certainly affected by the troubled atmosphere in her home, showing classic gastrointestinal problems as a result of emotional distress. I prescribed anti-anxiety medication for Brittany and suggested to Lisa that she see her own doctor to help with her emotional distress until the situation was resolved. Shortly afterward, Lisa left her husband and moved out of town, but before she left, she called to tell me that Brittany's vomiting had become less frequent now that her home life was again stable.

Brittany, Shawnee, and hundreds of other pets I have treated all bear witness to the incredible power of the link between the mind and body. The take-home lesson is that what is going on in our animals' minds influences everything I do in the practice of medicine and everything you do when you care for your pet. It may not be a major contributor in all cases, but even when emotions play no role in the cause of a disease, you should take full advantage of the mind/body connection to help your pet recover from illness by minimizing unpleasant emotional influences and promoting pleasant emotions.

Mind and Body: The Bottom Line

When it comes down to it, I can summarize the links between mind and body (in animals and people), and the way those links influence health, in four simple statements:

1. All body systems communicate with and influence each other.

2. Mind and body are inseparable.

3. Mental states have a complex and profound connection with health and disease.

4. Health care must focus on mental factors to be complete and effective.

HEALTH AND HAPPINESS

Just as unpleasant emotions can make your pet sick, there is evidence to suggest that pleasant emotions can benefit your pet's well-being. Obviously, pleasant emotions move your pet toward pleasure on the Pleasure/Discomfort Scale and make him feel better. (See Chapter 3 for an explanation and diagram of the scale.) But they also may play in important role in helping animals regain and maintain health.

Given the extensive experimental evidence of the link between mind and body, you would expect scientists to investigate possible connections between pleasant emotions and good health. After all, if the unpleasant emotions are so extensively linked to adverse health effects, it seems logical—and an obvious area for research—that pleasant emotions would promote health. Curiously, there has been very little research into the beneficial health effects of pleasant emotions in humans or animals.

In one of the very few studies on this topic, researchers at the Purdue University School of Veterinary Medicine recently reported an interesting association between positive emotional states and improved health in dogs. They were studying the factors that contribute to gastric bloat, one of the most dreaded canine diseases, in which a dog's stomach quickly fills with air. If not recognized and treated quickly, this condition can rapidly progress and kill the dog.

When the researchers looked at the personality traits of dogs, they consistently found that there was a decreased risk of bloat in dogs who were judged by their owners to be "happy." In fact, one study showed the risk of bloat in happy dogs was decreased by 78 percent, compared with dogs not judged to be happy. In just one of the many parallels between animal and human studies, this canine study shows remarkable similarities to a human study done at the University of Texas. Nearly 2,500 people older than 64 years of age were studied over a period of 6 years. The results showed that the people who scored high on the happiness questionnaire had a dramatically decreased risk of stroke than the people who had lower happiness scores. Associations such as these do not prove that dogs' and humans' emotional states are the cause of their superior health status, but such intriguing evidence certainly warrants further research on the effects of pleasant emotions.

THE HAPPINESS FACTOR

A little kitten gave us what may be the best look at a clinical case of this effect. Some years ago, a young man rushed into our hospital carrying a small, motionless, 6-month-old black male kitten. "I found him lying on the side of the road," the man, a Good Samaritan in the truest sense, told us. "I think he was hit by a car."

On first glance at this bedraggled little creature, which was in obvious distress, I agreed with the opinion of his rescuer. But tests and x-rays revealed it was not an injury that was hurting the kitten, but that he had ingested automobile antifreeze, an extremely toxic substance that causes severe kidney failure. I shook my head in sympathy. With the condition the kitten was in, I judged his chances for survival to be no higher than 10 percent.

Nevertheless, we proceeded to try to save him. We named the kitten Phoenix, with the hope that he would soon rise from his own figurative ashes. We began immediate treatment, but he remained extremely ill and refused to eat. As the days went on, I became more and more attached to him, especially knowing that he had no one else in the world to look after him. So I began to spend more time with him, just petting and talking to him. I soon noticed that he seemed to enjoy my company, especially when I petted him. After a few days, he still wasn't interested in eating, but when I turned up the petting to more vigorous scratching, I detected a slight purring sound.

The next day, Phoenix again refused the food my staff offered him, but I decided to try something different. I started scratching him until I got his purr going full throttle, then placed the food in front of him, continuing the scratching. Lo and behold, he chowed down right away! For the next several days, Phoenix continued to refuse food offered in the normal way, but ate avidly while I scratched him. This response was so reliable that my staff made sure I was free to do the scratching during the kitten's feeding time. Gradually, Phoenix became stronger and stronger, recovered completely, and was eventually adopted by a wonderful woman who sees him for the loving ball of fur that he is.

THE HUMAN TOUCH

I'm sure you've seen reports that people with pets have better health and may even live longer than those who don't. For example, having a family pet is associated with increased survival rates in people with heart disease, and blood pressure is lower in children when a dog is present. Even observing aquarium fish can lower blood pressure in many people. Studies have also shown mental health benefits for people with pets, including lower incidence of clinical depression and anxiety.

What is not so well-known is that the reverse is also true: Loving human contact can have a very beneficial effect on the health and mental state of animals.

For example, numerous studies have shown that the gentle touch of a person can improve numerous health conditions in pets and other animals. In dogs and horses, for example, petting is associated with dramatic decreases in heart rate. Rats that are gently handled and petted have a

Phoenix and the PAW Treatment

My patients have taught me some wonderful things over the years, but I have little Phoenix, the bedraggled black kitten, to thank for one of the most valuable lessons. (For Phoenix's story, see page 197.) When Phoenix was recovering, it occurred to me that I should find a way to write a prescription for happiness into his treatment plan. For example, if I could write on the plan "Make happy q 6 hr" (every 6 hours), just as I write "IV fluids @ 15 cc/hr," then I could institute emotional support alongside the standard medical treatment. But how would my staff follow an order to make a pet happy?

Then I realized that Phoenix had already showed me the answer. To make a pet happy, make a feline patient purr. And, of course, make a dog wag his tail. Even though there is only meager scientific evidence of its health benefits (so far, that is), I believe that the more minutes in a day an ill cat purrs or a sick dog wags, the better they will feel emotionally and, most likely, physically. I regard this as no different from going to a "regular" hospital to cheer a patient up by providing emotional support.

I started asking my staff to provide this additional treatment right away. Of course, many veterinary patients are too weak and ill to purr or wag, but that doesn't really matter—the treatment plan calls for doing those things that would normally make a cat purr and a dog wag his tail. Things like gentle, friendly, soothing, and cheerful voices; petting and scratching, especially in the "favorite spots" like over the rump; and gentle stroking. "Treatment" continues for just as much time as the patient load permits. We also strongly encourage visitation by the pet's owner, a very effective method for eliciting purrs and wags. My "purr and wag" treatment order soon became the shorthand acronym "PAW" and is now entered right into the treatment orders next to all the "scientific" treatments.

---

higher survival rate after surgery. Human contact causes major beneficial changes in blood pressure and blood flow to the heart in dogs.

A well-known study conducted by researcher Robert Nerem and his colleagues demonstrated a remarkable effect of gentle human contact in rabbits. The rabbits were divided into two separate groups and fed high-cholesterol diets. One group was given standard laboratory animal care, while the other group was given daily doses of petting, stroking, being talked to, and being played with. After 6 weeks, it was found that the rabbits in the gently petted group developed less than half the degree of atherosclerosis (hardening of the arteries) as the rabbits given standard laboratory care. Somehow, the gentle human contact slowed the progression of disease in these rabbits.

Farm animals also appear to benefit from caring human contact: Cows produce more milk when dairy farmers touch them and speak to them, and female pigs become more fertile. Even chickens are healthier when humans talk to them and handle them gently. I often see the positive effect of human contact in my veterinary clinic; the presence of their human companions has, at the minimum, a calming effect on sick, frightened animals.

Not all animals respond beneficially to human contact, of course. Animals who are untamed (feral) and animals that have been abused by people will often show the opposite reaction to the presence of humans. In general, three factors influence the effect of human contact on a pet: her socialization (the extent of social contact the pet has had with people in the past) and her familiarity with the particular person; the quality of the contact (obviously, gentle, compassionate contact causes very different effects than harsh, stressful contact); and the genetics of the individual animal (some dog breeds react more positively to people than others).

TOUCH AND HEALING

No one knows exactly how human contact exerts its benefit. Presumably the animal feels more confident and secure—and less anxious—

when a familiar person is present. Some researchers believe that gentle human contact works by lessening the intensity of unpleasant emotions ("stress"). As far as your own cat or dog is concerned, it's extremely important to maintain a loving relationship with lots of physical contact, and this is even more true when she is sick. If she needs to stay in the veterinary hospital overnight, as long as her condition wouldn't be harmed by your presence, try to arrange with her veterinarian to visit her, so you can touch and reassure her. I will have more to say about this topic in Chapter 10, "The Veterinarian's Role."

Although no scientific research has confirmed this, I believe that some of the benefits of human contact may be simulated by placing items that carry the owner's smell in a sick animal's enclosure. Blankets, towels, and clothing (all unwashed) as well as familiar toys, seem to be reassuring and comforting to many pets. If you have to leave your pet alone during the day, or at an animal hospital while you're on vacation, leaving some of your own much-handled objects with him may help him cope better with your temporary absence.

THE PLACEBO EFFECT

In people, the best-known evidence of the mind/body connection is the placebo effect: If a person thinks a particular treatment will be effective, that treatment often shows a positive result, even without the person receiving the actual active component of the treatment. The most widely known form of this is a pill—a "sugar pill"—that looks like the actual drug but lacks the active component of the real medicine. This is the placebo. It is believed that when a placebo is used, the patient's thought process itself actually induces the physical effect.

Mind over Medicine?

Some experimental findings raise the tantalizing possibility that the healing powers of the mind may someday be able to replace such traditional medical procedures as drugs and vaccinations. In one experiment, researchers used their fingers to gently scratch the skin of guinea pigs while simultaneously injecting bacteria into the animals' bodies. The bacteria caused a rapid and pronounced immune response in the guinea pigs, just as a vaccine provokes an immune response in the person or animal that is vaccinated.

Intriguingly, the researchers found that if injections of bacteria were given repeatedly at the same time as the gentle skin scratch, eventually the skin scratch alone—now acting as a placebo—provoked the very same immune response. The mechanism behind this placebo response is believed to be the same as certain placebo mechanisms in humans, such as when the mere sight of a doctor in a white coat prompts healing effects in some people.

Innovative studies like these demonstrate the health-promoting abilities of the brain and suggest that if we can harness these mental powers, we may be able to use them to replace the use of some standard medical treatments. For example, if we knew how to apply the guinea pig study, which involved a stimulation of the immune system, to our current methods of immunizations, it might become possible to administer the first few immunizations in an animal's life with true vaccines, then boost his immunity each year after that by using a placebo.

It is important to understand that the placebo effect is a real, not imagined, effect in the body. You have probably heard doctors, scientists, or even acquaintances comment about a treatment, "That's just a placebo effect," implying that it is somehow less real or less effective than an actual drug effect. It's not. The effect is in fact an actual change in the body (and mind, when it involves pain relief and some other conditions) that can be a useful medical therapy.

While the placebo effect is well-known in humans, most people—including veterinarians—assume that it is not possible in animals, due to their presumed inability to understand the concepts of disease and treatment. After all, how could an animal know what the treatment is for, let alone expect to get better?

However, amazingly, a number of experiments have demonstrated that the placebo effect does indeed work in animals. For example, in a fascinating experiment, dogs were given a series of insulin injections, and then given a placebo injection of water. The dogs showed the same response to the placebo that they did to the active insulin.

Another study evaluating the effects of a pain medicine for arthritis in dogs found that more than half of the placebo-treated dogs showed a response comparable with the pain relief achieved in the group of dogs given the actual drug. Several other studies of animal drugs have unexpectedly revealed a substantial positive response in the placebo-treated animals. I find these sorts of studies exciting—they indicate that the mind may hold immense, even unimaginable, powers for improving the health of animals with less reliance on drugs and surgeries, and perhaps even eventually replacing such forms of treatment.

Unfortunately, our understanding of the mental processes involved in the placebo effect is at pretty much the same stage as Ben Franklin was with electricity—he proved it was there, and immensely powerful, but had no idea how to harness that awesome power. We're not yet ready to start curing your cat or dog through mental forces, but it is certainly within the realm of possibility for the future.

BIOFEEDBACK: MIND OVER MATTER

Biofeedback is another area just beginning to be studied in animals. For years, it has been demonstrated that people can learn the ability to

What's Making Your Pet Sick?

If your cat or dog currently has any medical problems, the following questions can help you find potential psychological or emotional problems that are contributing to the condition.

1. Does the household contain any potential sources of anxiety or fear ("stress")? Examples include loud noises, construction work, disruptions in normal daily routines, tension or ongoing arguments in the house, moving, aggravation from children or other people, the addition of another person or pet to the household, bullying by other pets, and threats from the sight or smells of animals outdoors (such as through the screen door or window).

2. Does your pet spend long portions of the day alone? Does she seem overly dependent or clingy when you are home with her? Do the human members of the household frequently go out of town?

3. Has there been any potential source of grief or depression from loss of a close companion—human or animal?

4. On an average day, how much interaction ("quality time") does your pet have with you?

acquire conscious control over certain bodily functions, such as heart rate and blood pressure. Recent research indicates that biofeedback may also be applicable to health care in animals.

Through special training techniques, a variety of animal species have shown the ability to exert voluntary control over such bodily processes as blood pressure, rate of urine production, and heart rate. This is probably the most striking and conclusive evidence of the mind/body connection, for it shows that "mere" thoughts are able to exert important physical changes throughout the body. The potential for this literal mind-over-matter power

5. Is there any possibility that your pet is bored? When you are away from the house, does your pet have anything to interest him, to engage and stimulate his mind, to *do*?

6. How many enjoyable activities does your pet engage in every day?

7. On an average day, how much playtime does your pet get? Do you feel that you meet your pet's desires for interaction and play?

8. For cats: Is your cat indoors only, or allowed to go outdoors?

9. For dogs: How many walks does your dog receive on an average day?

10. What do you think your pet would want that he or she is not currently getting enough of?

When you have finished answering the questions, examine your answers for clues to potential emotional upsets or unmet needs that may be contributing to your pet's medical condition. Be sure to discuss your findings with your veterinarian. Together, you can find ways to alleviate the upsets, which may help prevent, improve, or even cure a troublesome medical condition.

may be virtually limitless. It is not unreasonable to envision, for example, cats with high blood pressure learning to will their pressures into the normal range and bring about health naturally, without reliance on drugs.

MIND + BODY = PET

The large body of research on the mind/body connection has shown that any line drawn between the mental and the physical is artificial. For pets as well as for people, as long as a conscious mind is connected to a living body, the whole organism functions as a single system. Trying to understand an animal by looking at the mind and body separately is like trying to understand the rainforest by examining its plant and animal life as two unconnected and separate entities.

In the next chapter, I'll show you how you can use this perspective to help shape a long and happy life for your pet.

Chapter 9

A LONG AND HAPPY
LIFE

IF A PERSON WHO HIRES HERSELF OUT as a cat sitter said to you, "I don't care for dogs," what would she mean? That she dislikes dogs? Or could she be a dog lover who has simply tailored her pet-sitting job to be exclusively for cats? What, exactly, does it mean to *care* for a pet?

As it involves animals, the word "care" is defined in two ways. One is to look after or provide for, to tend to an animal; the other is to feel concern about and have regard for, to be fond of an animal and having an interest in what happens to her. The second definition includes empathy, the ability to share another's emotions, thoughts, or feelings.

It is perfectly possible for someone to care *for* an animal without caring *about* him. When I speak of animal care, I mean the word in both senses: caring *for* and caring *about* animals. This is compassionate care.

The ultimate goal of compassionate pet care is to maximize the well-being of the pet under all conditions, in sickness and in health, from earliest puppy- or kittenhood to (hopefully) old age. In this chapter, I offer a plan for doing just that.

THE WORLD THROUGH YOUR PET'S EYES

You're probably used to observing all aspects of your pet's life from your own point of view. Consider your pet cat, "Samantha," who sheds all over the new bedspread, can never decide whether to go outside or come in, and scratched the groomer when he trimmed her nails. This is what you see; it is also essential to try to see the world from *her* viewpoint.

Compassionate care means looking at every problematic situation from the perspective of your pet, keeping in mind that she may not understand what is happening, that she may be reacting from strong self-protective motives, and that her view of the situation will be profoundly influenced by past experiences. In Samantha's eyes, the new bedspread is a lovely rough surface that loosens her excess hair and gives her pleasurable feelings when she rubs against it. She may stand indecisively in the doorway because of something she smells or hears that is beyond your senses; and she may have scratched the groomer because she saw his actions as threatening or likely to cause the same pain she felt when a nail was cut too short during a previous nail trimming.

A good example of using this perspective for understanding is the situation of a dog who has bitten someone. Most experts agree that, with very few exceptions, all dog bites can be explained if the dog's perspective is considered, because dogs do not act out of malice or randomly. Perhaps the dog felt threatened or challenged. Perhaps he thought that the person was trying to invade his territory or steal his food.

Remember Shep, the sheepdog whose story was told in Chapter 4? Although he didn't actually bite anyone, Shep had been uncharacteristically snapping at everyone who came near him. The mystery of this dog's behavior was solved only when I looked at things from his perspective and realized that Shep's recent haircut had given him a new, very scary view of the world. He now saw each person who approached him as a threat and reacted to those threats in what was to him a very natural manner.

In my animal hospital, the animal's view of what is happening is our sole guide as to how the animal is cared for. Putting yourself in the animal's place puts everything in the only perspective that matters—that of the often frightened, frequently wary, and always uncertain pet. Looking at everything through the pet's eyes makes it so easy to explain and understand anything he does, whether it's freezing motionlessly, trying to bite or scratch, struggling to escape, or resisting in any other way.

When you're trying to understand your pet's feelings, it's always important to take her individual past experiences into account. As perhaps the most prominent example, everyone's fears and anxieties are strongly shaped by experiences throughout life. Two different cats housed in the groomer's cages near barking dogs will have very different views and responses to their grooming experience if one cat lives in a home with three dogs, while the other has never before seen or heard a dog.

MENTAL AND EMOTIONAL HEALTH

Mental health in animals has received little attention in the popular or veterinary medical publications, except when it contributes to behavior problems. But as you know from previous chapters, mental health and well-being in your pet encompass much more than behavior problems. They also include positive experiences, emotional fulfillment, happiness, and life satisfaction.

We've all known cats and dogs who acted crazy. As with virtually every other "misbehavior," an emotionally troubled cat or dog is probably enduring unpleasant feelings that may not be evident to outside observers. An animal's "crazy" behavior is simply his attempt—often sadly misguided and ineffective—to return to his Comfort Zone. Animal behaviorists have recently started to look at behavioral problems in terms of emotional disturbances the pet may be experiencing. Although we are a long way from having collies lie down on a psychoanalyst's couch, treatment for emotional disturbances in pets is the beginning of a whole new field to make distressed animals feel good again.

Just as you devote time and resources to caring for your pet's physical health, it's important to focus on her mental and emotional health as well. This focus isn't just for animals with behavior problems, but for all pets, well-behaved or not. The way current research on animal emotions is progressing, it's entirely possible that the care of your pet's mental and emotional health will actually turn out to be *more* important to her than the care of her physical health. A program designed to promote good mental and emotional health—a mental wellness program—has the potential to vastly enrich the life of your pet, providing her with the opportunity for maximum enjoyment of life, from puppy- or kittenhood through old age.

You can start a mental wellness program for your pet at any age, but it's best to start when your cat or dog is very young—from the earliest days, if possible. I recommend a three-part approach, to promote, maintain, and maximize the mental health and well-being of your pet throughout her lifetime. Much of this program focuses on a preventive approach. Think of it as no different from the routine vaccinations and high-quality food that you regularly provide for your pet to maintain good physical health and well-being. The aim of a mental wellness program is to give your pet the greatest opportunities, means, and resources to achieve the greatest happiness in life.

GEORGE'S STORY

Morgan, a musician friend, tells a sad story of how mistreatment can permanently harm a pet's mental well-being. A lifelong fancier of French bulldogs, Morgan was devastated by the sudden loss of his 8-year-old bulldog, and he immediately sought a replacement. A breeder put him in touch with a family who wanted to get rid of a pup they'd recently bought because he had bitten one of the children.

"I found out that the parents had acquired the dog over their son's objections," Morgan told me, "and that the child had repeatedly mistreated the animal by pinching, hitting, and kicking him. Eventually, the dog learned to fight back by biting. After that, whenever he felt threatened, he would bite anyone within reach."

Because he had a great deal of experience with dogs, Morgan was confident that with patience and love, he would be able to help the dog, whom he renamed George, to overcome his bad experiences. Unfortunately, George continued to feel threatened even when there was no threat. Because of George's proclivity for biting, Morgan could walk him only late at night when there were few other people on the street and had to shut him in another room when he had visitors. "It was a constant problem," Morgan said. "It was like having an unexploded land mine in the house."

George even bit Morgan more than once, leaving permanent scars. "You could tell he was suffering," Morgan explained. "Whenever he felt threatened, he would go rigid, growling fiercely and reacting to the slightest movement or sound in his vicinity. All you could do was wait until he regained control of himself and finally relaxed. Until then, watch out!"

After consulting with a dog trainer and an animal behaviorist, it became clear to Morgan that George would never be mentally healthy. However, Morgan kept him and continued to shower him with love and affection until he died several years later. "Under most circumstances, George was a truly lovable dog," Morgan says now, "and I did indeed love him. And, God bless him, his personality quirk certainly wasn't his fault. I'm just thankful, for both of our sakes, that we found each other."

THE THREE-STEP MENTAL WELLNESS PROGRAM

A mental wellness program for your pet can be summarized by the three Ps: prevention, protection, and promotion. This may sound cryptic, but it's an easy way to remember these vital aspects of your pet's care. Let's take a look at each part of the three-step program. Then, when you need a refresher, turn to this section to remind yourself of the keys to a happy and (mentally) healthy pet.

STEP 1: PREVENTION

Just as you vaccinate your new kitten or puppy to protect her from disease, you can also "vaccinate" your pet against mental and emotional problems in later life. Research has shown that in both animals and humans, the neurochemical foundation—the "wiring"—of the brain is laid down in infancy and early life. It is during this time that the most profound and long-lasting influences on mental health occur. Specific times during early life—called "sensitive periods"—play the most crucial roles in mental development. Positive and negative events that occur during these sensitive periods influence how an animal's emotions will function for his entire lifetime. Those of us who care for animals should take maximal advantage of the sensitive periods to help guide the development of our pet's mind, so she will have the greatest potential for a life of happiness and emotional fulfillment.

The Importance of Early Socialization

Among the sensitive periods, scientists have identified a brief span during which the young brain develops its wiring for the animal's social relationships throughout life. This period, known as the socialization period, occurs at about 3 to 12 weeks of age in puppies, and 2 to 7 weeks in kittens. During this time, the animal's brain is forming the mental patterns that will govern his social interactions and bonds.

In addition to the bonds formed with one's own kind, when an infant mammal of any species (including humans) is exposed to other species during the socialization period, the baby animal's brain develops such that throughout his life, he will be highly inclined to experience positive social relationships with other individuals of that species. Since infant mammals in their natural setting are always with their own kind (even if only their mother), they will naturally form an inclination for positive relationships with their own species. However, if a baby mammal does not get the opportunity to interact with other animals during the socialization period, its social relationships will very likely be troubled, unpleasant, and unsatisfactory throughout life.

For pets such as dogs and cats, exposure to people as well as their own species, is critically important. Cats and dogs gently handled by people at the earliest ages—before, during, and after the socialization period—grow up to be friendly and confident. Studies have shown that puppies can be adequately socialized with as little as 10 minutes of human companionship a day (although proper upbringing care involves far more than this!).

The fascinating thing about this mammalian trait is that the brain becomes wired for positive relationships with all species the young animal is socialized with. A young kitten raised with frequent (supervised!) contact with mice and rats, for example, will result in a cat that is inclined to befriend rather than harm rodents. This knowledge can be very helpful in raising kittens. If you don't want your cat to hunt and kill birds, frequent exposure to birds during the socialization period will make it far less likely that he will later harm them.

As amazing as this process is, however, everyone has read news accounts of its limits and failures. A wild animal, such as a Bengal tiger or grizzly bear, even when raised by human hands and receiving lots of loving human contact during its socialization period, will still develop such a strong predatory drive that the brain wiring for social relationships can often, and tragically, be overridden.

The socialization period is probably the single most important part of your pet's mental wellness program, since the effects of your actions during this brief time are lifelong. During this period, you should try to introduce your young pet to as many other people and animals as possible, always using common sense and taking appropriate precautions to avoid exposing your puppy or kitten to disease. (See "Exposing Puppies to the World" on page 217).

Even if your pet was inadequately socialized when young, gentle handling at any stage in his life will make him more likely to bond with you and may help make up for the deprivation he experienced during his socialization period. Animals that received no socialization during the sensitive period (such as feral cats) are frequently unable to ever form healthy and positive relationships with those species they weren't socialized to, including humans. For these unfortunate animals, people and other animals may be perpetual sources of fear rather than comfort.

Short-Circuiting Fear

The other key developments in a young animal's brain involve the emotion of fear. During early life, from birth to around 4 months of age, the animal brain learns what to fear and what not to fear. Within this time frame, virtually anything the young animal is exposed to—as long as it doesn't frighten the youngster—will cause a desensitization to that object or event. This desensitization eliminates (or greatly reduces) the animal's fear response to that object or event, so the animal can live in comfort when she encounters it later in life.

If you can manage it, try to carefully expose your young pet to any-

Nutrition and Mental Well-Being

A growing number of studies suggest that nutrition plays an important role in maintaining the mental health and well-being of your pet. For example, researchers at Tufts University found that certain forms of fear-based aggression in dogs are reduced on a lower-protein diet. In other studies, dogs with age-related cognitive decline (a condition resembling Alzheimer's disease in people) have had much of their mental abilities restored by eating a special diet containing a unique blend of antioxidants and other nutrients. Several pet-food manufacturers are now incorporating this promising new research into their pet foods, making nutrition an increasingly important part of a complete mental wellness program for elderly pets.

In an earlier chapter, we talked about the health consequences of obesity in pets and how it detracts from quality of life. If your pet is overweight, her capacity to enjoy life can be severely diminished by joint pain and decreased stamina. But as we saw in Chapter 6 when we discussed overeating and comfort food, one of the most important aspects of obesity is that it may itself be a signal that your pet's mental well-being is diminished. Just as in people, many cases of overeating in cats and dogs may be a result of boredom, frustration, or loneliness, so the first question you should ask yourself if your pet is overweight is what unpleasant emotions may be at work.

---

thing that might frighten her at some later time during her life, including car and air travel, thunderstorms, fireworks, children (*very* important), gunfire, and elevators. This is also the ideal time to let her get used to medical and grooming procedures. If possible, give your puppy or kitten a gentle introduction to such procedures as nail-trimming, combing, bathing, fur-trimming with electric clippers, ear manipulations, temperature-taking, tooth-brushing, and pill-giving.

The other side of the coin, unfortunately, is that anything that severely frightens an animal at this age can cause a long-lasting and sometimes permanent fear of that object or event. Because during this sensitive period, a young animal's brain is extremely receptive to learned fear responses, be very careful and gentle with all learning experiences. Interactions with people (especially children, who don't always understand the need for gentleness) and other animals as well as events such as a trip to the vet or groomer, must be as emotionally positive (or at least neutral) as possible. Any emotional traumas, such as attacks by aggressive animals or painful medical procedures, could have a lasting negative effect on your cat's or dog's long-term emotional health.

At this time, it's also important to gently handle your pup or kitten frequently (during her waking hours) to accustom her to the soothing effects of gentle human touch. Research spanning several decades indicates that human touch has lasting physical as well as mental health benefits. Studies have shown, for example, that kittens who are handled develop more quickly than kittens raised without human contact. These same kittens as adults are also better able to cope with "stress" and learn more quickly.

STEP 2: PROTECTION

Throughout your pet's life, do your best to protect her from unpleasant physical and emotional feelings, and provide her with the tools to effectively cope with stressful events.

The best way to minimize unpleasant feelings is to meet your pet's emotional needs. Specific measures you can take throughout your pet's life include all the Happiness Boosters (see page 170). For example:

❖ As much as possible, minimize sources of fear and anxiety, such as loud noises, threatening animals, household tension and turmoil, unpredictability in the daily routine, and mistreatment or abuse.

- Provide mental stimulation in the form of play, games, interactive toys, recreation, challenges, opportunities for exploration, variety, and novelty.

- Provide adequate social companionship.

Exposing Puppies to the World

The standard guidelines for raising puppies have remained essentially unchanged for decades and have not kept pace with the rapid progress in our understanding of the mental and cognitive development of growing dogs. The new scientific understanding of canine social emotions tells us the old way is not the best way.

The traditional advice for new puppy owners has been to keep your puppy away from other dogs until he's received all his puppy vaccines, at about 16 weeks of age. New puppy owners are even told to not let their puppy outside until the last puppy shot has been given. However, with what we now know about emotional development in animals, this advice actually lessens your dog's potential for happiness throughout his life.

Because the earliest weeks are the time when puppies are forming the mental framework that will govern their social relationships throughout life, it's important and beneficial for the pup's future emotional well-being for him to interact with other dogs (and cats, other animals, and people) during his socialization period. In addition to the healthy dogs of your relatives and friends, check to see if there are puppy socialization classes or "doggy day care" programs in your area. Both of these can give your pup positive experiences with other dogs and people.

You must of course take proper precautions not to expose him to contagious diseases or parasites, so until your pup is older, avoid dog parks and contact with dogs whose background you don't know. Instead, make sure he socializes with healthy, well-cared-for dogs. Bearing that caution in mind, for the happiest and most well-adjusted dog, early experience and socialization with other animals is a must.

❖ Provide your pet with a sense of control through meaningful choices and a Safe Haven. (See page 101 for more on Safe Havens and how to create one for your pet.)

Other ways to protect your pet from unpleasant feelings are not so obvious or straightforward. For example, because dogs are highly social animals, their mental well-being depends on a recognizable and stable dominance hierarchy that serves to minimize conflict, uncertainty, and anxiety. In other words, they need to know who's "top dog" in the family and where they fit in.

It is a very good idea to enroll your dog (and yourself) in obedience training to establish a clear hierarchy among the human and canine members of your family. This will result in a smoother and more trouble-free relationship between your pet and every member of the family, human and otherwise—including you. You can also protect your pet from a wide variety of unpleasant feelings by having him, or her, neutered or spayed (See "Neutering and Quality of Life" on page 220).

Another unfortunately common emotional distress that can easily be prevented is that of separation between your pet and his bonded human (you) due to his becoming lost. It is essential to make sure that your home and yard are secure to prevent your pet from running off and not being able to find her way back home (or worse, being pet-napped). If your dog or cat should become lost, providing her with identification tags, tattoos, and a microchip implant will help anyone who finds her to quickly locate you and prevent her from suffering the trauma of permanent separation from the security and comfort of her family.

STEP 3: PROMOTION

The final aspect of a mental wellness program is to promote pleasurable feelings. Since your pet's quality of life is related to the amount of time she spends experiencing good feelings, make sure that she has plenty of play and opportunities for mental stimulation, exploring new objects and places, social interaction, tasty foods and treats, and—very important— meaningful contact with you and other people.

Among the many ways to provide your pet with enjoyable experiences are taking her for walks, runs, and trips to a dog park (for dogs); and walks on a harness or supervised visits outdoors (for indoor cats). Make an effort to give your pet your undivided attention during at least part of the day. Use that special time for interactive play and fun activities. If she is not interested in play, pet and stroke her while talking to her.

Always remember that your pet should also have plenty of opportunities to play, have fun, explore, and generally enjoy life when you're not around. Provide interactive toys, an ongoing supply of novel objects to explore, visual stimulation, and, if at all possible, a pet door with access to the outdoors. To help her keep herself entertained when you're unable to play with her yourself, especially for indoor cats, introduce boxes, tree branches, paper bags, and anything else that has new smells and exploratory potential. Provide interesting videos and windows for peeking out of. For more ideas on ways to enhance your pet's mental health, see previous chapters, especially Chapter 7, "The Best Quality of Life."

HOW TO MAKE A SICK PET FEEL BETTER

In keeping with The Pet Pleasure Principle, you want to do everything you can to minimize unpleasant feelings in your cat or dog. Sometimes there is little you can do about certain unpleasant feelings—say, pain from a healing wound or feelings of sickness from a viral infection. In those cases, you can still help maximize your pet's quality of life by providing her with even more pleasurable experiences, tipping the quality of life

Neutering and Quality of Life

Sexual activity and nurturing young are among the survival-promoting pleasures your pet evolved to seek, so it may seem that neutering, by eliminating those activities, might diminish your dog's or cat's quality of life. However, if the pleasurable feelings associated with an activity are outweighed by unpleasant feelings, then the result is tipping of the quality-of-life scales to the unpleasant side. This is the way reproductive-associated activities appear to be in pet animals. The pleasures obtained by mating are greatly outweighed by the serious negative consequences of not being neutered.

In considering this issue, keep in mind that successful reproduction is believed to be the sole driving force in the evolutionary process of natural selection, and that the sex drive is presumed to have been around for well over 100 million years. It's easy to forget that after that enormous period of time, it wasn't until about 50 years ago that dogs and cats became "house pets" who were no longer free to roam the neighborhood and satisfy their sexual urges.

The sex drive that had been refined, strengthened, and enormously effective for millions of years didn't vanish once we began housing animals indoors. Feeling this extremely powerful impulse and being unable to act on it in any way would seem to have great potential to create strong unpleasant feelings of frustration and unsatisfied urges.

Spaying and neutering not only eliminates that cause of potential discomfort, it also dramatically reduces the occurrence of many health disorders. In neutered females, the chances of having infections of the uterus,

---

scales further toward pleasant feelings. This is, after all, what pampering is: a way of flooding your beloved pet with pleasurable feelings.

So, by all means give your sick kitty or pooch lots of love and attention and as much mental stimulation as is suitable for her health condition including challenges, chasing and pouncing, play with interactive

hormonal disorders, and mammary cancer are all but eliminated. Neutering males makes infections, cysts, and cancer of the prostate and testicles extremely unlikely to occur.

Neutering also greatly reduces fighting among males (because they will not be competing for females). It will also reduce your pet's chances of being exposed to disease from close contact with other animals.

There's another quality-of-life issue to consider here, and it's a big one. Every responsible pet owner would agree that it would be wrong to try to improve a pet's quality of life at the expense of the quality of life of other animals. You wouldn't, for example, allow a pet dog who might enjoy attacking cats to run free and cause severe harm to neighbors' cats. The same applies to the unplanned litters of puppies and kittens produced by unspayed and nonneutered dogs and cats.

Consider the quality of life these poor infant animals have! Hundreds of millions are hauled to the pound and euthanized each year or left to roam the streets and countrysides, scrounging for morsels of food. And even when homes are found for these unplanned kittens and puppies, every one of those placed animals takes a potential home away from a lonely, frightened animal in the shelter, thus dramatically affecting *their* quality of life.

Any caring person can easily see that spaying and neutering plays an enormous role in the quality of life of animals—those animals you see as well as those you don't see. With spaying and neutering readily available, there is no excuse for even one pet to have an unwanted litter.

toys, outings, or whatever lifts her spirits. Be sure to provide food treats if her condition permits. Because quality of life is so individualized, you, as the person who knows your pet best, can choose the things that will give her the greatest pleasure and improve her current quality of life.

One way a disability or chronic illness diminishes quality of life is by

The Three-Step Mental Wellness Program for Pets

Here's an at-a-glance recap of my three-step program. If you do these three things, your pet will have the best life you could possibly give him.

1. **Prevention:** Prevent future problems by socializing young pets and desensitizing them to potential sources of fear.

2. **Protection:** Protect your pets from unpleasant feelings throughout life.

3. **Promotion:** Promote your pets' pleasurable feelings throughout life.

lessening the opportunities to experience pleasures such as chasing, running, and playing. In these situations, a key method to restore a good quality of life is to try to replace what has been lost. For example, a dog that has become paralyzed in the rear legs can regain the lost mobility through the use of specially made carts and handheld slings. Paralyzed dogs fitted with carts—which are basically canine wheelchairs—are often described by their caregivers as being unaware that they are even disabled. Watching these animals chase balls and go on walks confirms that they show all the signs of being very happy dogs. You can compensate for the disability experienced by deaf animals through the use of hand signals, and you can aid the visually impaired by making their home environment and walk routes relatively constant so that the pet develops a sense of security and a dependable feel for where things are.

It's always important to choose pleasant activities that are suitable for the specific disease or disability. Chasing a ball, for example, may be inappropriate for dogs with severe arthritis, but they may still be able to enjoy a gentle walk. Pets with advanced heart or respiratory disease should not be encouraged to do anything requiring major physical exertion.

When choosing pleasures for your cat or dog, make certain the activity promotes pleasurable feelings with the minimum amount of increased discomfort, so that the end result of the activity is an increase in pleasure. For example, Juicy, an aging golden retriever with arthritis of the hips, has difficulty walking even with medication for his pain, as evidenced by his limping and halting gait. However, as his mistress, Chloe, puts it, "He loves the walks so much—the sniffing and greeting other dogs—that I really think he forgets about the pain." For Juicy, the pleasures of the walk apparently outweigh the discomforts of the arthritis. At some point, Juicy's arthritis may worsen to the point where the discomfort of the arthritis will outweigh the pleasure of the walks, but for the time being, the walk brings about an overall increase in his pleasure.

WHEN YOU MUST BE AWAY

Confining your pet in a strange place is almost always frightening and anxiety-producing for her, and it may even lead to adverse health effects. Being in a kennel can cause fear, loneliness, and separation anxiety for many pets. On the other hand, some pets, especially dogs, seem to like going to boarding kennels. They enjoy the excitement and interaction with the other dogs. If your pet reacts negatively to boarding away from home, try to find alternative solutions when you need to leave town.

Among the most workable and accessible solutions is to find someone who can pet-sit in your home. Your pet will be in familiar, comfortable surroundings (her Safe Haven) and will therefore experience a minimum of negative emotions. If no one familiar is available, ask your veterinarian to recommend someone. Many veterinary technicians provide pet-sitting for a fee. Professional pet-sitters are increasingly available throughout the country. Try to find one a trusted friend or coworker

The Human Security Blanket

When I entered the examination room for routine examination of a new patient, Ollie, the young Lab mix immediately scurried behind his mistress's legs. I leaned down to one side to extend my hand in greeting, but Ollie quickly scurried around behind the other leg to stay out of my reach. This quite common scenario is often repeated during my day of seeing patients. Other dogs try other tactics—a small dog may jump into his owner's lap and try to bury his head beneath the owner's arms. One small Siamese cat always tries to crawl beneath her companion's shirt, apparently hoping that she will make herself invisible.

What's going on with these pets, as with cats and dogs who must travel or who experience other emotionally disturbing situations, is that the animals' caregivers provide a calming sense of safety and security for their pet companions. To your dog or cat, you are a security blanket, Valium, and bodyguard all in one.

As we discussed in earlier chapters, social bonds are extremely important in your cat's or dog's life. A body of research has revealed that for humans and animals alike, one of the best tools to counteract stressful feelings is contact with and support of a close social companion. Studies show that dogs exhibit both less fear and less pain when they are petted gently by a person. In a way, this is the flip side of the unpleasant emotion of separation distress—the physical closeness between you and your pet provides comfort and a calming influence—for both of you.

---

has been satisfied with. Check to make sure that anyone you hire is bonded, and ask for and check references.

If you must board your cat or dog, there are steps you can take to make the stay less upsetting. If you have two dogs or two cats, it is often beneficial to both if they are housed together at the boarding facility. The social contact with a bonded companion can serve as a powerful buffer against stress-related emotions. (However, sometimes the stresses of boarding can cause friendly companions to fight, using one another as outlets for frustration, which may make this solution unworkable.)

There are a number of things you can do to help relieve your pet's anxiety and fear when you need to leave him in a strange place. Providing him with items from home, such as favorite toys, a blanket, or a piece of clothing with your scent on it, seems to help. If he is to be boarded or must spend some time in an animal hospital, talk with the staff to see if it is possible to provide a hiding place within the cage or kennel (a Safe Haven). This can be especially helpful for very small dogs or cats. If you plan to be out of town more than a day or two, make sure that the kennel has provisions for playtime and exercise.

If your veterinarian recommends hospitalizing your pet, find out first if there is any way that you can provide the necessary medical care at home. The emotional distress of hospitalization as well as the adverse mind/body effects on your pet's health must always be weighed against the health benefits of the animal being in the hospital. Very often, the need for hospitalization can be avoided or minimized; discuss all alternatives with your veterinarian.

If your cat or dog must be hospitalized, visit him as often and for as long as your animal hospital's visitation policy permits. Research suggests that the effects of your presence and touch can make a difference to your pet's recovery. (For more on minimizing the adverse emotional effects of hospitalization, see Chapter 10, "The Veterinarian's Role.")

GOLDEN AGERS

All animals, including humans, change as we get older. We find our needs and wants changing and becoming more suitable for a new time in life.

For example, as we age, our need for calories declines—often resulting in weight gain if we don't decrease our food intake or increase our exercise to compensate. Most significantly, activities that were important in early life, such as wearing the latest fashions, competing in sports, and going to rock concerts, become less important; while things such as socializing with family and friends become more important. Over time, our interests, values, and priorities change. So it is with our pets.

Wolfgang, a golden retriever who as a young dog spent many happy hours chasing and retrieving tennis balls, gradually gave up this activity and began to spend more time resting in the sun. "He'll still chase the ball if someone picks it up and throws it," says his owner, Damian, a

 ## "Uncooperative" Behavior

Does your sweet, affectionate, docile cat become a howling, raging tiger when she's taken to the vet? Does your friendly dog turn into a snapping, snarling cur when you board him?

The vast majority of these "uncooperative" behaviors, including barking, biting, attempts to escape, and scratching, especially in settings such as boarding kennels, groomers, and pet hospitals, can be attributed to fear, anxiety, or pain. When your pet experiences or anticipates any of these unpleasant feelings, he is simply doing his best to move himself from the discomfort side of the Pleasure/Discomfort Scale into his Comfort Zone.

As with all other emotional discomforts, the best treatment is to try to lessen or eliminate your pet's unpleasant feelings. If you always keep in mind that "uncooperative" behavior is nothing more and nothing less than your pet's effort to reach or stay in his Comfort Zone, his behavior will become understandable, predictable, and natural. He is doing exactly what we are always doing ourselves—striving for comfort.

lawyer. "But he doesn't usually start the game, and he's okay with only doing it a few times before stopping now."

Shalmaneser, the Siamese cat I mentioned in an earlier chapter, liked to chase his tail as a kitten and young cat. But gradually he stopped and, like Wolfgang, began to spend more time resting. "It's kind of sad," John, Shalmaneser's owner, told me. "He doesn't jump up on the refrigerator anymore, either. One by one, I'm seeing his old behaviors drop away. But he's still the same Shalmaneser, just quieter, and he sleeps more."

Just as with us, animals' interests in various aspects of life change over a lifetime. Some of these changes are due to physical processes of aging such as diminishing muscle strength, joint stiffness, and gradual hearing loss, but others appear to be the psychological changes of personal interests and priorities. These changes are normal aspects of aging, and they seem to have relatively minimal effects on the animal's overall quality of life. In other words, even as animals (and people) experience major changes over their lifetimes, quality of life seems to remain at right around the same level. Let's look at why this happens.

A MATTER OF ADAPTATION

Your aging cat or dog often lives a very different life than when he was very young. Just like us, pets experience a variety of age-related physical changes and problems. Bear in mind, though, that most of the changes you see have occurred gradually, and your pet has become accustomed to them through the critically important process of adaptation. Adaptation probably arose in evolution as a means for us to accept, over time, the things that happen to us. In this way, the inevitable changes over time do not cripple us with sadness, despair, and hopelessness.

When you look at an elderly person with vision impairment, difficulty walking, dentures, arthritis, urinary incontinence, and diabetes, you may feel that you would be miserable if you had all those afflictions. Yet the elderly person herself, when asked, will very often describe her quality of life as very good. As happens with aging pets, the elderly person experiences all these changes gradually, allowing her time to adapt and accept what would invariably be viewed by others as an extreme hardship. Many elderly people, including those who suffer major disabilities such as blindness, often report that their quality of life is even better than when they were younger.

BUTCH'S STORY

Butch, a neutered male bluepoint Siamese, had always slept in the bed with his mistress, Rona, a self-employed publicity agent. When I first met Butch and Rona, she laughingly told me that the cat was her "alarm clock," because he always awoke her at dawn by walking back and forth on her body. When she was out of bed, Butch eagerly followed her into the living room, where she spent a few minutes with him purring on her lap.

As Butch became older, his behavior changed, and Rona called me one day in distress. "Butch won't let me sleep at all anymore," she told me. "He starts walking on me around 3:00 in the morning, and if I don't get up and sit with him in the other room, he howls or knocks objects off the dresser. When I scold him or tell him to stop, he just keeps doing it. He'll be miserable if I lock him out of the bedroom, but I've got to get some sleep!"

I explained to Rona that during the night, Butch was almost certainly out of his Comfort Zone and trying to return himself to it—perhaps he felt bored, lonely, or possibly afraid. Or he might have been experiencing a physical discomfort, such as pain, headaches, or nausea. As is frequently the case in these types of situations, it was not obvious exactly which unpleasant feelings were provoking Butch's nighttime restlessness. But we are safe to assume that sitting in Rona's lap moved him toward pleasure

With pets, just as with elderly people, the things that go into making a good quality of life change with age. Because of this remarkable psychological trait of adaptation, the *level* of quality of life stays relatively constant. There are a number of steps you can take to help your cat or dog adapt to any changes brought on by aging and to help assure that her quality of life continues to be the best possible, from her point of view, for the rest of her days.

---

on the Pleasure/Discomfort Scale. "Nevertheless, you need to think of your own health," I told her.

Several medical disorders, such as high blood pressure, an overactive thyroid gland, and an Alzheimer's-like cognitive disorder could also explain Butch's behavior My first advice to all pet owners seeing this kind of problem is to have their pet examined by their veterinarian. Rona brought Butch in for a checkup, and after examining him and running tests to detect the more common illnesses in elderly animals, I found no apparent health problems.

With this knowledge in hand, I reassured Rona that there would probably be very little long-term impact in locking Butch out of the bedroom when he woke her too early. The important thing was for her give her cat plenty of affection and stimulation at other times to relieve his unpleasant feelings in a regular and enjoyable way.

A few weeks later, Rona told me that the problem was already much better. "After I locked Butch out for two nights, he calmed way down," she told me. "He still gets up early and walks on me a little, but not so much, because he knows it means he'll be put outside the door. Some nights, he lets me sleep all night. And I've started playing chase with him more in the evening, in the hopes of tiring him out before bedtime."

A Quality-of-Life Checklist for the Aging Pet

Although the mind's capacity for adaptation assures that your pet's quality of life stays relatively constant during the aging process, that doesn't mean an elderly pet's quality of life won't change when challenged. It also doesn't mean that her quality of life is unresponsive to your efforts to improve it. Fortunately, you can really make a difference to your aging pet's quality of life. Here's how.

- **Mental health care.** Any changes in your pet's mental attitude and skills (such as focused attention and memory), responses to people, emotional behavior such as increasing fears of being left alone or thunderstorms, elimination habits (such as no longer being housebroken), excessive vocalizing, and sleeping patterns should be investigated. Your veterinarian is the first person to contact; and she may want to refer you and your pet to an animal behaviorist.

- **Health care.** When you notice changes in your older pet's energy level, be sure to have your veterinarian check her over to see if the change is caused by a physical problem. New treatments enable many elderly pets with chronic disorders to feel good again. Take a preventive approach to head off health disorders before they cause problems. You should take your pet for checkups more frequently than when she was young—twice a year is a good schedule for elderly pets.

- **Food.** You will probably need to feed your cat or dog less as she grows older. Your veterinarian may recommend a lower-calorie diet for aging pets (a "senior" pet food) or a special formula for cats and dogs with specific health problems. Be sure to continue to give your pet his favorite treats, but not too many, and only those that are safe for any health conditions he may have.

- **Pleasures.** Continue to provide your pet with access to her favorite pleasures. If these change, and they frequently do, then concentrate on the new pleasures. For example, a dog who no longer wants to run in the dog park may still enjoy frequent leisurely walks or car rides. Many pets enjoy receiving massages. A number of books have been written describing the techniques for animal massage (see "Appendix" on page 280). Many elderly pets enjoy warmth to ease the pain of aching joints and as a comfort measure. A heating pad made especially for pets provides a pleasure that can be enjoyed by both cats and dogs (always be very careful with heating pads, as what feels to you like a good temperature can be warm enough to cause skin burns when animals lie on them). Finally, just as with many aging people, aging pets often enjoy increased social interaction and seem to take great pleasure in the company of your friends and even their pets.

❖ **Support for changes of aging.** Be aware that your pet may no longer have the agility to play as he did in the past. In some cases, you may need to make modifications in your home or routine. For example, Arnie, a dachshund who developed arthritis in his legs, was no longer able to negotiate the steps to his home's backyard. His owner, Carl, a kind and handy man, built a wooden ramp to the back door so that Arnie could continue to come and go as he pleased.

Witchie, a cat who had lived with her mistress for 18 years, could no longer leap onto her companion's bed at night. After some thought, her owner made a series of steps using discarded sofa pillows, allowing the cat to climb onto the bed. Any kind of incline or ramp up to your bed will allow your disabled or challenged pet to continue to enjoy your company throughout the night (see "Appendix" on page 280).

HOW TO RECOGNIZE A PET'S UNHAPPINESS

How can we make sure that our pets achieve the happiness we desire for ourselves? Sometimes it's easy to forget that, because we provide every aspect of their environment and care, our pets are almost entirely dependent on us to help protect them from things that detract from their

Where There's a Will

As a veterinarian, I often hear sad stories about cats and dogs whose owners have died and left their pets alone. These unfortunate pets not only have to deal with devastating feelings of grief and loneliness, they are often placed in the local animal shelter, where they may languish for days or weeks and may or may not find another loving human companion. Even worse, sometimes no one is aware of the pets that the deceased person was caring for. In all the turmoil surrounding the death and its aftermath, the pets can be forgotten and left behind in the house or apartment for days or weeks, to suffer and starve.

Because you certainly don't want such a tragic fate for your own beloved pet—in fact, you don't want even the slightest delay or confusion in getting your pets immediate attention and care—it's extremely important, no matter what your current age or health status, to make provisions for your cat or dog in the event of your death or incapacitation. This can be as informal as an agreement with someone you trust who knows both you and your pet, or as formal as a paragraph in your will, leaving the animal and whatever money you can provide for her care to a designated friend or relative. (But make sure they know you're making this arrangement and are willing and capable of taking on this responsibility.)

Some years ago, one of my clients—a probate lawyer himself—passed along a very good suggestion. In the event of your death, your pets will need immediate care, but any provisions you have included for them in

happiness. When discussing pets' emotional health and well-being, I've found that the single greatest misconception among my clients is that they can always tell when their pets are unhappy. In fact, many pet owners believe that if they can't see a visible sign that something is wrong, their pet is happy. Surprisingly, some pet owners have never even thought about the question of whether their pets are happy. And, worst of all, some are simply dismissive of the whole concept. "Sure, he's your will may not be acted upon until months later. He posted a sizable sheet of paper on his refrigerator (it can be in any prominently visible location) that gave instructions as to how many pets he had in his house and who should be immediately contacted for their care. The paper also noted that he had made arrangements for a sum of money to be immediately released to a particular person to assure that full care could begin right away and not have to wait until his estate was settled.

A growing number of animal welfare organizations provide a service whereby you will a certain amount of money to the organization, and they in turn promise to oversee quality care for your cat or dog for life. Some such organizations pledge to find a foster home, while others, such as some no-kill shelters, will take your animal into the shelter. Before signing an agreement with such an organization, be sure to visit it (in person or on their Web site) and inspect the facilities where your pet may spend the rest of his days. If you don't believe your pet will have a good quality of life there, then keep looking.

It's important to be sure that any organization or person to whom you entrust your pet will see that your cat or dog gets high-quality food, proper veterinary care, and loving companionship for the rest of her life. See "Appendix" on page 280 for more information on providing for your pet's care after your death.

stressed," an owner might say of a poodle who is miserable because of a new baby in the house. "But he'll get over it."

The poodle might or might not "get over" the unpleasant feelings caused by the new baby's arrival. But his owner's failure to recognize that his pet is unhappy is potentially an even bigger problem for the dog. Sadly, this sort of ignorance leaves many pets outside their Comfort Zone, leading to emotionally unfulfilled lives.

What about *your* pet? Read through the following list for common signs of unhappiness, indicating that your pet may be experiencing emotional discomforts.

- ☐ Excessive or diminished self-grooming
- ☐ Frequent or persistent tenseness, edginess, or jumpiness
- ☐ Excessive sleeping
- ☐ Unexplained changes in behavior
- ☐ Irritability
- ☐ Aggression toward people or other animals, or increased fighting with other pets
- ☐ Destructive behavior
- ☐ Urinating or defecating in inappropriate or unusual places
- ☐ Excessive vocalizing (meowing, barking, moaning, crying)
- ☐ Frequent or recurrent health problems
- ☐ Overeating, weight gain, or obesity
- ☐ Decreased appetite
- ☐ Excessive clinginess to you or other members of the household
- ☐ Lessened interest in interacting with you or other animals
- ☐ Loss of interest in play, toys, or other normally pleasurable activities
- ☐ Loss of curiosity
- ☐ Hiding much of the time

If you notice any of these signs in your pet, work with your veterinarian to determine whether the causes are physical or emotional, then follow the suggestions throughout this book for things you can do to move her back into her Comfort Zone.

In the next chapter, I'll take you inside my animal hospital and give you a look at the role of The Pet Pleasure Principle in veterinary medicine.

Chapter 10

THE VETERINARIAN'S ROLE

I STILL REMEMBER MY FIRST HOUSE CALL. It was a chilly autumn day, as most days are at this time of year in the lakeside community on Lake Erie where I lived at the time. I was fresh out of veterinary school, proud but a little nervous about this "doctor" attached to the front of my name. The animal hospital where I had just begun working received a call from a distraught pet owner, George Fillmore, and I was paged to take the call. He had heard a bloodcurdling scream when he tried to start his car, and knowing what that probably meant, he quickly opened the hood of his car.

Attracted by the heat of car engines, cats commonly crawl up inside the engine in order to keep warm in cold climates. They almost always lie in the little space where, when the engine is running, the fan blade spins. Tragically, if the engine is turned on when a cat is there, the blade begins its spin but can turn only until it meets the cat's body, usually with tragic results.

Mr. Fillmore instantly saw what he feared most: Jingles, his black-and-white male cat, was crying out in pain as the fan blade held him pinned tightly. "I can't get him out," Mr. Fillmore frantically told me over the phone. "Can you come out to help?" I told Mr. Fillmore I'd be there as fast as I could. I rushed to collect some things I'd need and then set out in my car. My goal was to extricate the cat and bring him back to the animal hospital for emergency treatment.

When I arrived a few minutes later, Mr. Fillmore was waiting by his car and waved wildly to me. I hurried to his car and peered into the engine. The fan blade had struck Jingles in the side of his chest, making it very difficult for him to draw in a breath. Poor Jingles lay trapped, gazing at me with terror in his eyes as he gasped, trying hard to breathe. His look said it all: He was frightened and in terrible pain, and those eyes were begging me to help him.

I immediately started to pull at the fan blade to release the pressure on the cat's chest, but no matter how hard I pulled, the blade wouldn't budge. I tried again and again. I couldn't release the pressure. My mind was racing, aware every passing second that Jingles was enduring the worst kind of suffering: in pain *and* unable to get a breath, the two things that cause the greatest fear and panic in any animal or human being. I knew there was only one thing I could do, and I turned to Mr. Fillmore and spoke the words I knew he, like any loving pet owner, would never want to hear: "I can't save him. We have to end his suffering. There's only one way—to humanely end his life."

Jingles—and his family—had been dealt a cruel blow, and there was no time for deliberation. Mr. Fillmore said nothing. He looked at his wife and two children, who had come outside by now, and they all nodded while tears began to flow down their cheeks.

I drew the euthanasia solution into a syringe as the Fillmores, fighting hard to maintain their composure, leaned over Jingles and uttered a brief and truly heartbreaking goodbye. I gave the injection to little Jingles, who, with what looked to me to be a huge sigh of relief, took one final breath and then lay quiet. His unpleasant feelings were gone—the suffering was over. Jingles, still pinned by the fan blade, now lay in peace and comfort. The feelings of tension and extreme urgency in all of us were immediately washed away by a feeling of relief.

I removed Jingles' lifeless body from the car and gently placed him in a small box I had brought with me. As we all stood there with tears in our eyes, the Fillmores each thanked me, then I returned to the animal hospital.

For the next several days, I thought about what had happened with Jingles. What was it that had made everything so urgent? Why did we all feel such distress? Why did all the urgency end—and our relief set in—the instant Jingles breathed his last breath? And what was my real role in all of this? It came to me in one word: *comfort.*

Jingles had suddenly and powerfully been burdened with the most intense form of discomfort—suffering—and it was this feeling that had put us all in an extremely tense race to help him. He had wanted just one thing: relief from these unpleasant feelings. Jingles wanted to feel good again. It was the intensity of his suffering that had evoked our own sense of urgency, our empathy, and our efforts. And the instant his unpleasant feelings stopped hurting him, the urgency ended.

A VETERINARIAN'S GOAL

When your pet is sick or injured, he wants just one thing: to feel good. As we have already seen, unpleasant feelings are unpleasant feelings, regardless of whether they are physical or emotional. Your pet doesn't care if his unpleasant feelings come from a viral infection, a broken bone, an anxiety disorder, loneliness, hunger, or any other cause. All he wants is for them to go away. As with any other situation in his life, if something—such as a disease—inflicts feelings of discomfort, your pet wants nothing more than to move back into his Comfort Zone.

The discomforts of disease and injury place your pet on the discomfort side of the Pleasure/Discomfort Scale. The further toward discomfort the disorder places a pet, the more urgent is our task to move her out of discomfort and back toward pleasure. In the case of Jingles, the cold northern Ohio temperature had placed him in a bit of discomfort. In an effort to move himself back into his Comfort Zone, he sought to warm himself up by the heat of the car engine.

While Jingles was resting peacefully in his Comfort Zone, Mr. Fillmore got into his car and started the engine. In one horrific split second, Jingles was catapulted from his Comfort Zone to the most extreme discomfort on the Pleasure/Discomfort Scale. It was because he was thrown so far into distress that everything became so urgent for those of us trying to tend to him. When I could not change his position on the Pleasure/Discomfort Scale—I couldn't move him even a little toward his Comfort Zone—I was left with only euthanasia to relieve his discomfort.

Feeling Good

When I am treating a cat or dog for a physical or emotional disorder, my only goal is to make him feel good again. If I'm seeing an animal for a behavior "problem," I aim to relieve any emotional pain that is causing the undesired behavior. If he came to the hospital because of a physical disease or injury, my goal is to eliminate the unpleasant feelings that the disease or injury is causing.

Every day, all day long, I strive for one goal with every animal I see: to move him back into his Comfort Zone. As a way to stay focused on the goal, after I have listened to the owner's concerns and completed my examination, I look each pet in the eyes and promise, "Don't worry, we're going to make you feel good again."

Traditionally, the primary goal of medical practice—both for humans and animals—has been seen as curing illness and maintaining health. Comfort has always been viewed as important in health care, but only in a supporting role, and as a goal separate from the treatment of disease. Comfort is usually regarded as a fallback position, an outcome to seek when medical intervention is unsuccessful.

I believe that this traditional view is mistaken, and that comfort, rather than being a secondary goal, is in fact the primary objective in medical practice. Comfort, after all, is a matter of feelings, and as every word in this book has demonstrated, feelings are what matter to the pets that share our homes and our lives. We, as well as our pets, desire health, because to be healthy is to be comfortable. In other words, health is a means to the end of comfort, but comfort is an end in itself.

This is why my role as a veterinarian is centered directly on that mental location, the Comfort Zone. When the goal of veterinary medicine is viewed this way, it becomes clear that many other aspects of animal care share the same goal. The companies that manufacture antibiotics and the companies that manufacture plush beds for pets are actually making the same thing: tools to put your pet in his Comfort Zone.

By the same token, the veterinary surgeon is doing the same thing as the dog walker. The actions of the rescue workers who save a horse that has fallen into an icy lake are no different than those of the kind lady who adopts a lonely and scared dog from the animal shelter. The kennel owner who soundproofs kennel rooms to lower the noise level is doing the same thing as the zookeeper who provides toys and activities for the

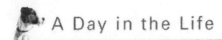
A Day in the Life

Here's a portion of a typical day at my animal hospital. You'll see the types of patients I see and what I view as my goals throughout the day.

- A limping dog: My goal is to stop the discomfort causing the limp.

- A dog with separation anxiety: My goal is to relieve the unpleasant emotional feelings the dog is experiencing.

- An overweight cat: My goals are to relieve any emotional discomforts, such as boredom, that may be contributing to overeating and weight gain; to stop or prevent discomfort in the cat's joints caused by carrying the extra weight; and to prevent the discomfort of diseases that the extra weight may contribute to (liver disease, pancreatic disease, diabetes, and heart disease).

- A dog brought in for routine vaccinations: My goal is to prevent the discomfort of contagious diseases.

- A scraggly, emaciated cat brought in by a woman who tells me the cat's family moved away 2 months ago and left the cat behind to fend for itself: My goal is to relieve the discomforts of hunger, any diseases, fear, unprotected exposure to the elements, and lack of human companionship.

- An itchy dog: My goal is to relieve the unpleasant itchy feelings.

animals in his care. In all cases, the goal is to put animals in their Comfort Zone and keep them there.

THE COMFORT TEAM

Because of the common view in the health profession that providing comfort is somehow separate from treating disease, the person actually

- A dog who has been vomiting and, when he arrives at my office, begins trembling in fear: My goal is to relieve the discomfort of his feeling of nausea and try to minimize the discomfort of his hospital-induced fear.

- A new kitten: My goal is to prevent emotional and physical discomfort throughout life by way of good nutrition, vaccinations, mental wellness care, and emotional fulfillment, achieved by counseling the kitten's new owner.

- A cat urinating all over the house since a new baby arrived: My goal is to relieve the unpleasant emotional feelings—anxiety, the loss of attention and affection—that the cat is experiencing because of the presence of the baby.

- A dog being treated for heart disease whose condition has worsened and who is now having trouble breathing: My goal is to make the necessary changes in his treatment to stop the breathing discomfort.

My goal for each of these patients is to relieve or prevent discomfort: to do everything I can to get this pet into his Comfort Zone and keep him there. It doesn't matter what the sources of the unpleasant feelings are—emotional, physical, or some combination of the two—my job is to eliminate these feelings to the best of my ability.

treating the illness, the doctor, is often assumed not to be a part of the effort to provide comfort. When people think of comfort, they think of the caring nurse or parent, not the doctor. Yet because the main discomfort during illness or injury comes from the medical condition itself, the treatment of disease—what people view as the doctor's role—is actually the single most important part of eliminating discomfort.

In the animal hospital, every member of the health-care team contributes to the same goal of delivering comfort; each simply delivers comfort differently by virtue of his training. Thus, the doctor, the nurse, the receptionist, the lab technician, and all others involved in the pet's care work as a cooperative unit to restore comfort to the patient. The health-care team is actually a comfort team.

EQUAL PARTNERS

You as your pet's guardian are a central part of the comfort team, too. You and the veterinarian have the exact same goal, and you should view yourself as an equal partner in this endeavor. The veterinarian is more knowledgeable in health-care matters, but you are the one who knows your pet best.

For example, a pet owner might worry that her dog's quality of life would be poor if his front leg with cancer were amputated. But the veterinarian, who has more information from personal experience and from the medical literature, knows that pets who have had amputations routinely live very normal and happy lives after the surgery. In this case, the owner's attempts to protect her pet may be based on unfounded fears, while the veterinarian's knowledge and expertise can indicate the likely outcome of the available treatments.

On the other hand, the pet owner's knowledge of her own pet should weigh heavily in the team effort to protect the pet from unpleasant feelings. For example, if the pet owner knows that a stay in the hospital will be a severe emotional trauma for her pet, alternatives to hospitalization should be considered.

This team approach is very important, and I take it very seriously. When I promise my animal patients that we will make them feel better, the "we" is intended to mean both me and the pet's caregiver. The pet is depending on both of us to protect him from the hurts of illness, not just me.

But what if you and your vet can't agree about the best way to protect your pet from discomfort? Since we can never know exactly how your pet's feelings will be affected by medical decisions, it is reasonable that any two people might disagree on how to achieve the most pleasurable feelings for a pet. As a veterinarian, my duty to your pet is always to offer my best medical opinion, based on what I believe is most likely to result in the greatest shift toward pleasure on the Pleasure/Discomfort Scale.

Your duty, on the other hand, is to use your knowledge of your pet's personality to offer your best personal opinion of what you believe will result in the greatest shift toward pleasure. I've found that when I explain this to a pet owner—that we are both striving for the exact same goal— any disagreement we have is much more easily resolved. Very often, it is because the owner has given me important information about her pet's emotional nature that I wouldn't have otherwise known, and I become convinced that her idea will more likely result in the greatest movement toward pleasure. On the other hand, owners often become convinced that my plan is the best for achieving our common goal. Many times it's a compromise, where we incorporate each other's ideas into the best plan.

COOPERATION

Although there are exceptions, most of the cats and dogs that I see in the animal hospital don't want to be there. Some react with sheer terror, as exemplified by Bonkers, a huge orange long-haired cat who digs in and does his best to remain in his carrier, no matter how gently and firmly his mistress and I try to extract him. Others show nervousness, which I always see with Pinto, a young Chihuahua who dances nervously on the examining table, his entire body trembling when I enter the room. Still

BENJAMIN'S STORY

Mrs. Albertson's little white Poodle, Benjamin, had stones in his bladder, which caused him discomfort whenever he tried to urinate. There are two ways to treat this condition: remove the stones through surgery, or try to dissolve them with a special food. When the dietary treatment works (and it doesn't always), it can take several months for the bladder stones to resolve. This means that Benjamin would feel this discomfort for a relatively long period of time. If we found out after that time that the diet was unsuccessful in dissolving the stones, then Benjamin would have spent all that time in discomfort and still have to go through the surgery. On the other hand, the surgery itself, while providing the quickest relief from the discomfort of the stones, would create its own unpleasant feelings during the week or so following the operation.

Although a successful outcome of the surgery would result in Benjamin returning to his Comfort Zone, the surgery option would actually move Benjamin further toward discomfort on the Pleasure/Discomfort Scale until the healing was complete. Our goal is always to protect Benjamin from discomfort and move him as far as we can toward the pleasure end of the scale. But which of these choices would best achieve this? Mrs. Albertson couldn't decide, and, in fact, neither could I. Sometimes there isn't an easy answer. (We eventually elected to do the surgery sooner rather than later, and Benjamin was his old happy self in just over a week's time. In this case, it looks as if we made the best decision.)

other pets experience general anxiety, as exemplified by Sherlock, a Beagle who whines in fear whenever any of our hospital workers approach him.

With each of these animals and many others, the fear has complex causes: They may be remembering a painful or otherwise unpleasant experience in this or another medical facility; the sounds and smells of other animals may be threatening to them; or there may be other fear-provoking cues that are beyond our human ability to sense, such as pheromones and ultrasonic sounds. Once an animal has learned to fear the vet's office, anything associated with it, such as being placed into the carrying case, the smells of the clinic, or the sight of a white coat or syringe, can reactivate the fear.

Veterinary medicine shares a problem with human pediatric medicine, which is that animals, like infants, don't understand our efforts to provide care. There is simply no way to explain to our patients that what we are doing is meant to help them, and as a result, our patients often fail to cooperate, no matter how gentle and compassionate we strive to be.

The term "cooperate," by the way, is misleading. As we usually use it, cooperate means that an animal behaves exactly in accordance with our human desires. Not cooperating, on the other hand, occurs when the animal does not do what we want him or her to do. Noncooperation, in other words, is not the animal's doing, but rather is defined by *our* desires. This seemingly small distinction is actually very important, since uncooperative animals are often seen as doing something wrong, when in fact they are doing whatever they can in order to move back into their Comfort Zone. From an evolutionary perspective, animal patients usually fail to cooperate with us when their survival-oriented feelings drive them to take self-protective actions that are inconsistent with the "cooperative" actions we want them to perform. Such "noncooperative" behavior is entirely normal and natural.

I see these self-protective actions many times every day in my veterinary practice. Common examples include the cat who tries to scratch when someone reaches into her cage, the dog that struggles as I palpate his painful abdomen, the dog who howls in terror while a technician trims his nails, and the cat who fights violently when placed on her side for x-rays (because pneumonia has already compromised her ability to breathe, and lying on her side makes breathing even more difficult). Other "uncooperative" behaviors include refusing to stand up, resisting being taken out of a carrier, snapping at the veterinary nurse who is trying to give an injection, frantically trying to escape, or hiding behind the owner's legs when the veterinarian stoops for an examination.

Sometimes an animal won't cooperate because he can't. For example, a dog may not stand up for an examination because he is too weak from anemia, may be unwilling to walk forward because she is blind, or may be unable to open her mouth because of a muscle disease that creates lockjaw. However, I would estimate that at least 95 percent of "uncooperative" behavior is due to fear and/or pain—two of the most powerful motivators of self-protective behavior. "Uncooperative," to me, equals "self-protective." In fact, the only thing I find surprising is how many patients *are* cooperative, given the fear and pain often experienced in the animal hospital.

Doing What Comes Naturally

It is also clear to me that no one—not the veterinarian or technician, not the pet's owner, and most especially not the patient himself—is to blame for "uncooperative" behavior. To take this one step further, because the dog or cat is doing what comes naturally—trying to return to her Comfort Zone—I see it as entirely wrong, unfair, and even harmful to try to scold, correct, or especially punish such behavior. To me, there is no justification, *ever*, for treating uncooperative animals roughly, striking them, shouting at them, or otherwise mistreating them.

In my hospital, everyone is taught to take a positive, understanding approach to all of their interactions with our animal patients. Anyone who experiences momentary feelings of frustration or anger at any animal's

behavior—uncooperative, aggressive, even vicious—is taught to immediately acknowledge their anger and adopt the viewpoint of the animal
(see "Compassionate Care" on page 248).

Habitually applying this attitude to frustrating situations makes
working with animals a consistent pleasure. Seeing the undesired behavior from the animal's perspective helps negative feelings give way to
understanding, while the frustrations associated with "uncooperative" patients are replaced by feelings of empathy and compassion. In the end,

When Force Is Needed

Although my staff and I always treat our patients as gently as possible, occasionally it is necessary to use some degree of force to carry out a necessary procedure, just as with human pediatric medicine and dentistry. For
example, we often have to snugly hold a cat or dog very still while a blood
sample is drawn or an x-ray taken, or gently but firmly remove a frightened cat from his carrier. In all such cases, it is only *gentle* force that is
used. When any force is needed, we always treat the patient with the same
care and respect as if he were a 6-month-old human infant and do our best
to keep the encounter from being emotionally upsetting.

On occasion, we need to take additional measures to minimize any
emotional unpleasantness the force might cause, using anti-anxiety medications, sedation, or anesthesia. Just as the standard pediatric practice of
having a parent present for medical procedures can calm a child, when
possible, we have the pet's owner present during procedures. Emotional
upsets can also be eased or avoided by performing procedures in a quiet
room, or, whenever possible, in the owner's home (a strong argument for
more house calls in veterinary medicine). In all cases, the force or restraint
used is the minimal amount needed to perform the treatment or test, and
we always keep in mind and respect the reason the animal is acting the
way he is.

animals can be counted on to behave exactly the way nature intended them to behave under these circumstances.

COMPASSIONATE CARE

Care of animals is partly action and partly attitude. Compassionate care involves every aspect of the animal hospital environment that the pet experiences, including handling, medicating, treating, housing, communicating, and all other ways of interacting with the animals we care for. This comprehensive approach to tending to pets promises that they will receive the kind actions and attitude of care that all animals deserve.

I spoke in the previous chapter of the importance of seeing events from the point of view of your pet. This is an attitude that permeates the atmosphere of my animal hospital, one that I instill into all the doctors, nurses, and technicians who work here. I remember Linda, a young and idealistic vet tech who worked in our hospital while studying for her undergraduate degree in pre-veterinary studies. Although Linda clearly had a deep love for animals, she found many of her chores difficult, and she often became stressed and even angry.

One day, I saw Linda become impatient and upset after repeated attempts to draw blood from the neck vein of a Pekingese dog named Oscar, who was a longtime patient of mine. Oscar, clearly emotionally distressed himself, nipped Linda after the third unsuccessful attempt, at which time she sharply snapped, "Bad dog!" Quickly, she turned to me and exclaimed, "This dog won't hold still, and he just bit me!"

I took over and drew the sample of blood, then gently took Linda aside. "Oscar had every reason to bite," I told her, "if you just see things from his point of view. Imagine yourself in his position. Think about being in a strange place, with someone much larger and stronger than you holding your head in an uncomfortable position. And then, for no reason you can see, another large person begins to repeatedly stab a sharp object into your neck. What would *you* do?"

Linda was silent a moment, then she gave a small, wan laugh. "I see what you mean, Dr. McMillan," she told me. "I guess I owe Oscar an apology."

BEYOND COMFORT

You may be wondering why I haven't mentioned trying to move my patients as far as possible toward the positive side of the Pleasure/Discomfort Scale. In other words, should medicine's goal be only to eliminate unpleasant feelings and put animals in their Comfort Zone, or should it also strive to increase pleasant feelings?

For every decision made in medical practice, there is more than one choice available. The bigger decisions involve such choices as whether or not to perform diagnostic tests, treat a condition or not treat it, perform surgery or treat with medicine, do a radical mastectomy or a much less involved lumpectomy. Smaller decisions involve such routine matters as taking an x-ray or doing an ultrasound, running a simple or an extensive blood analysis, or choosing which of two antibiotics to use. When faced with such an array of options, what is our guide for making the best choice?

Assuming that cost is not a factor, whenever therapeutic decisions must be made, we always choose the course that we believe has the greatest chance to

1. Place the animal in his Comfort Zone, and

2. Maximize his quality of life, which means to move the animal the furthest and for the longest time toward pleasure on the Pleasure/ Discomfort Scale.

Keeping these principles in mind makes it easier to see what's going on when a therapy decision is difficult. For example, if there is a choice between surgery or a noninvasive therapy like antibiotics, or choosing not to treat when only a moderately effective treatment is available, the indecision occurs because it is not clear—to the doctor or to you, the pet's closest companion—which of the available options is most likely to achieve our goals. And regarding the second goal, when it appears that multiple treatment options are likely to tip the quality-of-life scales to the same degree, it's harder to choose the best option.

Making Choices

Cheezer, a 14-year-old Siamese cat patient of mine, provides a good example of this conflict. Cynthia, Cheezer's human companion, told me that her cat had always had a sensitive stomach, and jokingly added that "throwing up is his hobby." She became concerned, however, when she noticed that Cheezer's incidents of vomiting had become more frequent. Cynthia also reported that although Cheezer was eating well—in fact, voraciously—he had been losing weight fairly rapidly in the past few weeks.

When Cynthia brought him in, Cheezer looked much thinner than when I had last seen him. Our scale showed he had lost 3 full pounds, which was 30 percent of his body weight. A series of tests revealed that he had a disorder called inflammatory bowel disease, or IBD, which prevented him from digesting and absorbing the food he was taking in. He continued to eat because his brain still told him he was hungry, but since the food essentially went right through him, he kept losing weight.

If not treated, IBD will cause progressive weight loss to the point where a pet is nothing but skin and bones. Fortunately, the anti-inflammatory drug cortisone has a very high success rate in controlling this disease. In Cheezer's case, however, there was a big catch. Cheezer was a borderline diabetic, and any aggravating cause could tip him into a full-blown state of diabetes—and cortisone was one of those aggravating causes. We faced quite a dilemma here: Which choice would result in the greatest and most enduring improvement in Cheezer's quality of life?

I discussed the options with Cynthia, and we agreed that because the diabetes could be treated if it were to develop, the greatest benefit for Cheezer's quality of life would be to vigorously treat his IBD. This story has a gratifying outcome: After several weeks on the cortisone and a special diet, Cheezer began to feel much better, gained weight, and his blood sugar level remained in the normal range. "It's truly amazing, Dr. Mac," Cynthia told me the last time we spoke. "Cheezer seems to have gained back the weight he lost. And he no longer seems hungry all the time."

PROACTIVE TREATMENT

Often, I diagnose a medical condition that has not yet caused an animal to suffer unpleasant feelings. One common example is running a blood test to look into an infection, and incidentally finding blood values indicating that a cat's kidneys are beginning to fail. But the best example that comes to mind occurred with my own dog, Dana, a beautiful, energetic, loving German shepherd mixed-breed (and in my totally objective opinion, probably the best dog in the universe), who was the picture of health when she was 8 years old.

One day when we were playing, Dana rolled onto her back, and for no particular reason, I started pressing on her belly, similarly to the way I conduct a medical exam on a patient. To my surprise and shock, I felt a huge, cantaloupe-size tumor. It was clear that this major health disorder had not, at this point, affected her quality of life. But because tumors like this sometimes rupture and can cause massive internal hemorrhage, taking action now would benefit her future quality of life.

(continued on page 254)

MAXIE'S STORY

Nobody is happy being sick in the hospital, and that includes our cats and dogs. Although hospitalization is sometimes necessary to restore health, even the best veterinary facilities add their own burden of discomforts to a pet already out of his Comfort Zone because of injury or illness. Among these discomforts are unfamiliar and possibly frightening sights, smells, and sounds, including those of other animals. Shy cats may be terrorized by the proximity of barking dogs, and almost all pets experience some degree of emotional distress when away from their human companions.

Happily, a growing number of animal hospitals, including mine in Los Angeles, encourage visits from pet owners. (See page 58 for a dramatic example of how an owner's visits improved her pet's health.) Many facilities still discourage owner visits, however, because of the outdated notion that such visits overly excite the pet, then cause depression when the owner leaves, hindering recovery. However, when visitations are conducted properly (you'd no more want to get an ill or recovering animal all excited and worked up than you would a hospitalized child—as with many other things in life, moderation is the key), it is highly unlikely that the emotional responses to visitation cause enough harm to worry about, especially in light of the potential benefits.

Hospital visits for ill and recuperating animals are still unheard of in many other parts of the world. A friend who lives in Germany had to overcome great resistance when he sought to visit his pet in the veterinary hospital. But he refused to take no for an answer and believes that his intervention literally saved the life of his little dachshund, Maxie. This is their story.

Albert, an American expatriate journalist who lives in Berlin, adopted Maxie 7 years ago after the death of his previous, much-beloved dog. On one of Albert's frequent trips out of town, Maxie, who was staying with a woman friend, suddenly began vomiting. When he didn't improve, his temporary caregiver took the dog to the university veterinary clinic, where doctors performed emergency surgery to remove a blockage in his intestines. (It turned out that Maxie had eaten several inches of drawstring cord from the draperies.)

When Albert arrived at the hospital, Maxie was in a bad way. "I found him quite literally more dead than alive," he told me later. "He barely responded at all to my presence. The manner of the people I talked with there gave me no reason to be optimistic."

Albert described the facility as a large room where students worked on animals under faculty supervision. Albert first spied Maxie lying on a blanket on the floor, surrounded by a number of operating tables. Immediately, Albert lay down beside him, nose to nose, petting and talking to his cherished pet.

The next day, Maxie was no better. "He couldn't even open his eyes," Albert said. "But when he heard my voice, and I petted him, he did manage to move the tip of his tail just a minuscule trifle."

Although Albert was allowed to continue to visit, he had to go through a complicated process of telephoning to make special arrangements before each visit. Confirming that old beliefs—even ones that were largely untrue to begin with—die hard, one veterinary student told Albert that visits were discouraged because they were too upsetting to the pets when their owners left. "Of the people I dealt with there," Albert told me, "I encountered no one who seemed to realize that a quadruped has a psyche."

Knowing what we now know about the benefits of human contact to animals, I think it's highly likely that Albert's visitation time with his beloved Maxie was a significant contributing factor to the dachshund's recovery. It's good to know that attitudes seem to be changing in Germany as well as the United States as more workers in animal health come to realize the importance of animal emotions and feelings in treating illness.

As for Maxie, after a long recovery, he was no worse for the experience. "It was a bad time for both of us," Albert told me. "But Maxie not only lived to tell the tale, he also, in the best dachshund tradition, has taken over total control of this entire area of Berlin." In the city, the little dachshund and his master are recognized by residents and shopkeepers alike on their daily walks.

The point here is that our actions to maximize quality of life don't always have to wait until the quality of life is impaired. Instead, when we can, we do things now to protect quality of life in the future. You frequently do this for yourself, by the way, whenever you get a vaccination, brush your teeth, or pay attention to good nutrition in your diet. Dana, you'll be happy to hear, had her tumor surgically removed and lived another seven healthy and happy years.

ALTERNATIVE MEDICINE

Just as with humans, alternative therapies such as acupuncture, homeopathy, chiropractic manipulation, and treatment with herbs and vitamins are becoming increasingly popular for pets. As with all medical decisions, I judge these therapies from the viewpoint of The Pet Pleasure Principle: Do they, in fact, move the animal further toward pleasure on the Pleasure/Discomfort Scale? If a sick animal is suffering, can, say, a homeopathic remedy (or other alternative treatment) restore him to his Comfort Zone? Can the treatment improve quality of life?

In my opinion, the critical—and *only*—factor is whether the alternative form of therapy can accomplish these goals as well as or better than conventional therapy. Thus, if the alternative treatment can move a pet into her Comfort Zone and tip her quality-of-life scales as far toward the positive side as standard medical care, I would find that therapy equally acceptable as traditional treatment.

When treating disease, whatever gets a pet into his Comfort Zone and has the greatest enduring benefit to his quality of life is the best treatment, whether it's a kidney transplant or a concoction of snake oil and eye of newt. Bear in mind, however, that if you try an unknown or unproven therapy, and it fails to help your pet as much as conventional medical therapy can, your pet is the one who suffers.

THE IDEAL VETERINARY HOSPITAL

I've done everything I can to make my veterinary hospital a place where pet lovers can bring their cherished companions with confidence. I want owners to feel that my staff and I will do everything possible to alleviate their pets' physical and emotional discomforts, restoring them to their Comfort Zones and even to a state of pleasure whenever possible. Our hospital isn't perfect (there's probably no such thing as the perfect animal hospital), but we practice the ideals that I believe all veterinary hospitals should try to achieve. Though not all animal hospitals yet have all (or even most) of these features, when choosing a veterinarian, try to find one whose hospital doctors and staff demonstrate as many of these features as possible.

- **Show sensitivity toward and attention to the pet's emotions and feelings.** Because of the commanding role that feelings play in animals' lives, especially with matters of health care, the veterinarian and his staff should have an interest in, respect for, and desire to tend to all of your pet's feelings—emotional as well as physical.

- **Make efforts to minimize hospitalization.** Because hospitalization can cause fear, anxiety, and other emotional discomforts, health-care personnel should try to minimize the length of necessary hospital stays. Whenever possible, health care should be carried out in the most emotionally supportive atmosphere, which is usually the animal's home.

- **Promote owner visitation.** When hospitalization is necessary, your pet should be in a facility that permits—and preferably encourages—owners to visit and spend time with their ill pets. Keep in mind that any animal hospital has to place some limits on visits, since there just isn't room for every owner of every hospitalized pet to spend unlimited time in the hospital.

- ❖ **Make special provisions.** For the maximum comfort of sick pets, veterinary hospitals should provide a soothing atmosphere (calming music, a choice of interior lighting levels and interior colors), limited noise and odors, and, if possible, special rooms for owner visitations.

- ❖ **Provide emotionally supportive nursing care.** All nursing care should attend to pets' emotional as well as physical needs, offering social companionship, mental stimulation, and maximum efforts to prevent fear and anxiety.

- ❖ **Make house calls.** Although often very difficult to provide on a routine basis (and often necessarily more expensive when provided), house calls offer pets health care in the calm and supportive environment of their homes, thus minimizing the emotional distress of trips to the veterinary hospital.

When you bring your ailing cat or dog to the veterinary hospital, remember that she doesn't care about health—she only cares about how she feels. It doesn't matter to her what is causing her discomfort. She, like you and me, only wants to be rid of the unpleasant feelings, and my job as a health-care provider is to find ways to keep her feeling good.

For every patient we see in clinical practice, the veterinarian and everyone working in the animal hospital should ask: "Have we made the best possible choices to give this animal the best feelings possible?" If the answer is yes, then we can go home at the end of the day feeling good ourselves.

In the next chapter, we'll examine the difficult issues that arise when medical treatment can no longer restore comfort to your beloved pet and how to determine when it is time to say goodbye.

Chapter 11

A PEACEFUL END

THIS CHAPTER DEALS WITH probably the most emotional issue associated with animal care: euthanasia. In this chapter, I am going to share with you my thoughts on this very sensitive subject. Be aware as you read that these are my opinions. I do not claim to speak with any special authority, from a scientific, religious, moral, or ethical perspective.

There is room for differing opinions about this issue, and of course you have every right to disagree with what I say. It doesn't matter to me whether you share my opinions; all I care about is that you protect your pets from anything—and especially health problems—that can hurt them. If you have a way to protect your pet that equals the protection euthanasia assures, then by all means that is what you should do.

A COURAGEOUS AND LOVING DECISION

The one thing about our attachments to animals that seems horribly unfair is that we almost always outlive our pets. The short lifespan of cats and dogs virtually assures that you, the pet's guardian, will almost always face the loss of your beloved companion.

The decision to bring a beloved pet's life to an end is always painful, but we suffer much of that pain for the wrong reasons: worries about

(continued on page 260)

GOOBY'S STORY

Gooby, my male Balinese cat, had lived a very healthy life. But I noticed when he reached the age of about 15½ years that he seemed to look thinner. He acted healthy in all respects and seemed to be eating well. I ran some tests and found that his kidneys were not functioning properly, which is a common disorder in aging cats. I hospitalized him on intravenous fluids for 3 days, then brought him home and began treating him with a number of medications to counteract the ill feelings that kidney disease causes.

Gooby did amazingly well for the next 15 months. Then I noticed that he again looked thinner, and on retesting his blood found that his disease had progressed. From that point, his condition began to decline quickly. His weight dropped rapidly, and he became weaker. I could see some unsteady wobbling in his walk. If he shook his head, he lost his balance to the point of almost falling over. He wasn't eating well and had begun to cry out in the night with a type of cry I had never heard before. Gooby began to stay in my closet almost all the time, coming out only to drink and use the litter box, both of which he did frequently because of his failing kidneys. I had to face the fact that he was sick, and this time there was nothing more that I could do to make him feel better.

What was Gooby's life like? Was he suffering? If so, how severely? Since he couldn't tell me, I couldn't know for sure. But it's well-known that in terminal kidney failure, the patient feels very sick, including suffering from near-constant nausea. And it was clear from Gooby's attitude and behavior that there were fewer and fewer pleasures in his life now to keep his quality-of-life scales tipping toward the pleasant side.

On the morning after Gooby had a particularly difficult night, and I knew it was time to make a decision, I happened to turn on the TV. Charles Schulz, the famous cartoonist, who had recently announced the retirement of his "Peanuts" comic strip due to his battle with colon cancer, was being interviewed on the *Today Show*. Mr. Schulz was undergoing chemotherapy for his illness, and although he tried to put on a brave face, it was clear how much emotional and physical pain he was in.

When the interviewer asked Schulz how he was feeling, the cartoonist replied, "Not so good," and punctuated his comment with a quick, but hollow chuckle. It was painful for me to watch. When I turned toward Gooby he was looking right into my eyes. I knew right then what he wanted to tell me—"Dad, I don't feel so good."

As we sat there together and looked at each other, I thought about his life. He had always been so full of energy and enjoyed so much of what life—and I—had to offer him. But his illness had changed all that. I could see that Gooby had few pleasures left. He still wanted to go out on his walks, even though he wouldn't go far; he liked feeling the sunshine and lying down in it; and he purred when I petted him. This was important. I wanted to know that he had at least some pleasures. I didn't want to wait until his disease had stolen every last pleasure from him—because that would mean that the only feelings he was left with would be his unpleasant feelings.

With Gooby's unpleasant feelings so prominent, unrelievable, and worsening, and with his pleasant feelings still present though diminishing quickly, I had come to the point that so many of my pet owners had faced in my years in medical practice.

My duty as Gooby's guardian was to protect him from all hurts and discomforts, from all distress and suffering. Now he wanted nothing more than to have the sick feelings go away. He didn't have any ability to make this happen on his own. He counted on me for this, and I now had to protect him from the hurts of his illness, knowing that no medicine, no treatment, no medical technique, and not even my love for him could stop the hurts any more.

When he was the tiniest little kitten, I'd promised Gooby that I wouldn't let anything hurt him, that I would be his protector to the very end of his life. And now, almost 17 years later, in what was by far his greatest time of need, I was not going to let him down. But to protect Gooby, I would have to bring our 17-year companionship to a permanent end and say goodbye as I provided him with the ultimate protection.

In what was the most painful thing I have ever done in my life, I held Gooby on my lap as I injected the euthanasia solution into his vein. He fell peacefully asleep, never to awaken. I still miss him, but I will always feel good about having done the right thing. I had done what he depended on me to do, what I had vowed to do, when he needed it most. And wherever he is right now, I like to think that he is grateful for the choice I made.

"playing God," agonizing over the exact right time and not wanting to do it too early, struggling over whether euthanasia or natural death is better, and many other self-imposed miseries. At the time of euthanasia, I have so often heard loving owners tearfully utter these heartbreaking final words as their loving companion breathes his last: "I'm sorry."

In my opinion, these pet owners should not be apologizing; rather, they should be proud of the caring action they have courageously and compassionately chosen. Losing a cherished pet is anguish enough, but all the other emotions of doubt, second thoughts, and guilt are unfairly self-punishing.

In this chapter, I want to show you a new way to look at euthanasia, one that is based on The Pet Pleasure Principle. I think you will find that this new perspective will offer you immense help in dealing with all the doubts and painful emotions surrounding this most important time in caring for a pet. And if you have been already been through the difficult and sorrowful experience, I believe this perspective will give you a good measure of comfort, solace, and reassurance about the decision you made.

COMFORT IS THE OVERRIDING GOAL

I wish that I could promise a cure for all of the sick cats and dogs that I see. But one of the facts of life is that we can't always successfully restore or maintain health. Limitations in our understanding of disease processes, financial constraints, and the inevitability of the aging process all can prevent our objective of ensuring everlasting good health for all animals.

In the last chapter, I stressed that when a pet has an illness or injury, the first and foremost goal is to get him back into his Comfort Zone. I'd like to add this: Despite the common perception, when disease can't be cured in a patient, comfort remains the primary goal. Note that in the face of an incurable and terminal condition, it doesn't change and become a fallback role, as assumed in the common comment, "All we can do now is keep him comfortable." In other words, as it has been all along, comfort is the prime objective; it's just that now we are unable to use the elimination of disease to achieve it. Our efforts instead will be focused on identifying discomforts and using all the measures we can to minimize those that remain in our power to control.

When all efforts to relieve discomfort fail to provide a reasonable amount of comfort for a pet, it is time to consider euthanasia. This aspect of pet care—end-of-life care—is, like all others, guided by The Pet Pleasure Principle. Looking at it this way transforms the concept of euthanasia to a meaning very different from how it is usually viewed. In my opinion, and contrary to popular belief, euthanasia is *not* an act to end a life. That is not its purpose, and that is not the outcome we are striving to achieve. It is, rather, an act to end your pet's discomforts. There is a big difference.

While euthanasia has but one purpose—to end discomfort—it has two *outcomes*: the desired one of ending the discomfort, and the undesired one of ending life. For many medical and emotional disorders, we simply don't know yet how to separate those outcomes. We lack the ability to achieve the outcome we desire—ending discomfort—without also being forced to accept the outcome we don't want—ending a life.

Separating the two outcomes is dependent on technological developments. Whenever medical technology can uncouple the two, we always opt for the one we want: ending discomfort. For example, 30 years ago, dogs suffering from the uncontrollable, debilitating pain of osteoarthritis caused by severe hip dysplasia faced euthanasia. At that point in veterinary medicine, we didn't know how to end the discomfort without also ending the dog's life. The technological development of prosthetic hip implant surgery gave us the ability to separate the two outcomes. Today, dogs with this condition can be returned to full mobility and function. We can now choose to eliminate the discomfort without having to end life itself.

Antibiotics, chemotherapy, insulin, and many other therapeutic advances have made it possible for us to end a pet's discomfort and allow her to go on happily living. But for many conditions, a time comes when our best efforts to alleviate discomfort fail. When that time arrives, I believe we need to lovingly embrace our duty to protect our pet from hurts, and choose to end the discomfort with the only means remaining to us.

When Illness Grows Worse

Euthanasia can be thought of in many ways, but seeing it through the lens of The Pet Pleasure Principle has been the most helpful for my pet-owner clients. Since disease places your pet on the discomfort side of the Pleasure/Discomfort Scale, all forms of treating that disease are intended to move your pet back into his Comfort Zone. If the disease is curable or fully recoverable—meaning that all of the changes and effects of the disease are eliminated from the body—then the cure or recovery itself will move your pet back into his Comfort Zone. If the disease is not curable, then we use other means, such as pain medicine, anti-nausea drugs, and fluid therapy, to move him as close to the Comfort Zone as we can.

Whenever illness progresses, your pet's unpleasant feelings grow in intensity. And as you well know, many incurable illnesses left to progress will ultimately lead to death. As a veterinarian, I feel my obligation to maintain comfort takes on extraordinary importance in dying animals.

As the unpleasant feelings increase and the pleasant feelings decrease, there comes a time when the unpleasant feelings—the miseries—far outweigh the pleasurable experiences. Your pet's quality of life diminishes. Ultimately, the pleasant feelings disappear, leaving only unpleasant feelings. On the quality-of-life scales, it's easy to visualize how the growing discomfort causes the scales to tip further and further toward the unpleasant side. When pleasant feelings are insufficient to counterbalance the growing unpleasant feelings, quality of life is at its lowest possible point. This is a life of misery.

TOO EARLY, TOO LATE—OR THE RIGHT TIME?

For most pet owners, the most agonizing part of the decision to euthanize a beloved pet is deciding *when*. From my own experience, with my own pets as well as the countless patients I have treated, I look at it this way. There are only three times when euthanasia can be done: too early,

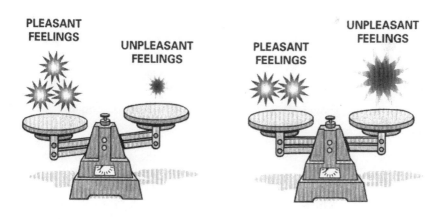

Before deciding whether it's time to euthanize, carefully assess your pet's pleasure and discomfort.

too late, and the exact right time. But there is no exact right time, and even if there were, we could never know when it was. So that option is out, leaving us with only two possible times for euthanasia: too early and too late.

Always keep in mind that your duty to your pet is to do everything possible to protect him from discomfort. This means you must do everything possible to prevent euthanasia from falling into the "too late" time period. Or look at it this way: Knowing that too early or too late are the only two choices you have, which would your pet want you to choose? Which would you yourself choose if the roles were reversed?

My feeling is that the answers to these questions mean that there is only one reasonable time for euthanasia. There is only one time that you, as a caring, compassionate, and loving pet owner can opt for. Sadly, it is the time most people fear the most: too early. Because it is the only compassionate time—the *only* time that assures you are providing the protection from suffering that your pet is counting on you for—no owner should fear it.

But can there be a *too* too early? Probably. If I take an x-ray of the spine of a dog with back pain and happen to notice the earliest signs of an incurable but very slowly progressive lung disease that the dog probably won't even know is there for another 2 years, euthanasia would seem for most to be premature. My view, *in general,* is that if you are acting out of the desire to protect your pet from hurts, then there really can't be a "*too* too early." However, we can once again rely on The Pet Pleasure Principle, and specifically the quality-of-life scales, to sort this out for us. While there are certainly some exceptions (such as when the only treatment available must begin immediately but is prohibitively expensive for you), a reasonable way to look at this issue is to say that if the disease has not yet had a meaningful effect on tipping the quality-of-life scales toward the unpleasant side, then it is probably *too* too early.

EUTHANASIA: BAXTER'S STORY

Baxter was a handsome 15-year-old male beagle who may well be the bravest dog I have ever known. I have never seen any living creature stand up against such a torrent of hardships, all the while maintaining his pride, dignity, and a never-say-die attitude . . . until the last few weeks of his life.

As he lay there on the living-room carpet in his home, Baxter was a

 When We Meet Again

You've already decided that when the misery of your pet's illness grows too great, you will not let him suffer anymore, and you will ask your veterinarian to put him into eternal rest. But you find yourself struggling with the common question: When is the right time? Here's a mental exercise that many of my pet-loving clients have found very helpful when making decisions about the timing of euthanasia.

Imagine that there is an afterlife where you will be rejoined with your loved ones, including your pets. (Whether you believe that an afterlife does or doesn't exist isn't important for the purpose of the exercise; for the moment, just pretend that it does.) Knowing that you will be meeting your pet again, you want to make all of your decisions now in a way such that when you are reunited with your pet, he will greet you joyously and thank you for the decisions you made, rather than asking, "What could you possibly have been thinking?"

Making your current decisions with the thought of a reunion in mind, it's very hard to make the wrong choice.

shell of his former self. He was so thin that each rib seemed to stick out an inch. He was so tired that he could barely lift his head. And the dark eyes that for years had held a magical sparkle now seemed to say, "I can't fight anymore. I have nothing left." And it was obvious why.

Seven months earlier, Francine—a soft-spoken special education teacher in her late 40s—brought Baxter in to see me. He had a swollen sore on his right hind leg that had been oozing blood and wasn't healing. Baxter was every bit as energetic and playful as I had known him to be throughout his life. He checked out fine except for this swelling on his leg. I told Francine that we should get a piece of the tissue for biopsy, and she quickly agreed.

Five days later, the biopsy report came back. It wasn't good news. Baxter had a malignant tumor called a squamous cell carcinoma, and the only treatment that could save his life would be for Baxter to have his hind leg amputated.

Francine was crushed to hear the news, but arranged for the surgery, and Baxter recovered speedily. In fact, he was ready to go home long before my entire staff—who loved this little guy—wanted to see him leave. Francine phoned me 2 weeks later to say the little Beagle was doing just great and was getting around on three legs better than most dogs get around on four.

Three months passed before I heard from Francine again. She called to say that Baxter hadn't been feeling well for the past few days and was looking thinner. When I saw Baxter in my office, I was a bit shocked. He had lost 7 pounds—over 30 percent of his body weight. I ran some blood tests and found that his kidneys were in an advanced state of degeneration.

I discussed with Francine the limited treatment options, the best of which was hospitalization on IV fluids and medicines to help flush out the toxic products accumulating in his blood. When she told me that she wanted to do "only the best thing for my Baxter," I cautioned her that in light of the severity of Baxter's kidney disease, I couldn't predict how successful the treatment would be, and it was possible that it wouldn't help at all. If that happened, her dog's condition would continue to deteriorate. I told her that she should begin to give thought to what she would want to do if Baxter did not respond to treatment.

Well, Baxter didn't have the reputation of being a fighter for no reason. He showed a fairly quick response to the fluid therapy and was discharged from the hospital 5 days later.

I continued to monitor Baxter's kidney function and body weight, and he was stable on both counts for about 2 months. Then a full month went by without a visit from Francine and Baxter, until one day when I received an urgent page from my front desk. I hurried up to the front of the hospital and saw Francine holding Baxter in her arms. "He can't walk, Dr. McMillan!" she exclaimed through tears. "I found him in the backyard, and he can't get up to walk!"

I took Francine and Baxter into the exam room and quickly found the problem. Baxter had torn the ligament in the knee joint of his remaining rear leg. Without this stabilizing ligament, he couldn't support any weight on the leg. Repairing the torn ligament would require orthopedic surgery. But there was worse news to come. His weight had dropped another 5 pounds. "He hasn't had much of an appetite for a couple of weeks," Francine told me tearfully. "Nothing seems to tempt him." I ordered some tests and found that only a tiny fraction of Baxter's kidneys were still functional.

I broke the bad news to Francine. Baxter would need surgery to ever walk again. With his kidneys now just barely functioning, he almost certainly wouldn't survive such a surgery. Even if we fitted him with a cart to hold up his hind end, there was probably less than a 5 percent chance that intravenous fluid therapy could make him feel well enough to eat. Without eating, he would literally waste away, feeling miserably sick the whole time.

I told Francine that Baxter was an amazing dog, but no matter how strong he had been throughout his life, he now was fighting a battle he could not win. And we had nothing left to help him in his battle. "It's horribly unfair," I concluded. "He's been dealt so many terrible blows in such a short time. First the cancer that took his leg, then kidney disease, and now the torn ligament. Baxter has been a strong and proud dog throughout all these hard times. But I'm afraid we have to admit defeat, Francine. He's dying."

I waited for Francine's response. After several minutes, during which she broke down in tears and then composed herself three or four times, she softly spoke, "Everything you've said is true. He's not going to beat this thing." Then she added, "I'm going to take him home where he can pass away peacefully. He should die where he is most comfortable."

Knowing that the dying process for Baxter would involve some of the most unpleasant sickly feelings and would probably take weeks, during which he would not be able to get up and walk, I felt compelled to open a discussion. "Francine," I began, "Baxter *should* die at home. And I can assure you he will. But we need to talk about your role in Baxter's life."

She looked at me, saying nothing. I went on: "Whether you ever thought about it or not, you've had one job the whole time Baxter's been in your care: to protect him from things in life that could hurt him. He has always counted on you for that. And he's never been hurt more than with what's happening to him right now." Francine's eyes opened wide. "We can stop this from hurting him," I went on. "That's the wonderful thing about euthanasia. Do you think that Baxter is still hoping you will protect him?"

Francine glanced down at Baxter, who feebly wagged his tail. "I'd never looked at it like that," she said. "Can I think about this?"

"Of course," I answered. "But for Baxter's sake, please don't take too long." Francine gently picked Baxter up off the floor and said goodbye to me. I hoped to hear from her soon.

And I did. Francine called me the first thing the next morning. "Can you come over today, Dr. McMillan? Baxter *is* counting on me. I can't let him go on feeling this way." I told her I'd be over in about an hour and hung up the phone.

An hour later, I was sitting in Francine's and Baxter's house, where this story began. Baxter lay on a blanket on the sofa while Francine and I sat on chairs nearby, Francine's fingers gently stroking her dog's flank. Francine told me what a loving dog Baxter had been, recounting some of the pranks he'd been up to through the years. I told her how much he had brightened the spirits of everyone at our hospital and how saddened we all were to know that he had been so ill.

"I've had him ever since he was a little puppy," Francine said, her voice breaking. "I've never had a dog that I loved so much."

When she had finished speaking, Francine and I knelt down next to Baxter. Minutes later, Baxter went peacefully to his eternal resting place—a place where no disease, or anything else, could ever hurt him again.

THE SPECIAL SIGNIFICANCE OF DEATH

For many people, the special significance of death provides a basis for the belief that natural death is preferable to euthanasia. There appears to

Is She in Pain?

One of the most frequent questions I hear from owners trying to decide whether or not to euthanize their pet is, "Is she in pain?"

Surprisingly, pain is a component of only a minority of terminal illnesses. My answer to this question, then, is almost always: "No, but pain is only one of the many unpleasant feelings that can cause distress and suffering. You must consider *all* of your pet's unpleasant feelings. I'm referring here to such things as difficulty breathing. Others include nausea, toxic feelings (from the buildup of toxins in the blood due to the impaired ability of diseased kidneys or liver to remove them from the body), nonspecific feelings of sickness (think of how you feel with a bad bout of the flu), fear, depression, and many others. Every one hurts her."

---

be a spiritual impulse to allow nature to "take its course" with one's pet. For many people, a natural death seems to make the pet once again a part of nature. But it's important to keep in mind that a "natural is best" philosophy would not, in almost any other instance, be acceptable for your pet.

In the wild, when nature takes its course, the results can be cruel. Consider the likely outcome for a deer that falls through the ice of a partially frozen pond, a bobcat who develops a severe pneumonia, a rabbit who is attacked by a coyote, and a baby bird that has fallen out of its nest. If, in these very natural situations, it were our pet who was the victim, we would never allow nature to take its course. Instead, we'd intervene for the sole purpose of *preventing* nature from taking its course. When natural processes create suffering in our pets that we can relieve, allowing that suffering to continue simply because it is natural seems exceptionally hard to justify.

There are many human beliefs and belief systems that guide peoples' decisions about euthanasia. Certainly, religious beliefs weigh strongly for many. For example, one frequently expressed belief is that we do not have the right to "play God." But my own opinion is that we should carefully consider whether these human beliefs—which animals know nothing of, and presumably do not care about—outweigh our primary duty to protect our pets from harm. We must also decide whether this duty is for any reason less strong for the dying animal.

HOW TO TELL WHEN YOUR PET'S LIFE IS APPROACHING THE END

It is not always clear when a sick or aging pet is approaching the end of life, but the following factors can help you determine when his unpleasant feelings are becoming greater than the pleasant feelings in his life.

 The Hardest Part of the Job?

Through my 23 years of practice, I long ago lost count of the number of pet owners who, around the time of their own struggle with the decision over euthanasia, say to me something like, "Boy, I don't know how you do this. Putting animals to sleep must be the hardest part of your job."

My response always goes something like this: "Yes, it sure is. But it's also the most deeply gratifying. I've been given the greatest privilege imaginable—the ability to totally protect Monroe from what his illness is doing to him. We're going to lay a protective blanket over him and put him in a place where nothing can hurt him. I know, as a pet owner as well as a doctor, that the pain of saying goodbye seems unbearable. But over time, that sadness gradually transforms into the deepest form of gratification you will ever know. And deep down, you know that that's true."

A Vow to Make to Your Pet on the Day of Adoption

"I will be your loyal companion from this day forward. Even more important, I will be your protector. You have my solemn promise that I will, to the absolute utmost that my strength and resources permit, protect you against all the hurts that life can hold, whether they be physical or emotional. You can depend on me for this. I will never let you down.

"And when any hurts become such that all of my efforts cannot effectively alleviate them, I will place your needs above mine, your suffering over my own, and use the only means left to protect you from those hurts. I will deliver you comfort by bringing your pains to an end, not because I will be ready to let go, but because, to protect you, I will have to say goodbye. I know you will count on me at that difficult time to protect you, and I will be there for you, right by your side.

"Should my passing come first, you need not worry, because I will have made all the provisions for your care, safekeeping, and happiness.

"Fear not, because when death ends our physical togetherness, our emotional bond will never end. You will be a part of my heart forever. I promise."

The minute you learn that your pet has an illness that will progress either to death or unrelievable discomfort, please repeat this vow to him. It is truly remarkable how good it will make you feel to know that your relationship with your beloved pet is cemented by such a loving pact.

- ❖ **Poor appetite.** A poor appetite tells you that your pet is feeling bad.

- ❖ **Weight loss.** Unintentional loss of weight is always a sign that something is amiss.

- ❖ **Lack of interest.** Loss of interest in formerly enjoyable activities such as play and going for walks is another sign that something has changed.

- ❖ **Change in socialization patterns.** Less desire to interact socially with the people or other animals in the house.

∴ **Lethargy or excessive sleeping.** This, too, is a sign that your pet isn't well.

When you notice any of these signs in your pet, or a combination of them, pay attention. Your pet is letting you know how he feels, in the only ways he can. This is a good time to retake the Quality-of-Life Questionnaire (presented in Chapter 7). I designed the questionnaire to clearly compare the "weight" of pleasant feelings with that of unpleasant feelings on the quality-of-life scales. As your pet's life approaches its end, the scales progressively tip toward the unpleasant side. When the unpleasant feelings strongly outweigh the pleasant, euthanasia is an appropriate course of action.

A JOURNEY ON TWO PATHS

All through your life together, your pet's interests and yours are essentially the same: to enjoy and maintain each other's companionship. But as a terminal illness progressively takes its toll, for the very first time, your interests start to diverge. Your own interest remains the same: You want to maintain the relationship you've always had with your pet. But your pet's interests are increasingly focused on the growing discomforts of his disease.

Your pet still wants your companionship, but as the intensity of his unpleasant feelings increases with the advancing disease, his primary interest focuses more and more on getting relief from his discomfort. In the end, his main—and ultimately sole—interest in life is being rid of the bad feelings.

In order to help your pet at this time, I feel your most caring option is to subordinate your own interests to his. You have to make his interests yours, and that's hard, because by doing so, you are making his comfort (which you promised you would do your best to give him) more important than the relationship itself. This change brings you the painful realization that you are letting go because you must: Protecting your pet from the unpleasant feelings comes first, absolutely, and unquestionably. This will cause you emotional pain, but as a loving and caring companion, you must come second. The key to accepting this sacrifice is to realize that your pet's needs really *are* your needs—that her desire to be free from discomfort is exactly what you want for her.

THE FINAL PROTECTION

I know that this is a very hard topic for pet owners to even read about, much less face. So let me summarize what I've said in this chapter for you here.

As with everything else in life that matters to your pet, euthanasia is all about feelings. When all other efforts fail to adequately protect your pet from a life dominated by persistent unpleasant feelings, we still have a tool that assures him full protection. We have the ability to provide this complete protection in a temporary way, which we call general anesthesia. When such complete protection is needed permanently, we call it euthanasia. It is the ultimate protection, and, when done for the right reasons, it is the kindest, most caring and loving gift that a person can bestow on his pet.

EPILOGUE: KEEPING ALL THINGS IN MIND

AT THE BEGINNING, I told you that this book had one basic theme: *feelings rule*. If I have persuaded you that nothing matters more in your pet's life than feelings, the book has fulfilled its purpose. After reading about the evidence supporting the existence of animal feelings, you might wonder how any scientist could still doubt that animals *have* feelings. Aside from those who have a vested interest in denying the existence of animal feelings (such as many of those who conduct research on animals), some scientists simply remain unconvinced that nonhuman species have the kind of consciousness that generates feelings. And the truth is, there is no conclusive *proof* that animals experience feelings, or, for that matter, possess consciousness. To most of us, the lack of definitive proof is unimportant because of our strong intuitive sense that animals are quite conscious and have many types of feelings.

But it is important to keep in mind that the "intuitiveness" and "obviousness" of animal emotions and feelings does not mean they exist. It is very easy—even natural—to ascribe feelings and other human mental attributes to animals, especially those that closely resemble us. Yet scientific honesty compels us to concede that making such attributions is not only fraught with risks, but it is indeed possible that making such a leap may actually be wrong. The story I told in Chapter 1 about what occurred on the set of *Dr. Dolittle,* when I briefly took an animatronic dog for a real one, illustrates the potential risks of blindly

RIBBY'S STORY

Louise, a friend of mine who had read the manuscript for this book in progress, told me the other day how applying The Pet Pleasure Principle had helped her make a difficult decision regarding her sick, elderly male domestic shorthair cat, Ribby.

"I was scheduled for a business trip that couldn't be postponed," she told me. "Ribby had to take two pills a day and wasn't doing so well. He'd lost so much weight, he looked like a little cat skeleton. To make matters worse, whenever he isn't with me, he gets depressed. The last time he had to stay at the vet after an operation, he refused to eat until I brought him home."

Louise's dilemma: what to do with Ribby while she was away. "My choices were to board him at the vet or hire a vet tech to come in once a day and give his pills and feed him. I kept thinking about all the pros and cons. I worried about his condition becoming worse while I was gone— wouldn't it be better to have him at the vet's, where he could be treated? But he hated it there so much. He'd be in a little cage, surrounded by scary smells and the sounds of barking dogs. On the other hand, I would never forgive myself if he needed emergency care but couldn't get it because no one was there at the right time."

Louise's other cat, Jillian, was healthy but, if anything, hated going to the vet more than Ribby. "I couldn't see putting both of them in a little cage at the vet's. But if I put only Ribby there, Jillian might feel she had been deserted by her whole family—both me and Ribby. The cats don't always get along, but they've been together a long time."

Louise told me she mulled the various possibilities over for several

following intuition. After all, there are even people who watch the Charlie Brown Christmas special and feel sorry for the little scraggly tree that nobody wants.

Some recent evidence suggests that ascribing feelings to other beings may be a part of human nature. Primate researcher Daniel J. Povinelli has days, till one morning she happened to walk past her cats, curled up on the carpet in a little pool of sunshine. "The expressions on both of their faces were blissful," she told me. "This was a picture of pure pleasure. At that moment, the lessons of your book flashed through my mind. I realized that all I needed to do was to apply The Pet Pleasure Principle to my problem and figure out what would result in the greatest net pleasure for both my cats."

Louise's reasoning went like this: *if Ribby alone boards at the vet, he will be miserable—he won't enjoy eating, if he eats at all, and he won't have access to anything he enjoys doing. In addition he will be frightened, lonely, and anxious. No pleasure. Although Jillian, at home, will have some pleasures including sunshine and her toys as well as access to her Safe Haven, she will be lonely and frightened with both me and Ribby away. Some pleasure, but counterbalanced by discomfort.*

If both cats board at the vet, they will be of some comfort to each other, but the amount of pleasure for either cat will be minimal, and probably outweighed by the ambient discomforts.

On the other hand, if I keep both cats at home with the vet tech to look in on them, both cats will have access to a number of pleasures. They will have the comfort of being together, and the great pleasure of curling up in the sunshine. They will have all their toys and their Safe Havens. They will have the comfort of being in a familiar place, even though I am gone. If Ribby has an emergency, the vet tech can always take him to the animal hospital.

Realizing that keeping both her cats at home would result in the greatest net pleasure for both cats, Louise made her decision with confidence.

proposed that humans have evolved an instinctual propensity to attribute emotion to other animals, even to inanimate objects. The robot dog manufactured by Sony, called AIBO (pronounced eye-bo), has acquired such a fanatic owner base that AIBO clubs exist all over the country and the internet. Club members freely admit that they regard their "dogs" as much more than machines, and they proudly talk about them as if they had actual personalities, emotions, and feelings.

Still, when we examine the evidence that seems to explain how the animal mind works, it overwhelmingly supports the notion that sentient animals behave in accordance with the pleasure principle, maximizing pleasure and minimizing discomfort. Does this mean that the whole system is hedonistic? Are animals' choices and actions based only on a selfish pleasure motive? To believe so wouldn't just miss the point, it would miss several points, and huge points at that. First, a remarkably effective motivational system based on pleasure appears to be the basic evolutionary construction of the brain of all sentient creatures, us included.

Second, as we have seen throughout this book, seeking pleasure and avoiding discomfort are a critical survival mechanism that protects animals from harm, keeps them on the right path, promotes their well-being, and offers the only possibility for enjoying life. An animal that violates the pleasure principle ignores nature's messages and foolishly places himself at risk, at the same time lowering his quality of life. Thus your pet—a product of millions of generations of genetic fine-tuning—acts on feelings that constantly inform him how best to act in his current circumstances. Understanding how this ancient system works is the essential element in helping your pet to live the highest-quality life.

Third, and most important, the pleasure principle does not diminish the meaning of any of the complex and wonderful emotions we sentient animals experience. In humans, love is no less beautiful just because it, like all feelings, operates according to the basic rule of the pleasure principle. Love is *meant* to feel good, and it does. The same is true of empathy, sympathy, and compassion. Recent research indicates that when one person cooperates with another person, brain scans of the cooperating person show heightened activity in the area associated with pleasure.

Does this mean that being kind and working with others is not noble, since it appears based in the hedonism of feeling good? Of course not.

The entire life experience of every sentient animal exists solely in the very small theater of the mind. Everything that an animal thinks, feels, remembers, or otherwise experiences all plays out only in that animal's mental space. The world outside of the animal mind has no meaning, no value, and indeed no existence for that animal until it flows through the filter of the mind. That is where the animal's world becomes reality. The mind *is* the animal's entire world. And now that you understand the importance of feelings and how they work in the animal mind, you can see that animals who receive mind-centered care have the greatest opportunity to live their lives with optimal pleasures, minimal discomforts, and the best quality of life. Once you focus on what your pet really wants, he will have the best chance to experience a life of emotional fulfillment, peace of mind, and happiness, which is exactly what we all want for ourselves.

APPENDIX

Many resources will help you to use The Pet Pleasure Principle to make your pet feel good and enjoy life. This appendix provides contact information for organizations and products that are all intended to help tip your pet's quality-of-life scales more toward the pleasant side.

RESOURCES FOR QUALITY-OF-LIFE ENHANCEMENT

Cat Walking Jackets
HDW Enterprises
www.hdw-inc.com/walkingjackets.htm
(916) 481-2287

"Wheelchair" Carts
Eddie's Wheels for Pets
www.eddieswheels.com
(888) 211-2700
K9 Carts
www.k9carts.com
(800) 578-6960
   These carts are for dogs and cats paralyzed or otherwise disabled in their rear legs.

Toys and Play Devices
Tennis Ball Throwing Machines for Dogs
http://tennis101.com/ball_throwing_machines_dogs/tennis_ball_machines_throwers_dogs.htm
(877) 836-6475
Nylabone Products
www.nylabone.com
(800) 631-2188
   This company sells premium dog chews and dog treats and virtually indestructible chew toys for puppies and adult dogs.
Pavlov's Cat Scratch Feeder
www.mktmkt.com/pavlovscat.html
(888) 818-6807
   This special scratching post rewards the cat with a treat for scratching on the post.
PetStages
www.petstages.com
   This company sells toys for dogs and cats, categorized according to the stages of the pet's life—youth, adult, and senior.

Treat-Dispensing Interactive Toys

Kong toys

The Kong Company

www.kongcompany.com

(303) 216-2626

These virtually indestructible toys are especially good for filling with a tasty treat (cream cheese, peanut butter, Kong Stuff'n treats) that your pet can work at getting out when you're away from the house.

Buster Cube

VoToys Pet Products

www.bustercube.com

This toy, which can be "programmed" with increasing levels of difficulty, will give your dog stimulation and something to engage his mind when left alone at home.

Busy Buddy toys

Premier Pet Products

www.premier.com

(888) 640-8840

Busy Buddy toys feature different types of chewing experiences to help redirect potentially destructive chewing behavior into positive playtime.

Pet Furniture

Cat furniture: cat trees, cat condos, scratch posts, and kitty gyms

www.7thheavencatfurniture.com

Dog furniture: dog couches and dog sofas

www.dogbedworks.com

Pet Ramps

Discount Ramps.com

www.discountramps.com/dog_ramps.htm

These devices make it easier for dogs and cats with weakness and discomforts (such as arthritis) to get up and down from beds and furniture and in and out of cars.

Books Describing the Techniques for Animal Massage

The Healing Touch for Dogs: The Proven Massage Program for Dogs, Revised Edition by Michael W. Fox, Newmarket Press: New York, 2004

The Healing Touch for Cats: The Proven Massage Program for Cats, Revised Edition by Michael W. Fox, Newmarket Press: New York, 2004

Cat Massage: A Whiskers-to-Tail Guide to Your Cat's Ultimate Petting Experience by Mary-jean Ballner, St. Martin's Press: New York, 1997

Dog Massage: A Whiskers-to-Tail Guide to Your Dog's Ultimate Petting Experience by Mary-jean Ballner, St. Martin's Press: New York, 1997

Animal Behavior Organizations

American College of Veterinary Behaviorists

(979) 845-2351

This is an organization for specialty training and board-certification of veterinarians in clinical animal behavior. Licensed veterinary behaviorists are the only behaviorists able to prescribe medications to help treat emotional disorders. The ACVB provides referrals for locating board-certified veterinary behaviorists nearest to you.

American Dog Trainers Network
www.inch.com/~dogs

The American Dog Trainers Network is a comprehensive resource for dog owners, dog trainers, and the media that offers dog training articles, safety tips, a list of recommended books, and free referrals to reputable dog trainers and pet care organizations throughout the United States.

American Veterinary Society of Animal Behavior (AVSAB)
www.avma.org/avsab

The American Veterinary Society of Animal Behavior includes members who range in interest from animal behavior to board-certified specialists. The group provides a locator service for behavior-oriented veterinarians.

Animal Behavior Society (ABS)
www.animalbehavior.org
(812) 856-5541

The ABS certifies individuals as Applied Animal Behaviorists and Associate Applied Animal Behaviorists and maintains a directory of Certified Applied Animal Behaviorists.

Animal Behavior and Training Associates (ABTA)
www.good-dawg.com
(800) 795-DAWG

The ABTA is a group of more than 500 professional trainers who are experts in obedience and problem solving.

Applied-Ethology
www.usask.ca/wcvm/herdmed/applied-ethology
(306) 966-7154

This Web site offers information and links dealing with applied animal behavior.

Association of Pet Dog Trainers (APDT)
www.apdt.com
(800) PET-DOGS

The APDT promotes public awareness of dog-friendly training techniques and encourages its members to make use of training methods that use reinforcement and rewards, not punishment, to achieve desired behavior. They provide a search service for locating trainers who are members of the organization.

RESOURCES FOR BEHAVIOR ADVICE

Note that these organizations offer advice for correcting undesired behavior in pets. Some are fee-based, but others don't charge.

Animal Behavior Associates
www.animalbehaviorassociates.com

Dumb Friends League/Humane Society of Denver
www.ddfl.org/tips.htm

Maricopa County Animal Care and Control—Animal Care and Behavior
www.maricopa.gov/pets/care_and_behavior.asp

Pet Behavior Problems
www.petbehaviorproblems.com

PetPlace
www.petplace.com

San Francisco SPCA
www.sfspca.org/behavior/dog_library/index_library.shtml

PRODUCTS FOR BEHAVIOR MODIFICATION AND CONTROL

Clicker Training
Karen Pryor Clicker Training
www.clickertraining.com
(800) 47-CLICK
This Web site is run by Karen Pryor, the most recognizable name associated with clicker training and the person most responsible for the popularity of this training method.

Electric Fencing
Invisible Fence
www.invisiblefence.com
(800) 578-DOGS
These electronic fences, with the special collars, elicit a small shock when the pet nears the underground "fence."
Radio Fence
http://radiofence.com/dog_fences_underground.htm

Gentle Leader/Promise System Canine Head Collar
Premier Pet Products
www.gentleleader.com
(888) 640-8840
This is a head collar and training system for dogs that uses a humane approach to un-desired behaviors such as jumping, pulling, barking, chewing, and begging.

Pheromone Products
Feliway
Farnum Companies, Inc.
www.feliway.com
www.farnampet.com/cat/feliway_home.htm
(800) 234-2269
According to Feliway's Web site, this product is a natural treatment developed to help prevent your cat from spraying urine or clawing furniture as well as coping with stressful situations.
Dog-Appeasing Pheromone (D.A.P.)
Farnum Companies, Inc.
www.feliway.com/html/comfortzone-with-dap.php3
www.farnampet.com/product/products.asp?product_id5100659
(800) 234-2269
According to the Web site, ComfortZone with D.A.P. is a natural treatment to help with inappropriate dog behaviors and to ease training a new puppy.

Snappy Trainer
Interplanetary Pet Products
www.interplanetarypets.com/snappytrainer.html

This innovative training product uses a bright red paddle and loud snap to quickly and humanely teach pets to stay away from unwanted areas.

Special Organizations

Association of Housecall Veterinarians
www.athomevet.org

The American Association of Housecall Veterinarians is dedicated to assisting all pets in getting the highest quality veterinary care possible. The Web site can help you locate a veterinarian who will come to you.

Delta Society
www.deltasociety.org
(425) 226-7357

The Delta Society is the leading international resource for promotion of and information on the human-animal bond.

Humane Organizations

American Humane Association
www.americanhumane.org
(303) 792-9900

This organization promotes humane care of animals, including pet animal care, use of animals in entertainment, and spaying and neutering animals.

The American Society for the Prevention of Cruelty to Animals (ASPCA)
www.aspca.org
(212) 876-7700

The mission of the ASPCA is to provide effective means for the prevention of cruelty to animals throughout the United States.

Ethologists for the Ethical Treatment of Animals/Citizens for Responsible Animal Behavior Studies (EETA/CRABS)
www.ethologicalethics.org

Founded by Marc Bekoff (professor of biology at the University of Colorado, Boulder) and Jane Goodall (renowned chimpanzee researcher), this organization aims to develop and maintain the highest ethical standards in comparative ethological research in the field and in the laboratory. Scientists, non-scientists, teachers, and students are welcome to join.

Humane Society of the United States (HSUS)
www.hsus.org
(202) 452-1100

The HSUS is dedicated to creating a world where our relationship with animals is guided by compassion.

Caring for Your Pet after Your Death

Estate planning for pets
http://estateplanningforpets.org

This Web site provides a wide range of information and resources for pet owners in estate planning for their pets.

www.professorbeyer.com/Articles/Animals_More_Information.htm

This Web site offers a bibliography of books and articles about estate planning for pet care.

BIBLIOGRAPHY WITH RECOMMENDED READING

Key
S: written for the scientist
GR: written for the general reader
S,GR: written for the scientist but important points understandable to the general reader
GR,S: written for the general reader with information useful to scientists
Recommended reading is in bold print

CHAPTER 1

Obesity is often a result of emotional problems.
- Dallman MF, Pecoraro N, Akana SF, et al. Chronic stress and obesity: a new view of "comfort food". *Proceedings of the National Academy of Sciences of the United States of America* 100:11696-22701, 2003. [S,GR]
- Solomon MR. Eating as both coping and stressor in overweight control. *Journal of Advanced Nursing* 2001;36:563-572. [S,GR]

Feelings are the most prominent guides for human behavior.
- Higgins ET, Grant H, Shah J. Self-regulation and quality of life: emotional and non-emotional life experiences. In: Kahneman D, Diener E, Schwarz N (editors). *Well-being: The Foundations of Hedonic Psychology.* New York, Russell Sage Foundation, 1999: 244-266. [S,GR]
- Kahneman D. Objective happiness. In: Kahneman D, Diener E, Schwarz N (editors). *Well-being: The Foundations of Hedonic Psychology.* New York, Russell Sage Foundation, 1999: 3-25. [S,GR]
- Rozin P. Preadaptation and the puzzles and properties of pleasure. In: Kahneman D, Diener E, Schwarz N (editors). *Well-being: The Foundations of Hedonic Psychology.* New York, Russell Sage Foundation, 1999:109-133. [S,GR]

Recent books on animal emotions.
- **Bekoff M (editor). *The Smile of a Dolphin: Remarkable Accounts of Animal Emotions.* New York, Discovery Books, 2000. [GR]**
- **Bekoff M. *Minding Animals: Awareness, Emotions, and Heart.* Oxford, Oxford University Press, 2002. [GR]**
- **Dawkins MS. *Through Our Eyes Only? The Search for Animal Consciousness.* Oxford, W. H. Freeman and Company Limited, 1993. [GR]**
- **Dodman N. *The Dog Who Loved Too Much: Tales, Treatments, and the Psychology of Dogs.* New York, Bantam Books, 1996. [GR,S]**

- **Dodman N.** *The Cat Who Cried for Help: Attitudes, Emotions, and the Psychology of Cats.* New York, Bantam Books, 1997. [GR,S]
- Masson JM. *Dogs Never Lie About Love.* New York, Crown Publishers, 1997. [GR]
- Masson JM. *The Nine Emotional Lives of Cats.* New York, Ballantine Books, 2000. [GR]
- **Masson JM, McCarthy S.** *When Elephants Weep: The Emotional Lives of Animals.* New York, Delacorte Press, 1995. [GR,S]

Unpleasant feelings protect us from threats.

- **Nesse RM. What good is feeling bad? The evolutionary benefits of psychic pain.** *The Sciences* Nov/Dec 1991:30-37. [GR,S]
- Panksepp J. *Affective Neuroscience: The Foundations of Human and Animal Emotions.* New York, Oxford University Press, 1998. [S]

Feelings focus attention on matters of importance. The mind prioritizes matters through feelings.

- Cosmides L, Tooby J. Evolutionary psychology and the emotions. In: Lewis M, Haviland-Jones JM (editors). *Handbook of Emotions.* Second Edition. New York, The Guilford Press, 2000: 91-115. [S,GR]
- **Johnston VS.** *Why We Feel: The Science of Human Emotions.* Reading, Mass, Perseus Books, 1999. [GR,S]
- **Pinker S.** *How the Mind Works.* New York, W.W. Norton & Company, 1997. [GR,S]

Psychology's first century was dominated by studies of the negative life experiences.

- Myers DG. *The Pursuit of Happiness.* New York, Avon Books, 1992. [GR,S]

New books in the field of Positive Psychology.

- Baker D. *What Happy People Know: How the New Science of Happiness Can Change Your Life for the Better.* Emmaus, PA, Rodale Books, 2003. [GR,S]
- Kahneman D, Diener E, Schwarz N (editors). *Well-being: The Foundations of Hedonic Psychology.* New York, Russell Sage Foundation, 1999. [S,GR]
- Keyes CLM, Haidt J. *Flourishing: Positive Psychology and the Life Well-Lived.* Washington, DC, American Psychological Association, 2002. [GR,S]
- Seligman MEP. 2002. *Authentic Happiness: Using the New Positive Psychology to Realize Your Potential for Lasting Fulfillment.* New York, Simon & Schuster. [GR,S]

The value of unpleasant feelings is seen in people who lack the ability to feel pain.

- Eich E, Brodkin IA, Reeves JL, et al. Questions concerning pain. In: Kahneman D, Diener E, Schwarz N (editors). *Well-being: The Foundations of Hedonic Psychology.* New York, Russell Sage Foundation, 1999: 155-168. [S,GR]
- Nagasako EM, Oaklander AL, Dworkin RH. Congenital insensitivity to pain: an update. *Pain.* 2003;101:213-219. [S]

Feelings are the mind's risk-benefit calculations based on ancestral history of encounters with the present situation.

- Cosmides L, Tooby J. 2000. (cited earlier in this chapter)
- Pinker S. 1997. (cited earlier in this chapter)

J. B. Watson's advises the abandonment of vague and nonscientific concepts such as consciousness.

- Watson JB. Psychology as the behaviorist views it. *Psychological Review* 1913;20:158-164. [S]

CHAPTER 3

The Pleasure Principle originated with the work of Jeremy Bentham.
* Bentham J. *Principles of morals and legislation.* New York, Hafner. (Originally published in 1789.) [S,GR]

The Pleasure Principle can be used as a general guide to explain most, if not all, human behavior.
* Higgins ET, Grant H, Shah J. 1999. (see references for Chapter 1)
* Kahneman D. 1999. (see references for Chapter 1)
* Rozin P. 1999. (see references for Chapter 1)

The emotion of moral outrage helped social animals maintain societal order.
* **de Waal F. *Good Natured: The Origins of Right and Wrong in Humans and Other Animals.*** Cambridge, Mass, Harvard University Press, 1996. [GR,S]

Sweetness is instinctively craved by mammal babies.
* Panksepp J. 1998. (see references for Chapter 1)

The terror of a young foal separated from his mother (mammalian infant separation anxiety).
* Panksepp J. 1998. (see references for Chapter 1)

Michael Cabanac and colleagues propose that animals make choices on the basis of net pleasure.
* Balasko M, Cabanac M. Motivational conflict among water need, palatability, and cold discomfort in rats. *Physiology & Behavior* 1998;65:35-41. [S]
* Cabanac M. Sensory pleasure. *The Quarterly Review of Biology* 1979;52:1-29. [S]
* **Cabanac M. Pleasure: the common currency.** *Journal of Theoretical Biology* 1992;155:173-200. [S,GR]
* Cabanac M. What is emotion? *Behavioural Processes* 2002;60:69-83. [S,GR]
* Cabanac M, Johnson KG. Analysis of a conflict between palatability and cold exposure in rats. *Physiology & Behavior* 1983;31:249-253. [S]
* Ramirez LM, Cabanac M. Pleasure, the common currency of emotions. *Annals of the New York Academy of Sciences* 2003;1000:293-295. [S]

Scarlett's story.
* Martin J, Suares JC. *Scarlett Saves Her Family.* New York, Simon & Schuster, 1997. [GR]

Unpleasant feelings discourage animals from repeating behaviors that, on average in the ancestral past, have resulted in a decreased chance of survival and reproduction.
* Panksepp J. 1998. (see references for Chapter 1)
* Pinker S. 1997. (see references for Chapter 1)

Choosing the greater pleasure isn't always what is best for long-term benefit.
* **Dawkins MS. From an animal's point of view: motivation, fitness, and animal welfare.** *Behavioral and Brain Sciences* 1990;13:1-61. [S,GR]

Two sets of feelings promote social attachments.
* Panksepp J. 1998. (see references for Chapter 1)

CHAPTER 4

Joseph LeDoux writes on the survival value of fear.
* LeDoux J. *The Emotional Brain.* New York, Simon & Schuster, 1996. [GR,S]

Zookeepers are beginning to address boredom in captive animals.

- Shepherdson DJ, Mellen JD, Hutchins M (editors). *Second Nature: Environmental Enrichment for Captive Animals.* Washington, DC, Smithsonian Institute Press, 1998. [S,GR]

Mice kept in small cages while being used in research may develop emotional disturbances.

- Garner JP, Mason GJ. Evidence for a relationship between cage stereotypies and behavioural disinhibition in laboratory rodents. *Behavioural Brain Research* 2002;136:83–92. [S]
- **Yeoman B. Can we trust research done with lab mice?** *Discover* 2003;July:64–72. [GR,S]

All social attachments probably originated with the mother-infant bond.

- Hatfield E, Rapson R. Love and attachment processes. In: Lewis M, Haviland-Jones JM (editors). *Handbook of Emotions.* Second Edition. New York, The Guilford Press, 2000: 654–662. [S,GR]
- Panksepp J. 1998. (see references for Chapter 1)

Cynthia Moss writes of the elephant who regularly returned to the spot where her mother died.

- **Moss C. *Elephant Memories: Thirteen Years in the Life of an Elephant Family.*** New York, William Morrow & Co, 1988. [GR,S]

Karen Pryor writes of the dolphin who lost her companion.

- Pryor K. *Lads Before the Wind: Adventures in Porpoise Training.* New York, Harper & Row, 1975. [GR,S]

Angry dolphins slap their tails and make impressive sounds.

- **Howard CJ. *Dolphin Chronicles.*** New York, Bantam Books, 1996. [GR,S]

Domestication of the dog involved the process of neotony.

- Coren S. *The Intelligence of Dogs.* New York, Free Press, 1994. [GR]

CHAPTER 5

Tabitha's story.

- Timmel CA. *Tabitha: The Fabulous Flying Feline.* New York, Walker and Company, 1996. [GR]

What is stress? How does it differ from emotion?

- McMillan FD. Stress, distress, and emotion: distinctions and implications for animal well-being. In: McMillan FD (editor). *Mental Health and Well-being in Animals.* Ames, Iowa, Blackwell Publishing. (In press, due 2005) [S]

The stress response is one of the ways that the body maintains balance and efficiency.

- **Sapolsky RM. *Why Zebras Don't Get Ulcers: A Guide to Stress, Stress-Related Diseases, and Coping.*** New York, W.H. Freeman and Company, 1994. [GR,S]
- Moberg G, Mench JA (editors). *The biology of animal stress: basic principles and implications for animal welfare.* CABI Publishing, Wallingford, Oxon, UK, 2000. [S]

Research indicates that the feeling of "being stressed" comes from the underlying unpleasant emotion.

- McMillan FD. 1999. Stress, distress, and . . . (cited earlier in this chapter)

Habituation is one of the psychological methods used to relieve both animals and humans of fears.

- **Landsberg GM, Hunthausen W, Ackerman L. *Handbook of Behaviour Problems of the Dog and Cat.*** Oxford, Butterworth Heinemann, 1997. [S,GR]

The psychological impact of unpleasant feelings is greatly reduced when the animal has control over the situation.

- Broom DM. Animal welfare defined in terms of attempts to cope with the environment. *ACTA Agriculturae Scandinavica Section A – Animal Science Supplement* 1996;27:22-28. [S]
- Novak, MA, Suomi, SJ. Psychological well-being of primates in captivity. *American Psychologist* 43(10):765-773, 1988. [S,GR]
- Sackett GP. The human model of psychological well-being in primates. In: Novak MA, Petto AJ (editors). *Through the Looking Glass: Issues of Psychological Well-being in Captive Nonhuman Primates.* Washington, DC, American Psychological Association, 1991: 35-42. [S]
- Seligman ME. *Helplessness: On Depression, Development, and Death.* San Francisco, W.H. Freeman and Company, 1975. [GR,S]
- Thompson SC. 1981. Will it hurt less if I can control it? A complex answer to a simple question. *Psychological Bulletin* 90:89-101. [S,GR]

For people, a sense of control is one of the strongest predictors of positive feelings of well-being.

- Averill JR, More TA. Happiness. In: Lewis M, Haviland-Jones JM (editors). *Handbook of Emotions.* Second Edition. New York, The Guilford Press, 2000: 663-676. [S,GR]

Animals who can make changes in their living conditions appear much more active and content than animals with no such control.

- Fox MW. *Laboratory Animal Husbandry: Ethology, Welfare and Experimental Variables.* Albany, NY, State University of New York Press, 1986. [S,GR]

Many animals seem to enjoy a sense of control for its own sake.

- Kavanau JL. Behavior of captive white-footed mice. *Science* 1967;155:1623-39. [S]

When animals lose control they can lapse into a state of helplessness and hopelessness.

- Seligman ME. 1975. (cited earlier in this chapter)

Allowing control can be a problem for dogs with dominant personalities.

- Landsberg GM, Hunthausen W, Ackerman L. 1997. (cited earlier in this chapter)
- Overall KL. *Clinical Behavioral Medicine for Small Animals.* St. Louis, Mosby, 1997. [S,GR]

The latest research in animal psychology supports the idea that a dependable and secure place to retreat is the single most important element of mental health and comfort.

- Carlstead K. Determining the causes of stereotypic behaviors in zoos carnivores: toward appropriate enrichment strategies. Shepherdson DJ, Mellen JD, Hutchins M. Second nature: environmental enrichment for captive animals. Washington, DC: Smithsonian Institute Press;1998. 172-183. [S]
- Carlstead KJ, Brown J, Seidensticker J. Behavioral and adrenocortical responses to environmental changes in leopard cats (*Felis bengalensis*). *Zoo Biology* 1993;12:1-11. [S,GR]
- Carlstead K, Brown JL, Strawn W. Behavioral and physiological correlates of stress in laboratory cats. *Applied Animal Behaviour Science* 1993;38:143-158. [S,GR]

In zoos and animals shelters, providing animals with a place to hide markedly reduces the fear and anxiety.

- Anderson US, Benne M, Bloomsmith MA, et al. Retreat space and human visitor density moderate undesirable behavior in petting zoo animals. *Journal of Applied*

Animal Welfare Science 2002;5:125-137. [S,GR]
- Carlstead KJ, Brown J, Seidensticker J. 1993. (cited earlier in this chapter)
- Carlstead K, Brown JL, Strawn W. 1993. (cited earlier in this chapter)

The value of a Safe Haven in pet animals.
- **McMillan FD. Building confidence with a "safe haven."** *Animal Wellness Magazine* 2002;4(3):36-37. [GR]

CHAPTER 6

Drug therapy can be an important part of behavior-modification arsenal.
- Dodman NH, Shuster L (editors). *Psychopharmacology of Animal Behavior Disorders.* Malden, Mass, Blackwell Science, 1998. [S,GR]

Counterconditioning.
- **Wright JC, Lashnits JW.** *The Dog Who Would Be King.* Rodale Press, Emmaus, PA, 1999. [GR,S]

Desensitization.
- Landsberg GM, Hunthausen W, Ackerman L. 1997. (see references for Chapter 5)

Rats exposed to stress ate more "comfort food" than rats not experiencing stress. Obesity may result from eating caused by anxiety or other unpleasant emotions.
- Dallman MF, Pecoraro N, Akana SF, et al. 2003. (see references for Chapter 1)
- Levine AS, Morley JE. Stress-induced eating in rats. *American Journal of Physiology* 1981;241:R72-6. [S]
- Scalera G. Taste preferences, body weight gain, food and fluid intake in singly or group-housed rats. *Physiology and Behavior* 1992;52:935-943. [S]

Methods for altering undesired behaviors in cats.
- **Bohnenkamp G.** *From the Cat's Point of View.* San Francisco, Perfect Paws, Inc.,1991.
- **Church C.** *Housecat.* New York, Howell Book House, 1998.
- **Delzio S, Ribarich C.** *Felinestein: Pampering the Genius In Your Cat.* New York, HarperPerennial, 1999.

Emotional upsets are often associated with cats urinating outside of their litter boxes.
- Buffington CAT, Chew DJ, DiBartola SP. Interstitial cystitis in cats. *Veterinary Clinics North America: Small Animal Practice* 1996;26:317-326. [S]

CHAPTER 7

The first paper on animal quality of life.
- McMillan FD. Quality of life in animals. *Journal of the American Veterinary Medical Association* 2000;216:1904-1910. [S,GR]

The animal's quality of life is determined by his view of his life, not yours.
- Dawkins MS. 1990. (see references for Chapter 3)

David Myers writes that every desirable experience is transitory.
- Myers DG. 1992. (see references for Chapter 1)

David Lykken writes about the "happiness set point."
- Lykken D. *Happiness.* New York, Golden Books, 1999. [GR,S]

Owners of paralyzed dogs report the dogs to have good mental attitudes.
- Bauer M, Glickman N, Glickman L, et al. Follow-up study of owner attitudes toward home care of paraplegic dogs. *Journal of the American Veterinary Medical Association* 1992;200:1809-1816. [S,GR]

Marc Bekoff proposes that a major purpose of play is to establish the rules and guidelines that help mold the basic foundations of social conduct in life.

- Bekoff M. Social play behavior: cooperation, fairness, trust, and the evolution of morality. *Journal of Consciousness Studies* 2001;8:81-90. [S, GR]

Play is important for many species of animals.

- Bekoff M, Byers JA (editors). *Animal Play: Evolutionary, Comparative, and Ecological Perspectives.* Cambridge, Cambridge University Press, 1998. [S,GR]

Laboratory animals will run mazes for the reward of a brief period of play.

- Siviy SM. Neurobiological substrates of play behavior: glimpses into the structure and function of mammalian playfulness. In: Bekoff M, Byers JA (editors). *Animal Play: Evolutionary, Comparative, and Ecological perspectives.* Cambridge, Cambridge University Press, 1998: 221-242. [S,GR]

One study showed dogs spend approximately 25 percent of their time using toys.

- Houpt KA. *Domestic Animal Behavior for Veterinarians and Animals Scientists.* Third Edition. Ames, Iowa, Iowa State University Press, 1998. [S,GR]

In people, a major contributor to life satisfaction is active and challenging engagement in the world.

- Averill JR, More TA. 2000. (see references for Chapter 5)

White rats prevented from interacting with stimuli develop smaller brains.

- Wemelsfelder F. The concept of animal boredom and its relationship to stereo-typed behaviour. In: Lawrence AB, Rushen J (editors). *Stereotypic Animal Behaviour.* Wallingford, England, Cab International, 1993: 65-95. [S]

Animals seem to prefer to "work" for their food, even when they can get it for "free."

- Kuhovy M. On the pleasures of the mind. In: Kahneman D, Diener E, Schwarz N (editors). *Well-being: The Foundations of Hedonic Psychology.* New York, Russell Sage Foundation, 1999: 134-154. [S,GR]
- Wemelsfelder F. Boredom and laboratory animal welfare. In: Rollin BE, Kesel ML (editors). *The Experimental Animal in Biomedical Research.* Boca Raton, FL, CRC Press, 1990: 243-272. [S,GR]

James McBain's recounting of the performing seals story.

- McBain JF. Cetaceans in captivity: a discussion of welfare. *Journal of the American Veterinary Medical Association* 1999;214:1170-1174. [S,GR]

In people, the frequency and duration of pleasantness, rather than its intensity, is the factor most closely associated with overall happiness level.

- Diener E, Lucas RE. Subjective emotional well-being. In: Lewis M, Haviland-Jones JM (editors). *Handbook of Emotions.* Second Edition. New York, The Guilford Press, 2000: 325-337. [S,GR]

Scientists believe that animals live only in the present.

- Clark JD, Rager DR, Calpin JP. Animal well-being II. Stress and distress. *Laboratory Animal Science* 1997;47:571-579. [S]

Once the captive dolphins were released into the ocean they had much less interest in toys.

- Howard CJ. 1996. (see references for Chapter 4)

Methods for improving your cat's quality of life.

- Bohnenkamp G. 1991. (see references for Chapter 6)
- Church C. 1998. (see references for Chapter 6)
- Delzio S, Ribarich C. 1999. (see references for Chapter 6)

CHAPTER 8

General references for mind/body interactions in animals.
- **Damasio AR.** *Descartes' Error.* New York, G.P. Putnam's Sons, 1994. [GR,S]
- **Lappe M.** *Evolutionary Medicine.* San Francisco, Sierra Club Books, 1994. [GR,S]
- **McMillan FD. Influence of mental states on somatic health in animals.** *Journal of the American Veterinary Medical Association* 1999;214:1221-1225. [S,GR]
- **McMillan FD. Is your animal's health affected by his emotions?** *Animal Wellness Magazine* 2001;3(3):11-13. [GR]
- **Nesse RM, Williams GC.** *Why We Get Sick: The New Science of Darwinian Medicine.* New York, Times Books, 1994. [GR,S]

Premature labor resulting from emotional stress.
- Dole N, Savitz DA, Hertz-Picciotto I, et al. Maternal stress and preterm birth. *American Journal of Epidemiology* 2003;157:14-24. [S]

Emotions and physical stress can influence a wide array of illnesses.
- Leventhal H, Patrick-Miller L. Emotions and physical illness: causes and indicators of vulnerability. In: Lewis M, Haviland-Jones JM (editors). *Handbook of Emotions.* Second Edition. New York, The Guilford Press, 2000: 523-537. [S,GR]

Loneliness is linked to immune deficiencies in monkeys.
- Coe CL. Psychosocial factors and immunity in nonhuman primates: a review. *Psychosomatic Medicine* 1993;55:298-308. [S]
- Laudenslager ML, Boccia ML. Some observations on psychsocial stressors, immunity, and individual differences in nonhuman primates. *American Journal of Primatology* 1996;39:205-221. [S]

Anger is associated with heart disease in dogs.
- Verrier RL, Hagestad EL, Lown B. Delayed myocardial ischemia induced by anger. *Circulation* 1987;75:249-254. [S]

Fear appears to trigger a fatal thyroid condition in rabbits.
- Kracht J. Fright-thyrotoxicosis in the wild rabbit, a model of thyrotrophic alarm-reaction. *Acta Endocrinologica* 1954;15:355-367. [S]

Various diseases have been shown to be connected to emotional distress in animals.
- Buffington CAT, Chew DJ, DiBartola SP. 1996. (see references for Chapter 6)
- Riley V. Psychoneuroendocrine influences on immunocompetence and neoplasia. *Science* 1981;212:1100-1109. [S]
- Riley V, Fitzmaurice MA, Spackman DH. Psychoneuroimmunologic factors in neoplasia: studies in animals. In: Ader R (editor). *Psychoneuroimmunology.* New York, Academic Press, 1981: 31-102. [S]

When an animal is challenged by an environmental threat, this complex information system ensures that the animal will respond as a whole unit.
- Cunningham AJ. Mind, body, and immune response. In: Ader R (editor). *Psychoneuroimmunology.* New York, Academic Press, 1981: 609-617. [S]
- Damasio AR. 1994. (cited earlier in this chapter)
- Pert CB, Ruff MR, Weber RJ, et al. Neuropeptides and their receptors: a psychosomatic network. *Journal of Immunology* 1985;135(2):820-826. [S]

An increase in the number of cats with urinary tract disease after the earthquake.
- Buffington CAT, Chew DJ, DiBartola SP. 1996. (see references for Chapter 6)

Pavlov's experiments with dogs.

• Pavlov IP. *Conditioned Reflexes.* London, Oxford Press, 1927. [S]

The immune system can be trained in the same way.

• Ader R, Cohen N. Behaviorally conditioned immunosuppression. *Psychosomatic Medicine* 1975;37:333-340. [S]

• Solomon GS, Kay N, Morley JE. Endorphins: a link between personality, stress, emotions, immunity, and disease? In: Plotnikoff NP, Faith RE, Murgo AJ, et al, (editors). *Enkephalins and Endorphins: Stress and the Immune System.* New York, Plenum Press, 1986:129-137. [S]

Young elephants can die suddenly, in what is called "broken-heart syndrome."

• Adams J. *Wild Elephants in Captivity.* Dominguez Hills, Calif, Center for the Study of Elephants, 1981. [GR]

Purdue study shows decreased risk of bloat in dogs who were judged by their owners to be "happy."

• Glickman LT, Glickman NW, Schellenberg DB, Simpson K, Lantz GC. Multiple risk factors for the gastric dilatation-volvulus syndrome in dogs: a practitioner/owner case-control study. *Journal of the American Animal Hospital Association* 1997;33:197-204. [S,GR]

• Glickman LT, Glickman NW, Schellenberg DB, Raghaven M, Lee TL. Incidence of and breed-related risk factors for gastric dilatation-volvulus in dogs. *Journal of the American Veterinary Medical Association* 2000;216:40-45. [S,GR]

A University of Texas study showed a dramatically decreased risk of stroke in people who scored high on the happiness questionnaire.

• Ostir GV, Markides KS, Peek MK, Goodwin JS. The association between emotional well-being and the incidence of stroke in older adults. *Psychosomatic Medicine* 2001;63:210-215. [S]

Studies have also shown mental health benefits for people with pets.

• Becker M. *The Healing Power of Pets: Harnessing the Ability of Pets to Make and Keep People Happy and Healthy.* New York, Hyperion, 2002. [GR,S]

Numerous studies have shown that the gentle touch of a person can improve numerous health conditions in pets and other animals.

• Gantt WH, Newton JEO, Royer FL, et al. Effect of person. *Conditional Reflex* 1966;1:18-35. [S]

• **McMillan FD. Effects of human contact on animal health and well-being. *Journal of the American Veterinary Medical Association* 1999; 215:1592-1598. [S,GR]**

Robert Nerem and his colleagues demonstrate effect of gentle human contact in rabbits.

• Nerem RM, Levesque MJ, Cornhill JF. Social environment as a factor in diet-induced atherosclerosis. Science 1980;208:1475-1476. [S,GR]

Farm animals also appear to benefit from caring human contact.

• McMillan FD. 1999. Effects of human contact . . . (cited earlier in this chapter)

Factors influencing the effect of human contact on a pet: socialization and familiarity, quality of the contact, and genetics of the animal.

• McMillan FD. 1999. Effects of human contact . . . (cited earlier in this chapter)

Some researchers believe that gentle human contact works by lowering stress levels.

• Nerem RM, Georgia Institute of Technology, Atlanta, GA: Personal communication, 1998.

Numerous experiments have demonstrated a placebo effect in animals.

• McMillan FD. The placebo effect in animals. *Journal of the American Veterinary Medical Association* 1999;215:992-999. [S]

The dogs showed the same response to the placebo that they did to the active insulin.

• Siegel S. Conditioning insulin effects. *Journal of Comparative and Physiological Psychology* 1975;89:189-199. [S]

A study of the effects of a pain medicine for arthritis in dogs found a high rate of response in the placebo-treated dogs.

• Vasseur PB, Johnson AL, Budsberg SC, et al. Randomized, controlled trial of the efficacy of carprofen, a nonsteroidal anti-inflammatory drug, in the treatment of osteoarthritis in dogs. *Journal of the American Veterinary Medical Association* 1995;206(6):807-811. [S,GR]

Animals are able to exert voluntary control over certain bodily processes.

• McMillan FD. 1999. Influence of mental states . . . (cited earlier in this chapter)

Any line drawn between the mental and the physical is artificial.

• Damasio AR. 1994. (cited earlier in this chapter)

• **McMillan FD, Rollin BE. The presence of mind: on reunifying the animal mind and body.** *Journal of the American Veterinary Medical Association* 2001;218:1723-1727. [S,GR]

In one experiment, researchers gently scratched the skin of guinea pigs while simultaneously injecting bacteria into the animals' bodies.

• Metalnikov S, Chorine V. The role of conditioned reflexes in immunity. *Annals of the Pasteur Institute* 1926;40:893-900. [S]

CHAPTER 9

Dogs do not act out of malice or randomly.

• Daniels TJ. A study of dog bites on the Navajo reservation. *Public Health Report* 1986;101:50-59. [S,GR]

Treatment for emotional disturbances in pets is the beginning of a whole new field to make distressed animals feel good again.

• **McMillan, F.D. Emotional pain management.** *Veterinary Medicine* 2002;97:822-834. [S,GR]

• **McMillan FD. A world of hurts—is pain special?** *Journal of the American Veterinary Medical Association* 2003;223:183-186. [GR,S]

A program designed to promote good mental and emotional health.

• **McMillan FD. Development of a mental wellness program for animals.** *Journal of the American Veterinary Medical Association* 2002;220:965-972. [S,GR]

The ages when the socialization period occurs in puppies and kittens.

• Landsberg GM, Hunthausen W, Ackerman L. 1997. (see references for Chapter 5)

Puppies can be socialized with only 10 minutes of human companionship a day.

• Serpell J, Jagoe JA. Early experience and the development of behaviour. In: Serpell J (editor). *The Domestic Dog: Its Evolution, Behaviour and Interactions With People.* Cambridge, UK, Cambridge University Press, 1995: 79-102. [S,GR]

The sensitive period during which the animal brain learns what to fear and what not to fear. Fear desensitization occurs by exposure to objects or events.

• Overall KL. 1997. (see references for Chapter 5)

Sensitive period during which fearful experiences can create enduring fears.

• Luescher UA, McKeown DB, Halip J. Stereotypic or obsessive-compulsive disorders in dogs and cats. *Veterinary Clinics of North America – Small Animal Practice* 1991;21:401-413. [S,GR]

Handled kittens develop more quickly, are more stress resistant, and learn faster.

• McMillan FD. 1999. Effects of human contact . . . (see references for Chapter 8)

Dogs' mental well-being is dependent upon a stable dominance hierarchy.

• Overall KL. 1997. (see references for Chapter 5)

You can maximize your pet's quality of life by tipping the quality-of-life scales farther toward pleasant feelings.

• **McMillan FD. Maximizing quality of life in ill animals.** *Journal of the American Animal Hospital Association* 2003;39:227-235. [S,GR]

Research suggests that the effects of your presence and touch can make a difference to your pet's recovery.

• McMillan FD. 1999. Effects of human contact . . . (see references for Chapter 8)

As animals and people experience major changes over their lifetimes, quality of life seems to remain at right around the same level.

• Diener E, Lucas RE. 2000. (see references for Chapter 7)

Tufts University study found that certain forms of fear-based aggression in dogs are reduced on a lower-protein diet.

• Dodman NH, Reisner I, Shuster L, et al. Effect of dietary protein content on behavior in dogs. *Journal of the American Veterinary Medical Association* 1996;208:376-379. [S]

Dogs with cognitive decline had some mental abilities restored by eating a special diet containing a blend of antioxidants and other nutrients.

• Dodd CE, Zicker SC, Jewell DE, et al. Can a fortified food affect the behavioral manifestations of age-related cognitive decline in dogs? *Veterinary Medicine* 2003;98:396-408.

Social companionship in humans and animals counteracts/buffers stress-related emotions.

• Ray J, Sapolsky R. Styles of male social behavior and their endocrine correlates among high-ranking baboons. *American Journal of Primatology* 1992;28:231-240. [S]

• Sapolsky RM. The physiology and pathophysiology of unhappiness. In: Kahneman D, Diener E, Schwarz N (editors). *Well-being: The Foundations of Hedonic Psychology.* New York, Russell Sage Foundation, 1999: 453-469. [S,GR]

Fighting may occur between friendly companions who use one another as outlets for frustration (also, redirected aggression).

• Overall KL. 1997. (see references for Chapter 5)

• Sapolsky RM. 1994. (see references for Chapter 5)

Studies show that dogs exhibit both less fear and less pain when they are petted gently by a person.

• Wright EM, Marcella KL, Woodson JF. Animal pain: evaluation and control. *Lab Animal* 1985;14:20-36. [S]

• Smith AW, Houpt KA, Kitchell RL, et al. 1986 Report of the AVMA panel on euthanasia. *Journal of the American Veterinary Medical Association* 1986;188:253-268. [S]

Chapter 10

Comfort, rather than being a secondary goal, is in fact the primary objective in medical practice.

- **McMillan FD. Comfort as the primary goal in veterinary medical practice.** *Journal of the American Veterinary Medical Association* 1998;212(9):1370-1374. [S,GR]

Noncooperation, is not the animal's doing, but rather is defined by our desires.

- **McMillan FD. Compassionate animal care in veterinary practice. Parts 1 and 2.** *Veterinary Technician* 1996;17:169-174, 259-265. [GR]

Chapter 11

Euthanasia is not an act to end a life.

- **McMillan FD. Rethinking euthanasia: death as an unintentional outcome.** *Journal of the American Veterinary Medical Association* 2001;219:1204-1206. [S,GR]

Epilogue

Daniel J. Povinelli proposes that humans have an instinctual propensity to attribute emotion to other animals.

- Povenelli DJ. *Folk Physics for Apes: The Chimpanzee's Theory of How the World Works.* Oxford, Oxford University Press, 2003.

Brain scans of a cooperating person show changes in the area associated with pleasure.

- Rilling JK, Gutman DA, Zeh TR, et al.. A neural basis for social cooperation. *Neuron* 2002;35:395-405. [S]

General reference for animal mental health and well-being.

- **McMillan FD (editor). *Mental Health and Well-being in Animals.*** Ames, Iowa, Blackwell Publishing. (In press, due 2005) [S,GR]

INDEX

Boldface page references indicate illustrations.

<u>Underscored</u> references indicate boxed text.

A

Acclimatization, 136–37
Accomplishment, 176–77
Adaptation, 26, 94, 227–29
Adrenaline, 90, 92
Affection, dog's need for, <u>69</u>
Aggression
  to acquire control, 101
  displaced, <u>90–91</u>
  effect of diet on, <u>215</u>
  inability to change behavior, <u>130</u>
Aging
  adaptation, 227–29
  changing interests and behaviors,
    225–27, 230–31
  quality-of-life checklist, 230–31
AIBO robot dog, 277
Airplane, cat trapped on, 87–88, 92
Alertness, 65–66
Alternative medicine, 254–55
Aluminum foil, as scratching
    deterrent, 141
Anger
  at animal's behavior, 246–47
  causes in animals, 78, 79
  expressions of, 75, 78, 79
  moral, 41
  role in
    health, 187
    undesirable behaviors, <u>146–47</u>
Animal behaviorists
  desensitization therapy and, 135
  focus on observed behavior, <u>8–9</u>

Anthropomorphism, <u>9</u>
Anti-anxiety medication, 32, 63, <u>81</u>,
    <u>91</u>, 94, <u>123</u>, 134, 191, 192,
    195
Anti-bark collars, 126
Antidepressant, 133
Anxiety, 63. *See also* Fear
  boarding and, 223, 225
  reducing with
    comfort food, 138–40
    medication, 32, 63, <u>81</u>, 89, 94,
      <u>123</u>, 134, 191, 192, 195
    Safe Haven, 102, <u>103</u>, 104
  role in
    health, 192
    inappropriate elimination,
      144–45
    undesirable behaviors, <u>146–47</u>
  separation
    Clomicalm for, 89
    examples of, 68–70, 112–13
    relieving, 114
    responses to, <u>147</u>
    role in undesirable behaviors,
      <u>146–47</u>
    signs and causes, 70–71, <u>146</u>
Aristotle, 10
Arthritis, 203, 222–23, 261–62
Asthma, 93–94
Attention
  feelings and, 16–18, 21
  seeking behavior, 120–21
Autonomic nervous system, 90

B

Backup systems in nature, 52–53
Barking, 72, 109, 111, 118, 125–27,
    148, 150
Battered-wife syndrome, loneliness
    and, 71
Begging for food, 116–17
Behaviorism, 8
Behavior modification
  devices
    invisible electric fence, 127–28,
      128
    shock collars, 125–26, 128, **128**
  inability to change some
    behaviors, 130
  methods
    counterconditioning, 121, 124
    desensitization, 134–37
    drug therapy, 131–34
    elimination of discomfort, 114
    removing rewards, 116–20, **117**,
      119
    substitution of more pleasurable
      option, 114–16
Behavior problems, 109–150
  destructive behavior
    chewing, 141–42
    digging, 142–44, **143**
    scratching, 140–41
  inappropriate elimination, 144–45,
    148
  overeating, 138–40
  painful emotions responsible for,
    146–47
  too much noise, 148–49
  viewing as emotional disturbances,
    210
Bekoff, Marc (animal researcher),
    167, 173
Bentham, Jeremy (philosopher), 37
Biting, 208, 211
Black box of the mind, 8–9
Bladder stones, 244
Blood pressure, affected by
  biofeedback, 204–5
  touch, 198, 199

Boarding, 223–25
Boredom
  need for mental stimulation, 66–68
  power of, 63, 65
  relieving, 51, 114
  role in
    motivating animals, 65–66
    undesirable behaviors, 143, **143**,
      146–47
  signs of, 65, 68
  stress from, 91
Brain
  cost/benefit calculations by, 20
  evolution of, 11–12, 25
  mind differentiated from, 13
  neotony and, 69
  neurochemical development, 212
  wiring for social relationships,
    212–14
Broken-heart syndrome, 193

C

Cabanac, Michael (physiologist),
    44–45
Cancer, 266
Carrier, counterconditioning to
    remove fear of, 121, 124
Cars, fear of, 31–32, 80, 134, 135, 136
Chewing, 115–16, 141–42
Choice, importance of, 98–100
Citronella, 126
Clawing furniture, 116
Clicker training, 149–50
Clomicalm, 89
Cognitive dysfunction syndrome,
    144
Collar
  anti-bark (citronella), 126
  Elizabethan, 131
  shock, 125–26, 128, **128**
Comfort
  as primary objective in medical
    practice, 239
  team approach to providing,
    240–43

Comfort Zone, 24–36
  as alert system for
    needs, 28–31
    straightforward threats, 31–33
  definition, 26
  as goal for veterinary care, 239–40,
    241
  how it works, 28–34
  influenced by
    boredom, 66–67
    feelings of control, 96–97
    multiple discomforts, 33–34
    natural environment, 24–26
  as key to pet behavior, 34–36
  location of, 34
Comfort Zone Scale, 27–28, **28**,
  45–46
Companionship
  happiness boost from, 170
  need for, 122–23
  during socialization period, 213
Compassionate care
  meanings of, 207, 208
  pet's perspective on, 208–9
  in veterinary care, 248–49
Conditioned fear, 82–83
Confidence, loss of, 122–23
Confinement, effect on quality of
  life, 157–58
Congenital analgesia, 22
Consciousness, feelings and, 7–10,
  215
Control
  desire for, 99
  empowering by
    allowing choice, 98–100
    responding to requests, 100
  importance of, 96–97, 98–99
  limits on, 100–101
  removal of, 96
  role in
    coping, 95–96
    happiness, 170
    hope, 101
  Safe Haven and, 104
Coping, 95, 96, 99–100

Cost/benefit calculations, 20, 44–45
Counterconditioning, 121, 124, 136
Cravings, for
  food, 160, 161–62
  play, 161

D

Death. *See also* Euthanasia
  natural, 269–70
  special significance of, 269–71
Debarking, 126
Decision making
  feelings as guide for, 12–14
  Pet Pleasure Principle and, 51–54
  in veterinary care, 249–51, 254
Depression
  role in
    hopelessness, 101
    learned helplessness, 97
    undesirable behaviors, 146–47
  treatment, 89, 133
Descartes, Rene (philosopher), 6
Desensitization, 134–37
Destructive behavior
  caused by separation anxiety,
    68–70
  chewing, 115–16, 141–42
  digging, 109, 111, 115, 142–44,
    143
  scratching, 140–41
Diabetes, 35–36, 188
Diaries, of pet's symptoms, 4
Digging, 109, 111, 115, 142–44, **143**
Disability, 222
Discomfort
  on Comfort Zone Scale, 27–28, **28**
  intensity of, 28
  on Pleasure/Discomfort Scale,
    45–46, **46**, 48, 49–50, 52, 53
  relieving
    to change behavior, 114
    with euthanasia, 258–59,
      261–64
    with medication, 131–34
  signs of emotional discomfort, 234

Happiness
    boosters, 170–71, 172, 216–18
    cognitive and emotional
        components of, 184
    definitions of, 164
    health and, 171, 196–98, 199
    individuality of, 158
    in life overall, 166–67, 184
    play and, 172–76
    quality of life compared, 164–65
    recognizing unhappiness, 231–34
Health
    emotions' effects on, 187–98, 204–5
    happiness and, 171, 196–98, 199
    mind/body connection, 186–206
Heart rate, affected by
    biofeedback, 204
    petting, 198
Helplessness, learned, 97, 166
Hiding places, 102, 104
Hope, 101
Hormones, 188
Hospitalization, 225, 252–53, 255
House calls, 256
Housetraining, 55–56
Howard, Carol J. (marine biologist),
        78, 167
Howling, 98–99, 112, 132, 148
Human touch, 189, 198–201, 216

I

IBD. See Inflammatory bowel disease
Identification tags, 218
Immune system
    connection to the brain, 188, 193
    placebo effect and, 202
Indecision, 51
Inflammatory bowel disease (IBD),
        250–51
Insecurity, 30–31
Instinct
    forms of
        fear, 40
        maternal, 38–39, 42
        mating, 40

inability to change instinctive
        behaviors, 130
    relationship to emotions, 37,
        38–39, 40–42
Invisible electric fence, 127–28,
        128

J

Joy, 163
Jumping up
    on counters by cats, 118
    on people by dogs, 115, 124
Justice, sense of, 41

K

Kidney disease, 258, 266–68

L

Learned helplessness, 97, 166
Learning
    habituation, 94–95
    theory, 9
LeDoux, Joseph (neuroscientist), 62
Loneliness
    emotional pain of, 71–73
    reducing, 51
    role in
        health, 187
        separation anxiety, 70, 71, 114
        stress, 91
        undesirable behaviors,
            146–47
Lost pets, 218
Love, 70, 278

M

Macaque monkeys, 74
Mail carrier, counterconditioning
        response to, 124
Maternal instinct, 38–39, 42
McBain, James (marine-mammal
        veterinarian), 177, 180

Pet Pleasure Principle (*cont.*)
    behavior modification methods
        counterconditioning, 121, 124
        elimination of discomfort, 114
        removing rewards, 116–20, **117**,
            119
        substitution of more pleasurable
            option, 114–16
    downsides of, 47
    exceptions to, 47
    as guide of behavior, 37, 46–47,
        47, 56
    influence on
        decision-making, 51–54
        motivation level, 49–51
    origins of, 37
    Pleasure/Discomfort Scale, 45–46,
        46, 48, 49–50, 52, 53, **117**,
        128
    shock devices and, 125, 127–28
    use in
        changing behaviors, 112–25,
            128, 130, 137–45
        training, 149–50
    value system of the pet, 126
Pet-sitting, 223–24
Petting
    cravings for, 161
    positive effects on pet health, 189
Phobia, 135
Pilling, desensitization to, 136–37
Ping-Pong balls, 117
Pinker, Steven (psychologist), 20
Placebo effect, 201–3, 202
Play
    happiness and, 172–76
    promoting for mental wellness,
        219
    purpose of, 173
Pleasure
    in aging pets, 225–27, 230–31
    choosing, 42–45
    cost/benefit analysis, 44–45
    evolutionary value, 43
    health benefits of, 196–98, 199
    individuality of, 161–63

maximal, 160
promise to your pet, **185**
promoting for
    mental wellness, 218–19
    sick pet, 219–23
quality of life and, 159–63, **160**
sources, 43
use in changing behavior, 114–16
Pleasure/Discomfort Scale, 45–46,
    46, 48, 49–50, 52, 53, 238,
    262
Positive Psychology, 23
Positive reinforcement, 149
Post-traumatic stress, 80–81
Prevention, in mental health wellness
    program, 212–16, 222
Priorities, set by feelings, 19–21
Proactive treatment, 251, 254
Prozac, 89
Pryor, Karen (dolphin trainer), 73
Psychology
    Behaviorism, 8
    Positive, 23
Psychotherapy, 184
Psychotropic drugs, 131, 134
Punishments
    feelings as, 43
    inappropriateness of, 129
Puppies
    exposing to the world, 214–16,
        217
    socialization period, 212–14

Q

Quality of life, 151–85
    checklist for the aging pet, 230–31
    decision, 178–79
    euthanasia decision and, 263, 273
    feelings and, 153–55, **155**, 156,
        180–81
    as guide for animal care, 152–53
    happiness and, 158, 163–76
    individuality of, 156–58
    for indoor and outdoor cats,
        174–75

measuring, 158–61, 180–81
neutering and, <u>220–21</u>
questionnaire, 181–83
restoring for sick pet, 219–22
thermometer, 180–81

R

Rabbits, effect of touch on, 199–200
Reflex actions, 12
Repellant sprays, 142
Repetitive behavior, 67
Rescue of animals, 2–3
Restlessness, 65
Restraint, use of, <u>247</u>
Rewards
  competing, 118, 120
  doubling incentives, <u>124</u>
  feelings as, <u>43</u>
  food, <u>126</u>
  removing to change behavior,
    116–21, **117**, <u>119</u>
  unseen, <u>115</u>
  use in clicker training, 149–50
  value system, <u>126</u>

S

Safe Haven
  creating for pet, 105–8
  as happiness booster, <u>170</u>
  hiding places, 102, 104
  importance in multi-pet
    households, 104–5, 107–8
  rules for respecting pet's, <u>103</u>
Scars, emotional, 79–83
Scratching, 140–41
Scratching post, 116, 140–41
Security, of Safe Haven, 102, 104–5,
  107
Sensitive periods, 212, 214, 216
Separation anxiety
  Clomicalm for, 89
  examples of, 68–70, 112–13
  relieving, 114
  responses to, <u>147</u>

role in undesirable behaviors,
  <u>146–47</u>
signs and causes, 70–71, <u>146</u>
Sex drive, <u>53</u>, <u>220</u>
Shelters, <u>233</u>
Shock collars, 125–26, 128, **128**
Sick pets, caring for, 219–23
Slipped disc, 33–34, <u>178</u>
Social bonding
  consequences of disruption
    grief, 73–74
    loneliness, 71–73
    separation anxiety, 68–71
  formation during socialization
    period, 213
  function as
    happiness booster, <u>170</u>
    security blanket, <u>224</u>
  mother-infant bond, 70
  motivational forces for, <u>53</u>
  need for affection, <u>69</u>
Socialization, 200, 212–14, <u>217</u>
Social status, <u>166–67</u>
Sony (AIBO robot dog), 277
Spaying, <u>220–21</u>
Spraying urine, <u>115</u>
Sprays, pet-repellant, 142
Starvation, emotional, 83–85, <u>86</u>
Stereotypic behavior, 67
Stimulus-response reactions, <u>8–9</u>
Stress, 87–108
  dealing with, 94–95
  meanings of, 88–89
  of medical examination, 188
  positive aspects of, 90–92
  treatment of, 89, 92
  understanding causes in pets, 93–94
Stressor, 89
Stress response, 90–92, 104
Suffering
  on Comfort Zone Scale, 27–28, **28**
  effect on body systems, 193
  on Pleasure/Discomfort Scale, 46,
    46, 49–50
  positive aspect of, <u>22</u>
Sweets, cravings for, <u>160</u>

T

Territorial marking, <u>130</u>
Thermometer, quality of life, 180–81
Touch, 189, 198–201, 216
Training
    clicker, 149–50
    obedience, 218
    Pet Pleasure Principle use in,
        149–50
Treats. *See also* Rewards
    food, <u>126</u>
    placement on scratching post, 141
    use in clicker training, 149–50

U

Uncooperative behavior, <u>226</u>, 245–48
Unhappiness, recognizing in pets,
    231–34
Unpleasant feelings
    dealing with, by
        adaptation, 94
        coping, 95
        habituation, 94–95
        sense of control, 95–101
    discomfort, 26–26, <u>29</u>
    effect on euthanasia decision, <u>259</u>,
        262–65, <u>270</u>, 271–74
    evolution of, 59–60
    functions of
        attention focus, 16–18, 21
        priority setting, 19–21
        protection, 14–15, <u>22</u>
    origins of, <u>43</u>
    protection from, 216–18

stress associated with, 88–89,
    <u>90–91</u>, 92, 94
Urination, inappropriate, 144–45, 148

V

Valium, 89
Value system of the pet, <u>126</u>
Veterinary care. *See also* Euthanasia
    alternative medicine, 254–55
    compassionate care, 248–49
    delivery of comfort, 240–43
    goals, 237–40, <u>240–41</u>
    ideal veterinary hospital features,
        255–56
    noncooperation from pet, 245–48
    proactive treatment, 251, 254
    therapeutic decisions, 249–51, 254
    use of force, <u>247</u>
Visits, hospital, <u>252–53</u>, 255–56

W

Watson, J. B. (psychological theorist),
    <u>8</u>
Wills, <u>232–33</u>
Wool chewing, 142
Work, animals' desire for, 177

Z

Zoos
    boredom problems in, 66
    broken-heart syndrome, 193
    Safe Havens, 101–2